Marianne Jewell Memorial Library
Baker College of
Muskegon, Mich

BAKER COLLEGE

3 3504 00508 4282

MW00620576

HV 2561 .S74 J68 2004
Joyner, Hannah.
From pity to pride

DATE DUE

From Pity to Pride

From Pity to Pride

Growing Up Deaf in the Old South

Hannah Joyner

Gallaudet University Press
Washington, D.C.

Marianne Jewell Memorial Library
Baker College of Muskegon
Muskegon, Michigan 49442

Gallaudet University Press
Washington, D.C. 20002

http://gupress.gallaudet.edu

© 2004 by Gallaudet University
All rights reserved. Published 2004
Printed in the United States of America

Library of Congress Cataloging-in-Publication Data

Joyner, Hannah.

    From pity to pride : growing up deaf in the Old South / Hannah Joyner.

      p. cm.

    Includes bibliographical references and index.

    ISBN 1-56368-270-2 (cloth : alk. paper)

    1. Deaf—Southern States—History—19th century. 2. Deaf—Education—Southern States—History—19th century. 3. Deaf—Southern States—Social conditions. 4. Southern States—Social conditions—19th century. I. Title

HV2561.S74J68 2004

305.9′082′0977—dc22

                          2004043300

∞ The paper used in this publication meets the minimum requirements of American National Standard for Information Sciences—Permanence of Paper for Printed Library Materials, ANSI z39.48–1984.

I assure you that I never regret being deprived of my hearing in my life, as I trust that God knows what was best, and that I am as happy as you would wish.

If you ever visit one of the schools for the education of the Deaf and Dumb, you will find this unfortunate class of your fellow beings so happy as to make you forget that they are objects of pity.

I hate pity because it shows a want of good manners.

—Ellen Galt Martin to Elizabeth S. Martin,
23 August 1842, Elizabeth S. Martin Papers,
Southern Historical Collection, Wilson
Library, University of North Carolina,
Chapel Hill, NC

For David

CONTENTS

ACKNOWLEDGMENTS

In February of 1993 I had surgery for a non-cancerous brain tumor. Durng the surgery my acoustic-vestibular nerve was cut. I lost hearing in one ear and my balance was impaired. Rather than preparing for my Ph.D. exams scheduled for that spring at the University of Pennsylvania, I needed to learn to walk, use a fork and a pencil, and read again. In order to face my hearing loss and to provide therapy for my weakened right hand, I decided to take an introductory American Sign Language class. As my eyes began to focus, I started reading everything I could get my hands on about deafness and Deaf culture. I was fascinated. I discovered that what I had thought was a devastating loss instead offered me a new lens through which to see the world. Connections between deafness and my historical interest in discrimination and resistance became clear. I began a historical study addressing this idea. The next fall when Gallaudet University, a college designed for Deaf students, advertised a position in the history department, I applied. My campus interview was on the one-year anniversary of my surgery. I started teaching there the next fall.

As this book developed, being on the Gallaudet campus gave me further insight into the issues I was studying. I would like to thank all the students who patiently taught me about Deaf language and culture. Thanks to all in the history department, especially those who shared their interests in Deaf history and Deaf culture: Barry Bergen, Joe Kinner, Mary Malzkuhn, Dave Penna, Donna Ryan, John Schuchman, Ausma Smits, and John Van Cleve. Almost since the beginning of this project, Susan Burch at Gallaudet has been an enthusiastic critic, a thoughtful collaborator, and a great friend.

Thanks also to my department chair Russ Olson for his support and to the department secretary Lynne Payne.

As I was exploring the connections between deafness and southern history, I found a handful of other historians interested in disability and the South. Thanks to Peter McCandless, Steven Noll, Penny Richards, and Peter Wallenstein for their input and camaraderie. Thanks also to Bertram Wyatt-Brown, Steven Stowe, Sally McMillen, Katherine Ott, and Brenda Brueggemann for their advice and encouragement. The larger community of researchers in disability studies has made this work possible.

Thanks to the archivists and librarians who made researching this book possible: the staffs of the Virginia Historical Society, the Southern Historical Collection at the University of North Carolina, the Caroliniana Library at the University of South Carolina, the manuscript department at Duke University, and the Volta Bureau. Michael Olson and Ulf Hedberg from the archives at Gallaudet University saw me through the very beginning of this project and also pointed me toward manuscripts that proved essential to finishing it. I would also like to thank Reggie Boyd at www.deafhistory.org, Todd Lawrence at the Tillinghast Family Society, and especially Gary Wait at the American School for the Deaf. I extend my gratitude to the Montgomery County Public Library's Interlibrary Loan service and the staff at the Silver Spring branch, especially Adam Greene, who dedicated an entire hold shelf to me almost every week.

Gallaudet University Press has nurtured this project and helped it grow into a book. Special thanks go to John Vickrey Van Cleve, Ivey Pittle Wallace, Deirdre Mullervy, Alexa Selph, and Gary Gore. Also, thanks to Douglas Baynton and Lauri Unmansky who served as manuscript readers for the press. They provided suggestions that enriched the book immeasurably.

My interest in history has been nurtured by many people. Thanks to Drew Faust, my primary advisor at the University of Pennsylvania. She is a role model in terms of teaching as well as scholarship. Thanks also to the other members of my dissertation committee, Michael Katz and Charles Rosenberg, for their insights, challenges, and mentorship.

No one survives graduate school alone. I was blessed with a terrific cohort of fellow scholars at the University of Pennsylvania, including Beth

Clement, Russ Kazal, Roseanne Adderly, Steve Conn, Abby Schrader, Marc Stein, Ed Baptist, Michael Kahan, and Kirsten Wood. We shared many meals, editing sessions, relationship woes and joys, high-minded debates, costume parties, and April Fool's jokes. While jobs have taken us to all corners of North America, they are never far from my mind.

Before Penn, I studied at the University of North Carolina with Jacquelyn Dowd Hall. I am grateful for her generosity as well as her skill as an advisor. Harry Watson taught my first graduate class at UNC and convinced me that I had made the right decision to become a historian. In that class were Marla Miller, Anne Mitchell, and Laura Moore. There is no poverty in grad school with friends like these.

College friends have also helped me on this path. George Waldrep shared his love of southern history with me and introduced me to the exhilaration of teaching. Chad Heap studied both history and poetry with me, helped me celebrate my birthday in grand style, and spent days at the Library of Congress with me as I worked through the final draft of this book. Thanks also to Michael Alterman for his continuing friendship.

This book could not have been completed without the support of people outside my academic programs. First I want to thank my dissertation group. Who would have thought that four women in four different fields from three different schools could find each other in suburban Washington and fit together so well? Alex Carter, Sharon Groves, and Susan Miller (and their partners and pets) offered insightful advice, great snacks, and loving support.

Watching my friends complete books of their own served as inspiration. In addition to my college and graduate school friends, Maxine Grossman and Hayim Lapin have been terrific role models as well as wonderful company. And thanks to Stu Sheifer, Karin Twilde-Sheifer, and their children Madeleine and Daniel; Ellen Daniels, Adam Frank, and their daughter Zahava; and Margaret Newman-Balfe, Kevin Balfe, and their son Matt for reminding me that there is life outside of writing. We have shared homes, holidays, families, and friendship.

My parents Charles Joyner and Jean Dusenbury Joyner taught me, through their involvement in the Civil Rights movement and with their other commitments, how important the struggle for justice is. They also showed me how that fight can be carried out using a typewriter. My father's work continues to remind me that the study and teaching of history can fill the mind and the heart. Thanks also to my brother Wesley Joyner. His curiosity and knowledge about other cultures and languages makes him a thought-provoking sparring partner. I welcome him to the world of history and historians.

I owe a special debt to my Meyers family. Jay and Susan Meyers listened patiently to my ramblings about this book, believed enthusiastically that I could finish this project, and entertained their grandchild while I did. Eliot Meyers has offered me his kindness and love. All three have warmly welcomed me into their family, giving me another place to call home.

In the fall of 1999, I left Gallaudet to stay home with my new son Abraham. While I finished my dissertation, he watched from a spot on my lap and occasionally assisted in some editorial work. As the dissertation grew into a book, Abraham grew into a little boy. He recycles manuscript drafts by drawing pictures on them, builds castles out of stacks of history books, and teaches me the meaning of family every day.

My greatest debts by far are owed to my partner David Meyers. We met in 1990 while teaching at TIP, a program at Duke University for teenagers. The evening we met we stayed up talking all night, and we haven't stopped since. This book took shape as our relationship did. David is undoubtedly the second most knowledgeable scholar of Deaf family history in the mid-nineteenth-century South. He has traveled to archives with me, deciphered antebellum handwriting, bought tens of printer ribbons, and boiled thousands of pots of tea. And he has debated every point with me. His dedication to this project knows no bounds. On our honeymoon he even agreed to stop at the Virginia School for the Deaf and the Blind. David learned American Sign Language at the same time I did and is therefore able to offer his Deaf patients a chance to communicate directly with their physician. His commitment to justice inspires me daily. I cannot express how much he means to me.

As a Prisoner Escaped, a Sick Man Cured

IN VIRGINIA IN 1877, Edward Pye Chamberlayne was killed when he was hit by a train. During the late nineteenth century many Deaf people across the nation came to their deaths in this way. But Edward, as his brother John Hampden Chamberlayne (Ham) noted, was "always cautious" and "furnished accurately with the time" so he could avoid the tracks when the train was due. On the day of his death, however, Edward crossed the train's path during a storm that had delayed the scheduled train. The wind obscured the vibrations of the coming train and prevented Edward from feeling, as his brother wrote, "the jar of the moving weight." Edward's eyes did not serve him either, for the train came from behind, "turning a sharp corner on a down-grade." The train struck him, lifted his body from where he stood, and threw him clear of the track. He was unconscious by the time he landed. "Death was almost instantaneous, and wholly without pain," wrote his brother Ham, wishfully. "This was the manner of it."[1]

In reality, Edward was still alive. When the train came to a stop, Edward's unconscious body was "lifted tenderly" from the ground by the conductor, and "borne to the station, where kind friends tended him." There, "still unconscious of what was done," Edward took his last breath. His brother Ham was summoned by telegraph. Before he arrived at the train station, Edward's friends stayed with the body. When Ham first arrived, friends had already "decently clothed" Edward's body in "his working garments, clean, but only such as he daily wore at work." Although first shocked to see his brother without the trappings of class appropriate to his

1

family's station, Ham quickly changed his mind. "I thought it was well done to lay him to rest in the armor of his daily fight," said Ham, "like a true soldier as he was, who fought a battle always."[2]

Edward's friends placed his lifeless body in "its last resting place." They lifted the "simple wooden coffin, where the body may soonest be resolved to its parent clay," onto a railroad car for its return to his family's home in Richmond. The Deaf man's friends went with Ham to the town, where his coffin would have to be transferred from one train to the next. As Ham explained, their labor meant that "all was done by love and respect from the touch of death to the decent burial in the sweet earth." Ham was comforted that "no servile hands" touched his brother's body.[3]

Despite his family's aristocratic background, Edward was not a man of great fortune. As Ham said, "He was a man denied from birth man's chief sense." The limits of his deafness, Ham felt, meant his independent brother lived much of his life "in grinding poverty, working for poorest wages." Edward had "nothing but an inborn worth," said Ham, but he knew that was a treasure "the world seldom recognizes." It was the "nobleness of his character" that allowed Edward to endure, in his brother's mind, "a life desolate and solitary."[4]

Both Ham and the brothers' mother were relieved, they claimed, that Edward had been "delivered from a present labor and sorrow, and from a future infinitely dark, where age and want and natural infirmity marched against him." Edward's deafness, as his hearing mother and brother understood it, was "surely the hardest [experience] ever laid on mortals." Edward's "sudden, providential translation" from an earthly life to a heavenly one "unstopped the ears that never heard, and loosed the tongue which never spoke." The two family members felt that Edward's death had been a blessing. Ham told his family that he thought of his dead brother "wholly as a prisoner escaped, a sick man cured."[5]

The church where the funeral was held was "filled with men and women" mourning for Ham's brother. Edward's death precipitated the "true grief" of the large congregation of mourners. Ham was surprised by the deep connection that Edward's friends had. The deep sense of loss they were now feeling "seemed strange" to him.[6]

Within hours of his death, Edward's classmates from the Deaf school he had attended forty years before began to arrive at his home. Others of the group that Ham referred to in his letter were his brother's Deaf acquaintances from across the country—perhaps people he had met at national conventions of teachers of the Deaf. At the funeral were Deaf people who valued sign language and Deaf identity. Their deep sense of community was not something Ham and his hearing family members had understood before. They could see now that while Edward did not enjoy all of the privileges of his hearing family's station, his life was far from desolate or solitary. His was an unusually strong and nationwide community. Although mainstream culture saw deafness as a deep misfortune and Deaf people as the objects of pity, Deaf people themselves constructed a different world. Rather than seeking charity, they viewed their struggle as one for self-determination and community. Rather than seeing deafness as a source of pity, they construed it to be a source of pride.

ℰ

Today's Deaf community shares much with the world of Edward Pye Chamberlayne and his nineteenth-century friends. To a significant degree, the political-cultural (rather than the medical-audiological) meaning of Deafness has produced an exceptionally cohesive community. Prelingually deafened children are often sent to residential schools where they form bonds of culture and language. They are unified by common experiences in these residential schools and in their dealings with hearing majority culture. They develop values and specific cultural modes of expression that respond to such experiences. When they graduate from the schools, Deaf people frequently choose to marry each other, live near each other, and work together. These community members see deafness as a natural and essential part of who they are. Most have no desire to become hearing, and many hope their children will be like them and share their deafness.[7]

The primary unifying force in the Deaf community is the use of a distinct language. Linguists have shown that babies easily learn the language of their parents simply by exposure to its daily use. Just as hearing infants can pick up oral language from their speaking parents, infants (deaf and hearing) can acquire visual language from their signing parents. But 90 percent of deaf infants are born to hearing parents. Because they do not hear, profoundly deaf infants born to nonsigning parents are unable to acquire spontaneously their family's language. They do not learn to speak, but the problem is more complex: these young children do not learn structured language at all unless they are exposed to a visual language.

The United States Deaf community uses American Sign Language, a language with a grammatical structure quite different from English. Much of the grammar stems from its visual mode. Other aspects of the grammar of ASL are, due to the history of American Deaf education, rooted in nineteenth-century French educational sign language, influenced by spoken French rather than spoken English.[8]

Because Deaf children cannot easily learn English until they begin to read (when they are school-aged rather than infants), they usually learn it at the level of a second language. Learning written language is an especially difficult process for Deaf people because it must be learned without similar first-language grammatical structures or the support of phonetics. Even after serious efforts to learn written English, most Deaf children struggle mightily with speech. Through concerted effort, some Deaf children learn to reproduce the lip, tongue, and breath movements that produce sounds, but because they hear neither the vocal models nor their own productions, articulation is extremely difficult for most people deafened before they learn to speak.

Because communication between Deaf people and hearing people is usually strained, Deaf people in the United States gravitate toward others who use American Sign Language. Users of ASL have formed a community with shared values. Hearing people who know little about the Deaf community see deafness as a handicap because Deaf people, even those with clear speech and strong speechreading skills, still seem impaired to hearing people. Most Deaf people have experienced intolerance and misunderstanding or worse in their efforts to communicate with the hearing.[9]

With other signers, Deaf people need not make the concerted effort to produce spoken words they cannot hear or to stare at people's faces to try to speechread. Sign language offers a communication style requiring no intense concentration or special effort on the part of Deaf individuals, allowing them to focus on the meaning, rather than the production, of their words.

Deaf people emphasize the cultural and linguistic bonds that unite the community. That is, instead of defining deafness merely as an absence of hearing, Deaf people also define it by the use of a signed language. From this perspective, any "handicap" or "disability" that the Deaf community experiences is simply the result of oppression, be it unintended or deliberate, by the hearing establishment. Deaf people recognize that deafness is not a medical condition but a social and political position. Inside the Deaf community, the handicap of deafness completely disappears.[10]

ℯ

The cultural meanings of deafness are always created within a particular time and place. The Deaf children in this book grew up in the South before the Civil War. During this period the South was a place set apart from the rest of the country by its "peculiar institution" of chattel slavery and by the distinct social, cultural, political, and economic systems that grew up in its shadow. While the North was developing an industrial society based on wage labor, becoming more urban, incorporating a great variety of immigrants, and articulating (to a sometimes limited degree) an antislavery position, the South was solidifying its system of plantation agriculture based on the servitude of African American slaves. Class structure and relationships, gender construction, religious expression, and political affiliation were among the aspects of society that varied according to sectional identity.[11]

The experiences of Deaf individuals and their families in the South could vary widely, depending on their race, class, and gender identities. Enslaved African American men and women, poor white men and women, male and female members of the middling yeomen class, and plantation masters and mistresses almost certainly saw Deaf people in quite distinct ways. Likewise, Deaf members of those groups grew up with extremely different experiences.

This book will examine the formative experiences of a particular group of Deaf people during the mid-nineteenth century. The people I discuss are from wealthy white families. Some lived on rural plantations, while others were more urban, but all were from slaveholding families. Almost all of the individuals discussed in this book were male.[12]

Elite families in the antebellum South adhered to a southern identity predicated on both mastery and dependency. A small number of privileged white men were masters, the holders of wealth and authority. Dependents included African Americans, poor whites, women, and, although not previously discussed by historians of the antebellum period, many people with disabilities. Had they been hearing, the young men growing up Deaf that I discuss in this book would have been the masters of their society. Instead, they were treated as inferiors in need of assistance. As one Deaf man said while thinking back on his life, "I sometimes fancy some people to treat me as they would a child to whom they were kind."[13]

Although Deaf people in the North also faced discrimination by hearing society, the culture of paternalism and dependency in the South codified a rigid system of oppression and hierarchy that left little room for self-determination for Deaf southerners. At least some of these elite Deaf people rejected their family's (and their society's) belief that deafness was a terrible misfortune and that Deaf people were unable to become fully independent members of southern society. They developed a very different understanding of their deafness. They viewed themselves as competent and complete. And as they came to adulthood, they joined together with other Deaf Americans, both southern and northern, to form communities that would understand their inherent worth and allow their independence. Although they often had to break from the traditions of their families (and the traditions of the southern elite as a whole) to do it, the Deaf boys in this book grew up to become proud and self-sufficient men.

Part I. Responses to Deafness

Most hearing southerners believed that children who could not hear should be deeply pitied. Because southerners (and indeed almost all Americans) saw deafness as a desperate and despicable condition, medical experts sought ways to cure deafness. Because physicians felt that the horrors of deafness were worse than any medical treatment, they were willing to operate experimentally on Deaf children. These negative social and medical attitudes toward deafness and Deaf people affected individual families. The diagnosis of a child's deafness was usually a great disappointment and a shock for hearing parents. Because of social and familial fears about deafness, Deaf children were dragged to doctors for experimental treatments. But parents' searches for cures reinforced their belief that their children's deafness was a terrible misfortune. These same attempts at fixes served to alienate their Deaf children.

Deaf children and their hearing family members found communication difficult. They often could not talk about anything other than the most concrete daily situations. Although families developed a form of communication called home sign, hearing parents had trouble expressing complex thoughts and understanding their children's increasingly rapid and complex sign language. Deaf children often felt isolated within the family as events transpired that no one could explain to the youngsters. Their frustration was shared by their hearing parents.

Because educational leaders believed deeply in the transformative power of education for the Deaf, southern families explored educational options for their Deaf youngsters. Some mothers investigated pedagogical techniques and tried to educate their Deaf and hearing children together. Others hired graduates of Deaf schools to teach their Deaf youngsters. The vast majority of these efforts met with limited success and ended in varying degrees of frustration. The Deaf children were still isolated and unable to communicate successfully with the community surrounding them. As their children grew to the age of eight to twelve years old, many parents chose to enroll them in large state-sponsored schools for the Deaf in their home states, in nearby southern states, or in the North.

$\mathcal{C}\curvearrowright$ *The Peculiar Misfortune*

IN THE ANTEBELLUM AMERICAN SOUTH, the inability to hear was seen by most of society as a great calamity. Southerners did not understand why some people were Deaf, but they sought an explanation in their larger worldview: either "nature and her caprice" or "God in His wisdom" had denied the sense of hearing to individuals. Many Americans felt that Deaf people were suffering greatly from their condition. The life of "the poor mute" was the "peculiar misfortune" of the "most unfortunate class of our fellow creatures." Hearing southerners concluded that "the condition of the uneducated deaf and dumb [was] lamentable beyond degree."[1]

In the first book published in the United States about "the Deaf and Dumb, those most unfortunate beings," author John Burnet posited that without education, Deaf people were condemned to live in "silent darkness." By using these two descriptives, the author was following the social convention of referring to deafness as not only an absence of sound but, metaphorically, an absence of sight. This chapter will discuss how these two choices of imagery created and reinforced society's cultural attitudes toward Deaf people.[2]

Deaf children were frequently designated as "children of silence." The phrase seemed a natural one: prelingually deaf people could neither hear nor speak and therefore lived in a world rooted in vision, not sound. Although most people realized that "even silence has its charms," many of them thought that deafness destroyed those charms: "the world of sound" was for Deaf people "a tuneless void." Hearing southerners felt that

momentary silence was peaceful, but for Deaf people, life was "one unbro-
ken silence from the cradle to the grave." A life of silence, they imagined,
was a "boundless, dreary and silent Sahara." Hearing southerners believed
that Deaf people were forced to "ever wander on in a voiceless, silent solitude."[3]

Living in a world of silence, thought many hearing southerners, left
Deaf people miserable. Said one observer, "The crushing load of misfortune . . . weighs down the sorrow-stricken . . . Deaf and Dumb." Their lives
were dreary, gloomy, cheerless, and full of "human woe." The central reason for their supposed unhappiness, according to hearing observers, was
the fact that Deaf people were cut off from nature and from their families.
Some writers catalogued the sounds of nature and imagined that the inability to hear them would leave Deaf people lonely. As one writer said,
"The bright fields and waving groves may echo the notes of the feathered
songster, yet they heed them not." With the exception of the sounds of
birds, these images were visual and perfectly accessible to Deaf people, but
hearing people often could not imagine any pleasure in a world without
"all the varied music of Nature." As one wrote, "The Song of bird and bee /
The chorus of breezes, streams, and groves / All the grand music to which
nature moves / Are wasted melody." In short, hearing southerners thought
that for Deaf people, "the world and all its dazzling pomp" was "an unmeaning show."[4]

In addition to their separation from nature, Deaf people were removed
from the family circle, according to hearing observers. Deaf people knew
"nothing of the relations of father and mother, sister and brother; of family
affections and ties of kindred, that highest link in the chain of human connections." Not only were they "ignorant . . . of the names of . . . parents,
brothers and sisters," but they could never even hear their friends and relatives: they were "never . . . cheered by the fond voices of parents and
friends." Many hearing southerners assumed that Deaf people's inability to
hear their parents meant that they were unable to understand that their
families loved them. One observer said that "the voice of affection, though
falling from a mother's sacred lips, excites no emotions in their unim-
pressed hearts." Another said, "No word of human kindness nor voice of
human love, ever found its peaceful way to their hearts."[5]

Because Deaf people could neither hear nor speak loving words to their families, hearing people thought they were "cut off from . . . social intercourse" and therefore "outcast[s] from society." Although a deaf person could see "fellow human beings communicate in some mysterious way with one another" with their mouths, it was "a painful enigma" to understand how it was done. Therefore, the gates of successful communication were locked. "A mighty chasm" stood between Deaf and hearing people.[6]

Hearing people could understand Deaf people no better than they imagined Deaf people could understand them. Deaf people were "perfect blanks in the community" and a total cipher to hearing society. In short, a Deaf person was "with them, but not of them." Even family members, when Deaf, were "strangers and aliens."[7]

In addition to metaphors of silence, comparisons between deafness and the inability to see were commonly used to describe deafness, even though they were obviously not literal. In the space of three pages, author John Burnet, Deaf himself, made reference to the "utter darkness," "chaotic darkness," and "solitary darkness" in which uneducated Deaf people lived. Southerners usually assumed that Deaf people's "condition by nature is . . . dark and miserable." Sometimes the metaphorical blindness was seen as an obstruction between Deaf people and the world: "the veil which shrouded his eyes" and the "films of ignorance for ages deemed impenetrable." Hearing people felt that Deaf people were made to "grope" their path "in silent darkness from the cradle to the grave," or "from their mother's arms to the cold embrace of death."[8]

The metaphor of darkness highlighted, or perhaps even encouraged, many social beliefs about deafness. One was that Deaf people were cursed to live in "mental darkness." Many southerners felt that Deaf people's "dark minds" were "locked in hopeless ignorance" because they could not receive knowledge by the channel used by most young children: their ears. Unlike hearing children, Deaf children could not learn from their parents' oral conversations with each other. Although they were "surrounded by every species of intellectual food," their inability to hear meant they were "debarred the very crumbs of knowledge." Rather than recognizing that the eye could replace the ear as the channel for learning, many hearing people assumed that spoken language was the only true "channel of thought" and, therefore, that "the mind of the uneducated deaf mute is shut out from all those sources of light and development." Deaf people who were not educated would "sink into the most repulsive ignorance, their minds enfeebling till they become driveling simpletons." Many southerners believed that Deaf people were "the most totally ignorant of all knowledge . . . of the entire race of man."[9]

Describing deafness as a form of darkness, despite the fact that Deaf people were by necessity fundamentally visual, made sense to hearing southerners partly because the metaphor of darkness was already part of the cultural currency. For example, in the creation story of Genesis 1, God said on the first day, "'Let there be light,'" where before there was "darkness" and a "void." But not until the fourth day were "the lights in the firmament of the heavens" created "to separate the day from the night" and "to give light upon the earth." So what was the light of the first day? Perhaps, thought readers, it represented understanding and knowledge. Because this "light" required "hearing" the word of God, blindness and deafness were conflated to mean lack of religious awareness.[10]

Hearing society's belief in Deaf people's "moral darkness" or "spiritual darkness" was central to the negative view of deafness in the antebellum world. One hearing observer summarized a general assumption: to Deaf people, "no light of truth has been sent" because they could not hear the word of God. Therefore, hearing observers assumed that Deaf people could know nothing of "God, of [the] soul, or of the immortality that awaits." They remained untouched by "the rays of the Star of Bethlehem." Not only could Deaf people not receive God's word; the human practice of religion eluded them. Although Deaf children might routinely attend both community religious services and daily familial devotions, Deaf children were, according to hearing observers, "wholly ignorant of the object of all these forms."[11]

Because Deaf people could not receive the word of God, many hearing southerners felt they were morally irresponsible. They lived in an "awful moral . . . desolation." For Deaf people, "the handiwork of God" did not "create an idea of moral responsibility." They were, thought many hearing southerners, exempt from moral obligation. Asked one, "Can beings so ignorant [of God's word] be held morally accountable for their conduct?"[12]

Discussions of mental and moral darkness eased into comparisons of Deaf people with the heathens and savages of supposedly "dark" lands. One writer suggested that a Deaf person's isolation and ignorance was "like the darkness of Egypt." Another stated that Deaf people lived with "all the miseries of a mind shrouded in worse than Egyptian darkness." Such racial discourse was commonly applied to Deaf people, whatever their race, because of their separation from the Christian community. "Even in this land of Christianity and civilization," said author John Burnet, uneducated Deaf people were "condemned for life to a lot worse than that of the most ignorant savage." They were "sunk in . . . heathenism" because of their separation from the Christian community. Some southerners felt that a so-called savage had an advantage over a Deaf person: "The Hottentot or Digger Indian were rather to be envied than he, because the Hottentot and Digger were utterly ignorant of the existence of countless objects, which the eye had revealed to the deaf mute" but which the Deaf person could still not understand. Others felt that Deaf people were even more separated from God than the so-called savages: Deaf people were "entirely destitute of a knowledge of even natural religion, with which the most abandoned tribes of the heathen, it is believed, have some acquaintance." As one writer said, "the benighted heathen" had received God's message in a limited way and had "from the tradition of his ancestors . . . learned enough to lead him to the contemplation of the Supreme"—but Deaf people could not even imagine a world other than the concrete one in front of their eyes.[13]

Some hearing writers felt that Deaf people were not even fully human. Deaf people, wrote one observer, were "not much above the animal creation." For these writers, a Deaf person was "a creature . . . limitedly endowed" and simply "little removed from other dumb creatures." An uneducated Deaf person was "barely admitted to sit down at [humanity's] threshold."[14]

Hearing writers often expressed concern about the "dark" personalities of Deaf people as well. Although few people blamed the Deaf people themselves, many felt that either overindulgence or outright abuse by parents would leave Deaf children with damaged characters. Because of the "fatal effects" of "the almost unrestrained indulgence of his whims at home," Deaf children became unbridled and willful. Because of the difficulties of communication, hearing parents often did not explain proper behavior to their Deaf children. "Too often the love which the family bear him denigrates into a morbid affection," said one writer. "How wrong!" Because of a "want of proper control," uneducated Deaf people acquired a "violent temper and refractory disposition." Other writers claimed that Deaf people became passionate and obstinate, selfish and suspicious, and irritable. Because of their unpleasant personalities, according to hearing observers, Deaf people became "object[s] of aversion and dislike." They were "almost a certain source of misery to themselves and family" and "a pest, if not a curse."[15]

Some hearing observers felt Deaf individuals were helpless. Deaf people would lead, thought hearing observers, "an idle, immoral, and vagrant life" in constant poverty. Because they would be unable to work to support themselves, they would always be "dependent on charity, the grudged assistance of others." Their dependency would make them "a burden to themselves, their friends, and to the community" and "a standing tax upon the public" for their entire lives.[16]

Because physicians as well as parents were bombarded with images and stereotypes of the dependent, defective, and deviant Deaf, many felt that any possibility of a cure, no matter how unlikely, was worth the effort. "Any prospect," said one expert, "of relieving this afflicted portion of our race, must be received as a boon to humanity." The doctor continued, "if only a small number of these can be relieved, it is imperative on the medical man" to try to cure "the class of cases in which treatment promises to be successful." Physicians realized that congenitally Deaf people, who had never experienced hearing, were often unaware of their loss, but hearing society nevertheless felt that Deaf individuals were suffering from a terrible calamity that should be alleviated at all costs.[17]

The only significant attempt to cure congenital sensorineural deafness during the antebellum years was by the use of electric shocks sent through opening of the ear, down the auditory canal, and through the eustachian tube. Many people expressed doubts about the safety of the treatment, especially because the danger of "tampering with so important an organ as the ear, situated as it is so close to the brain." But others felt that this use of electricity would eventually "be numbered amongst one of the boons to humanity."[18]

Many nineteenth-century doctors felt that noncongenital deafness, acquired by accident or disease, could be cured more easily. They believed it the result of a blockage caused by hardened mucus or some other substance. Because of the obstruction between the mouth and the ear, communication was interrupted. Doctors attempted several methods to clear the eustachian tube. One of the most common was to catheterize the ear, accomplished with either air, water, or ether. To accomplish the procedure, the doctor needed "an inflexible silver catheter, about six inches long" along with a "calibre, varying from the size of a crow quill to that of a large goose quill." The physician would thread the "warmed and oiled" catheter through the patient's nose, "along the floor of the nostril." As the catheter reached the "mouth of the Eustachian tube," the doctor would turn the catheter into the "orifice of the canal."[19]

When an air-douche was the treatment of choice, the physician would simply blow through the catheter or an attached syringe, or use an air pump. Although experts admitted that "sometimes no relief is given," or even "at other times the deafness is increased," one physician noted that occasionally "on the first introduction of air, it seems as *if the deafness was literally blown away.*"[20]

Other physicians preferred rinsing the eardrum or eustachian tube with either plain or salt water. A third option was to douche with ether in either fluid or gas form. "Five minims" of acetic ether could be mixed with an ounce of warm water and rinsed through the catheter once a day. Or, the physician might choose to put a few drops of ether in a glass along with the end of the catheter tube, then heat the glass until "vapours" rose into the tube.[21]

In order to clear obstructions in the eustachian tube, some doctors turned to experimental surgery. One physician suggested that in cases of "an inflamed state of the throat," the tonsils could be "scarified" or, in extreme cases, "removed with a pair of scissors." In addition to the surgical removal of tonsils, physicians sought to remove the polyps they found in some individuals' auditory canals. Rather than using a dangerous caustic fluid, one expert suggested that doctors use surgery; they could "easily remove" the polyps with a knife, at least in cases where the tumors were accessible and could be "laid hold of."[22]

Antebellum medical journals in the South published very little information about the cure of deafness. One article, published in Louisville, Kentucky, in 1841, described the remarkable surgery of John Washington. Although Washington was a northerner who had received his education at
the American Asylum in Connecticut, his story captured the imagination
of a medical journal in a slave state.[23]

Author and physician S. M. Knapp stated in his introduction to Washington's story that he had examined the young Deaf man, and that he
thought he could "be successful in bringing him to his hearing" by piercing
his eardrum. Other northern physicians commonly supported this kind of
surgery as well. If "the Eustachian tube is permanently obstructed" and
"the catheter cannot be introduced" in order to flush out the passageway,
the "mymbrana tympani should be perforated" in order to allow "air,
which could not find entrance by the tube," to pass through the eustachian
tube. The membrane needed to be pierced while the child was still young,
to assure that the "acoustic nerve has been allowed to remain active."[24]

Despite Knapp's examination and high hopes for the operation, the
physician "shrank from the responsibility" and never performed the surgery. Young Washington did not give up his conviction to have the surgery,
nor did he seek another physician to perform the operation. Instead, Washington "resolved to operate upon himself."[25]

Knapp allowed Washington to present his story in his own words. John
said that his deafness was caused "by a preternatural membrane" covering
the tympanum, which he claimed was the most common obstruction causing deafness in children. Washington read medical texts and studied the
procedure purported to cure such deafness. He prepared tools for the operation, including "a common thumb lancet, ground down to about one
third of its original width," then fit the blade into "a common silver pencil
case, with the point protruding about a line and a half." He would use this
instrument to pierce both his eardrum and the covering membrane, then
insert in the hole a tube designed to drain the pus blocking his eustachian
tube.[26]

Washington failed at his first attempts at the surgery. Because "the pain
was so excruciating," he "was forced to desist." In order to prepare himself

for the operation, he "injected daily oleum amygdalae and black drop" in order to "soften the parts" of his ear. He also "used every precaution" to keep his "nervous system in a state of rest." Finally, a week after his first attempt, Washington calmed his nerves by "taking a common half-pint tumbler about two-thirds full of Holland gin," and closed himself in a room alone where he intended to carry out the operation.[27]

John Washington prepared himself to perform the surgery by "tying a bandage round my head in order to open the lobe of the ear and confine it back close to the head," so he could see inside his ear "by casting my eyes upon a looking glass obliquely." He inserted the tube, then through it the bladed instrument. He held them in the opening of his ear for a moment, then, "summoning all my energies, I plunged it in." After the blade pierced the covering, Washington found a small cavity between it and the actual eardrum. But he continued pushing until he "pushed the lancet firmly through" the eardrum. He was surprised by its resistance, which was, as he said, "greater than I expected." After making one incision, he "turned the tube around and made another," crossing the first cut. He then drew the lancet out of his ear.[28]

Although Washington intended to push the tube, still in his ear canal, "between the lips of the incision," he found he was unable to accomplish the task. As he explained, "the pain of the operation, together with the sudden admission of air, threw me into a series of fainting fits," and he was later told, "a number of slight spasms" or seizures. Someone came into his room to help him. With a "tight bandage" over his head and the tube still in his ear, he went to bed. Although he tried to sleep, "amid such agony" he could not. As he suffered through the night, a "slight discharge" of pus and blood came through the tube, but this was the least of his symptoms. He was beset with "a whirling and dizziness" in his head, accompanied by "flashes of light" and "explosive noise" in his head. The noise that night was all "blended into one distracting tumult."[29]

The next morning he knew he needed medical care and decided to put himself under the care of a physician. Washington felt "a peculiar itching, tingling sensation" in his ear canal, reported the physician, as well as "a feeling as if the upper part of the cranium were gone." He continued to hear "acute noises." The doctor also noted that Washington was "feverish and somewhat delirious." He was also "troubled . . . with a profuse sweating" on one side of his body, the side of the surgery.[30]

Although in his own account of his story, John Washington never comments on his perception of the success or failure of the operation, the doctor who treated him after the surgery clearly felt that, despite its dangers, the surgery was a complete success. Quickly the young man learned to distinguish between sounds, improving his skills "from hour to hour." Before Washington's surgery, the doctor had seen Washington "attempt to make a noise resembling his own name." After the operation, the doctor could "pronounce it upon his ear" (instead of in front of his eyes) and hear Washington repeat it "in a full, deep, sonorous tone, that sounded like a voice from the grave." What had been long dead had come back to life.[31]

The doctor claimed that by the fourth day, Washington "was able to hold a metaphysical argument," and that he could now "clothe his ideas in such a language as to convey every shade of thought and emotion." The doctor suggested that, in addition to improving the quality of his thinking, the surgery had improved the man's moral state. He claimed that Washington's "eyes acquired a new expression; his lips became thickened and chiselled; his temper has become subdued; and his whole bearing is changed into something characteristic and commanding." John Washington's physical sufferings, felt the doctor, were more than adequately rewarded by not only his ability to hear, but by the improvement of his person.[32]

By piercing the eardrum or otherwise gaining access to the supposedly blocked passageway, doctors hoped to clear out the area so communication could take place. Procedures like Washington's may or may not have worked for children with hearing damaged by ear infections or colds, but for many children the operations could cause pain, infection, or even additional hearing loss. For congenital or sensorineural deafness, medical procedures were almost always useless, as doctors often confessed. According to one report, "The restoration of a person naturally, or by disease, deaf and dumb, has been accomplished in very few well-authenticated cases." Nevertheless, the case of John Washington, because it was published in a widely distributed journal, surely persuaded or convinced some southern physicians of the possibility of the curing of deafness. Because they believed they might be able to make Deaf people hear, they poked and prodded—and sometimes caused great pain—to the Deaf children they purported to help.[33]

e⌒

Families also turned to home remedies in their search for cures for their children's deafness. Many therapies were rooted in the concept of opening blocked passageways. Some were meant to be decongestants, like the application of hot onion or cabbage. Tobacco smoke was also thought to clear the head. Purifying the body with a hot bath, sometimes using castile soap, was another suggestion. Deaf children were also encouraged to drink a large quantity of water to flush out their systems. Salt was another purifier, used either diluted in bath water, syringed into affected ears, or scrubbed into the scalp. Another proposed cure was to fill the Deaf child's ear with fluid, presumably to soften obstructions. Healers suggested using almond oil, walnut oil, turkey buzzard oil, honey, alcohol, and even laudanum. Protecting the ears from cold air, either by the wearing of a tight cap or by plugging the ears with fabric, was another therapy. Some suggestions for cure were harsher: blistering the child behind the ear, applying leeches behind the ear, and using purging were common suggestions. One commentator, recognizing the futility of parents' search for a cure for most Deaf children, suggested that "a pretty wife" would be just as effective.[34]

In addition to folk remedies, families with a Deaf child had access to vials of restorative tonic, advertised on broadsides to "have *improved* the Hearing in several *hundred* cases," including cases of congenital deafness. The unidentified fluid had to be used according to directions: two drops were to be inserted into the child's ears twice a day, then it was to be stoppered with wool fabric. If the directions were followed, claimed the advertisement, the tonic could, "in *many instances*, [be] proven a *speedy* and *effectual* cure." The advertising broadside instructed people ordering by mail to enclose five dollars and "a *particular* description of the past and present sensations in the Ear or Ears." The description would help the sellers of the restorative tonic choose which variety of the tonic would be *"most likely* to effect a cure."* Family members of the Deaf child were to distinguish between deafness because of "a sense of fullness in the Ear, and an insensibility of the nerves," cases where deafness was *"produced* by *inflammatory* diseases of any kind, causing a *gathering* in, and discharge, from the Ear," situations where there was a "*violent* concussion of *air* . . . whereby the *nerves* have become *paralyzed*," deafness due to the cessation of the "healthy secretion of wax," and cases "where the Nerves are debilitated"[35]

Folk remedies and marketed tonics were not any more effective than physicians' therapies to cure deafness. Parents turned to these treatments for the same reasons they consulted doctors. The social implications of deafness were so devastating that parents were willing to try useless or even dangerous treatments on their children. They felt that the possibility of curing their children's deafness, no matter how slim, was worth almost any risk.

CHAPTER 2

$\mathcal{C}\!\!\sim$ *Forget That They Are Objects of Pity*

GIVEN THE CULTURAL CLIMATE, the diagnosis of an individual child's deafness was a great disappointment and a shock for many hearing parents during the nineteenth century. According to John Burnet's 1835 study of American deafness, a Deaf child's mother would be horrified when she discovered her child could not hear. "When she makes the agonizing discovery that her child is deaf and will become dumb," said the study, "she thinks the misfortune irremediable." Parents, according to the author, would imagine an "appalling and all but impassable gulf" dividing them from their child.[1]

Like most hearing parents faced with the antebellum social meanings of deafness, the Tillinghast family of 1830s North Carolina grieved when they realized that their son Thomas, born in 1833, could not hear. They approached his diagnosis by taking him to northern experts in search of a cure. While on a business trip to New York, Tom's uncle approached two doctors about the boy's deafness. He reported to his sister (Tom's mother) that the two doctors did "not, I am sorry to say, give much encouragement." They suggested that Tom be brought to New York since "no positive opinion can be given without an examination." Despite the doctors' willingness to examine the boy, they warned that only "cases where the hearing is imperfect or has been impaired are often cured or benefited." They did "not seem to have much hope of doing anything for one born deaf."[2]

Twelve years later in 1845, Tom's younger brother David lost his hearing at the age of four. Although he had apparently been born hearing and soon began to babble and say a few words, after an extended illness he "seemed a little deaf." Because the possibility for finding a cure for David was more likely than it was in Tom's case (since David was not born deaf), the Tillinghasts were less willing to accept their younger son's deafness.[3]

William Tillinghast, one of Tom and David's hearing brothers, downplayed David's deafness in a letter to Tom, saying "I expect he will soon get over it." Robina Norwood, the boy's strong-willed grandmother, also hoped the deafness would not be long-term: "I am truly concerned to hear that poor David is threatened much by his deafness" but "I assume it is only temporary," she said, "as he certainly has had his hearing." Following the then-current beliefs about deafness, she stated that any serious blockage "surely can be removed."[4]

David's parents, however, quickly lost their optimism, even though they continued their quest. Almost six weeks before William's letter, Jane Tillinghast was already frustrated with their physician: "I see very little of the doctor, who continues to be much engaged." Even if the physician had spent more time with the Tillinghasts, he probably could do little. He informed them that he could "make nothing of David unless he had the proper instrument to examine his throat."[5]

After several months without cure, grandmother Robina continued to "hope and trust dear little David's deafness, as it certainly arose from some accidental or temporary cause, may be removed by the efforts of nature alone." But she also consulted local healers in her community. One man Robina consulted, "talking in a careless way," suggested that "if it is owing to inflammation from cold etc. which occasions the swelling of the tonsils, if it cannot be assuaged or does not subside, they might be cut away in part or even wholly." To reassure Robina, he told her the removal of tonsils was "a very easy operation, not so bad as pulling a tooth."[6]

Most of the doctors that Robina consulted were hesitant to state an opinion without seeing David: "To give an opinion that might be relied on, they ought either to have an opportunity of examining or have a very minute description and accurate account of all the symptoms from the beginning." Robina suggested that parents Jane and Samuel "write a particular account and of all the circumstances of the time when you first ob-

served it, whether you supposed it to be occasioned by cold and inflammation of the throat, swelling or other disorder of the ears, etc. etc."[7]

Knowing that Samuel and Jane were beginning to become desperate and
were looking everywhere, Robina tried to get her daughter and son-in-law
to continue the search for a cure in the South. She said, "I dare say he may
be cured without going to the North which as you observe would be attended with heavy expense." But their financial loss was not her prime concern: "As far as observation and experience, or rather recollection, goes, I
have been told to doubt the superior skill of Northern to Southern doctors
especially in regard to Southern patients and I think at least you ought to
try to get all the advice and information you can before you take that
step."[8]

A few months later, when the boy's deafness had not abated, Robina
shared her disappointment with David's parents. She said she still hoped
that better doctors might be able to cure his deafness. "I think it is very
strange that none of your Physicians can do anything for his relief," she
said. "I still trust that the obstruction, whatever it is, can be removed, as it
can be no defect in original formation." Perhaps Robina did not lose her
faith because she, unlike the child's mother, did not see experiment after
experiment fail. Or perhaps Robina did not truly believe David could be
cured; she only wanted to comfort her daughter. Jane and Samuel, however, seem to have given up the quest by the time of Robina's letter. As relatives realized that David would not be cured, they expressed their compas-
sion for his mother's grief: "Poor . . . Jane! She seems to have a pretty large
share of the troubles of this life."[9]

Tom, now away at the Virginia school for the Deaf, was told about his
brother's seemingly permanent deafness. Unlike his hearing family, he did
not respond with despair. He first wrote, "I was surprised that my brother
David is perfectly deaf." He began to be more curious about his Deaf
brother and to single out David from his hearing siblings in his letters
home: "I want to know how my dear Brother David is." As the years passed,
his feeling of affinity for his Deaf brother would grow.[10]

℘

Another southern family's experience of the diagnosis of their child's deafness resulted in similar bereavement, hope for cure, and disappointment. Virginia and Nicholas Trist of Virginia knew that their son Jefferson was a sickly child. In September 1829, Virginia informed her husband that "dear little Jefferson has been very sick." One month later, he was "very unwell again." Two weeks later he had "a bad cold." Every time one of the house servants took him out for a walk, the little boy returned with the "threat of croup." Because "the dampness of the river air disagrees with Jefferson," Virginia spent much of her time indoors with her sick child: "Jefferson's being so sick has made me live quite a secluded life, and now it is quite often a vexation for me to go out."[11]

During these months of sickness, the Trists began to notice that Jefferson was neither walking nor speaking yet. Although he displayed his talents at "standing alone" when he was seventeen months old, Jefferson did not "step about." Neither did he did "prattle" as their daughter did at a similar age. Virginia admitted her son's "extreme backwardness in walking and talking," but claimed that her son was "so *sensible* and conveys his meaning so perfectly by the significance of his signs, that he has no need for language." Although she knew that Jefferson was using gesture rather than voice to communicate with the family, neither she nor her husband realized that their son could not hear.[12]

Not until the next year was Jefferson's deafness fully recognized. The boy's parents told the extended family that they were "very uneasy" about the hearing of the "poor little fellow." They thought back on their early concerns about Jefferson: for a long time the family noticed that "when he was called he never turned his head, but if called repeatedly, would cry." Although his father considered that he might be not be able to hear, the boy's tears led Nicholas to suspect the real reason was Jefferson's "most singular temper." Virginia admitted that for a long time she "would not listen to the fears of the rest of the family on the subject," but was "obliged now to give them their due weight" and had "great cause to be alarmed."[13]

Upon the discovery of Jefferson's deafness, Virginia began to doubt that her two-year-old son could communicate. Earlier, "he appeared to understand what was said to him," but now that she knew he was deaf, she thought "he understands nothing but signs and uses them to express all his own ideas." To further her point, she ended a letter to her sister Jane, "I dare say Jeffie remembers [his cousin] and would be delighted to see him, but the dear little fellow has no means of expressing his remembrances." Jefferson's inability to communicate in spoken language meant that "he was very fond of sugar, but never learned to know its name" in spoken English. No longer did Virginia believe that gestures were her son's own style of communication and that he therefore had "no need for language." The social fear of deafness led Virginia to envision complete isolation of her son from his family and society.[14]

The Trists also began to treat their son as dependent and as an object of pity. When looking for a governess, Virginia acknowledged the responsibility involved. She felt "Jeffie cannot be given up to his own charge as he might if he could hear." Believing Jefferson's deafness the reason for his dependency, Virginia stated, "My poor little deaf boy requires more attention than he would do, I suppose, if he could hear." In short, his deafness "makes him backward." A family member pitied Jefferson's condition and wrote that his deafness "makes us all love him more than we should do if he was like other children."[15]

The family's concern about young Jefferson's supposed helplessness soon changed. He became a pest, too strong-willed for his own good. The boy's active nature and "independent habits" made him "so venturesome that he is never safe alone." Virginia reported that Jefferson could "now lock and unlock every door in the house." Once he disturbed the family "by locking himself up in a room alone," unable to hear their cries and unable to see their gestures explaining how to open the door. More often, said Virginia, "we . . . found *ourselves* bolted in the parlor by him." At other times he put himself in danger trying to descend into the cellar "in complete darkness and without banisters." His independence, however, merely confirmed the need for a good governess: "Poor little fellow, he is much more troublesome, and requires much more looking after than if he could hear."[16]

One of Jefferson's aunts expressed to the Trists that she hoped "most sincerely your fears about dear little Jefferson" and his inability to hear "may be unfounded." She rationalized that "children are often so slow in the development of their facilities that it is difficult to judge by ordinary appearances. There is a family in one of the country towns near Boston in which the children do not begin to articulate before they are four or five years old." She stated that she knew "an instance of one child, the son of a gentleman here, who at four years could not pronounce a word." Jefferson, she concluded, might eventually show that he could hear.[17]

By this time, however, Virginia and Nicholas Trist had become certain of their son's deafness. After conducting "various experiments . . . to ascertain the degree" of hearing loss, the Trists felt "there is still one hope to catch at—that his deafness proceeds from an obstruction in his ears which can be removed, and not from any defect in the nerve." Virginia requested that the relatives who knew Jefferson as an infant write if they or their servants remembered having "observed in the first month of his life any sign of deafness." She explained that she remembered nothing: "I had no fears then, but I took it for granted all was as I wished." She remembered "no circumstance to excite our suspicions about his ears—no eruption, no inflammation, and no discharge" that might have made his deafness apparent earlier.[18]

One of Virginia's sisters said she did not believe Jefferson was Deaf as an infant. She was "sure his attention was then attracted by sounds." Another family member felt "he was not *born* deaf," for she remembered Jefferson "starting at the clapping to of a door and the firing of a pistol in the yard." Although the Trists did not realize it, Jefferson's response to sounds may have been a Deaf child's reaction to vibration rather than sound. These anecdotes therefore could not demonstrate beyond doubt that his deafness was acquired rather than congenital.[19]

Claiming that Jefferson's deafness was acquired, whether true or not, allowed the Trists to believe that a cure could be found. They began to discuss Jefferson's case with doctors around the country. One physician from New York, upon the receipt of ten dollars "as a fee for advise respecting your son," suggested that Virginia and Nicholas tilt Jefferson's head to one side and, using a syringe, fill his ear with sweet almond oil. He added that "there are however no objections to syringing with soap-suds, which may sometimes be more convenient and agreeable." Virginia reported that at the onset of treatment, Jefferson "would lie quite still and close his eyes during the operation of the syringing." The oil allowed the "little scales and scabs to be extracted" from Jefferson's ears. The treatment, continued about a year, was finally abandoned when the boy "appeared to dislike it." Virginia suspected sometimes that the treatment "gave him pain."[20]

The Trists also tried the home therapy of rubbing table salt into Jefferson's hair. After massaging in the salt, Virginia would "bound a silk handkerchief around his head" and put him to bed. When he awoke in the morning, she "brushed out the salt." After eight months, "little blisters appeared on his head, which made it quite sore," so she discontinued the therapy. It too did not work.[21]

Soon, another therapy was sought. When Nicholas Trist took his daughter to Philadelphia to have her tonsils removed, the family decided he should also take Jefferson. They hoped the physician, Dr. Physick, who would treat Martha, might be able to help their little son as well. On the trip to Philadelphia to see the doctor, Jefferson was "lost in wonder, at the thousand new objects which have crowded upon him" and he "behaved to a charm." But the doctor was "too much engrossed" with Martha (called Pat and Pattie as a child) and her tonsils that he had little time for Jefferson. Nicholas wrote that the doctor had "not been able to give even a good look into Jefferson's ears." As Nicholas explained to his wife, the physician's "interest in Pat is enough for him to bear for the moment."[22]

When Pattie began to improve from tonsil surgery and Dr. Physick was "perfectly satisfied" with her case, he turned his attention to Jefferson. Because of the cloudy weather, he could not see well into the boy's ears. Nicholas reported to his wife that "the Dr. said 'it seems the sun is never going to shine again.' We shall have to wait for a change in this respect before this chance can be even looked into: and it is now raining." Virginia doubted the physician could cure Jefferson's deafness: "I fear nothing can be done to his poor ears." Although she had "little or no hope" that "anything can be done for Jeffie," she awaited the doctor's report with "suspense."[23]

When the weather improved, and "the sun shone into both Jefferson's ears," the doctor could "see the *drums,* which he had hoped he should not be able to do." If the eardrum had been blocked from view, the deafness might be the result of obstruction that could be removed. In that case, "there would have been some hope." Because he saw no obstruction, the doctor told Nicholas there was little possibility for cure. He also reprimanded him for not bringing Jefferson in sooner: "Could it have been known in time, it might possibly have been remedied."[24]

Dr. Physick suspected that Jefferson's deafness was caused by "the pressure of some of the secretion (when he had those violent colds in his head) upon his nerves, which have thus been destroyed," reported Nicholas. "The pressure was probably the cause of his fits of screaming." The physician claimed he had restored the hearing of another child who had lost it by the same means. He proposed to use "strong purgatives" to cure the case. Nicholas and Virginia apparently decided against the treatments. Similarly, although Nicholas asked Virginia to explore the possibility of "applying galvanism upon the ear," existing letters do not document any further conversation about it.[25]

e⁓

During the 1850s, Henry and Fanny Lawrence of Louisiana also responded to deafness in four of their children by searching for a cure. Family members and friends recommended a variety of doctors and particular remedies. Fanny's sister-in-law warned her that the doctor she knew of would be unable to cure the children, "although he can cure stammering and deafness from colds but not in natural deafness or mutes." Despite this warning, the Lawrences continued to search for a cure for another year. While Henry was traveling, he saw a report that seemed promising. "I send thee a letter about a Lady being cured of Blindness," he told Fanny. The doctor's cure of a sensory deficit like blindness, Henry thought, suggested that the doctor might be able to cure the children's deafness. Because of his hope, Henry wrote, "I shall go to see this man and have a talk with him." He took his two oldest sons with him. As the months passed, Henry's hopes turned sour. To Fanny he reported, "I hoped ere this that I should have had some good account to give thee about our little boys, but as yet I cannot see any change." The doctor suggested that the reason for his failure to cure the children was Henry's doubts: Henry explained that the doctor had "no doubt I have no faith at all but live on hope. But my fears are stronger than my faith." Although Henry felt that the doctor used "fairly rational means" and "ought to make them hear if there is anything to hear with," he could not let go of his suspicions: "I fear to say what I think of him." He decided to continue with the children's treatments. Although his belief in the treatments was failing, he did not yet abandon his dream: "I am sad but I hope on."[26]

ℰ

After years of research, the Lawrences and the Tillinghasts recognized that their efforts were not likely to be successful and that their hopes for hearing children must end. They decided to seek out educational opportunities for their Deaf children instead. But some families continued to search for cures even after their children had begun their education.

As Jefferson Trist's family began to explore the Pennsylvania school for the Deaf in Philadelphia, Nicholas and Virginia were still searching for a cure for their son's deafness. They investigated the promises of Dr. Togno of Philadelphia. Virginia told her husband, "He says he cures half the cases" of deaf children that come to him. A family friend who knew Togno insisted that the doctor was prone to exaggeration. As she reported to Virginia, Togno "had about a hundred" cases, but only "made two cures." When Virginia arranged her first meeting with Dr. Togno, he promised to bring "the little boy he has (he says) cured." She did not hide her skepticism from her husband.[27]

Dr. Togno was "deeply interested" and "extremely anxious" to "experiment upon" Jefferson, primarily because the boy was the great-grandson of Thomas Jefferson. Togno was interested in young Jefferson's case not because of some "disinterested administration that he feels for Mr. Jefferson," nor for financial reasons. Instead, he suspected that successfully treating the child would bring him fame and "eclat."[28]

At the first meeting with Dr. Togno, Virginia discovered that he refused to "attend a child placed at the asylum." He claimed that the directors of the school were "his enemies" and "inimical to him" because his cures would put the school out of business. "He fancies because of his business of curing the deaf," wrote Virginia, that he "would diminish the numbers that go to the asylum by fitting them for other schools." The doctor's defensive suspicions concerned Virginia: "This, I think, shows what sort of man he is." Nevertheless, she felt, considering her husband's hopes, that "if [Togno] can do Jefferson any good," it was worth the risk of dealing with the difficult man. The Trists determined to enroll Jefferson in the school for the Deaf for a few months. At some point Jefferson would be removed to undergo Togno's promised therapy, as yet still undiscussed with the Trists. Nicholas agreed to wait a few months until spring to begin Jefferson's treatment, as long as Togno would "*see* him and examine him once" before the wait.[29]

The evening before Jefferson was to enroll at the school for the Deaf, Virginia discussed his case with a family friend. The friend had previously met Alfred Greene, "the child Dr. Togno has cured of deafness," and found his case "a very interesting one." He advised Virginia not to enroll her Deaf son at the school quite yet, but meet with Dr. Togno "immediately."[30]

That evening, the doctor was invited to dinner with the Trist family. He explained his medical procedures to Virginia, who passed on the information to her husband: "Dr. Togno spoke of two operations, that of the eustachyon [*sic*] tube," with which she was familiar, "and another—I understand him piercing the tympanum." She was shocked by the violence of the procedure. Nicholas insisted that Virginia "let it be distinctly understood that there is to be no *experimenting*" in their son's case. Because there was no definitive treatment for deafness, Togno knew he *must* use experimental procedures. Friends in the medical profession urged her not to agree to the piercing of the eardrum, advising her "not to consent to anything but the operation on the eustachyon tube." Another urged her to "take the child at once to the asylum" rather than submit Jefferson to Togno's treatments.[31]

Virginia Trist considered the options. She determined to postpone Jefferson's treatments for at least a few months. Her decisions were based partly on the opinions of others, but also because she had strong doubts herself about Dr. Togno. She suspected that he was primarily interested in treating Jefferson because he wanted "to make a job of it," gaining both fame and fortune for himself. She also doubted his academic work. "I have read his last report," wrote Virginia, "but I am told he cannot be relied on for truth even in his publications." She also resented Togno's manipulation of her emotions. The doctor "claimed acquaintance" with her, although Virginia did not remember "ever to have seen him." Finally, she was furious that he claimed to be from Virginia even though she suspected Togno was "not a Virginian by *birth*." Her views, in sum, were that Togno "must be employed with caution, that the truth of his statements cannot be relied on, though published, and moreover that he wants to make a job and get as much money as he can out of us."[32]

Although Virginia was suspicious of the doctor and not very hopeful that he could cure her son's deafness, Nicholas continued to trust that Togno could change Jefferson into a hearing child. He instructed his wife to pay the man for any services he performed. "Should he effect a cure," wrote Nicholas to his wife, "I would without a grudge give him *thousands,* could I afford it." He continued, "Should he return Jefferson to hearing at all . . . and ask for not more than $500, pay it to him." If he should "*fail* to do anything for Jefferson," an unlikely outcome in his opinion, Nicholas instructed Virginia to ask her physician friends about the "propriety of the charge" before paying the bill.[33]

Virginia continued to be frustrated with Dr. Togno. She tried to explain to Nicholas that the physician "was thought to be an extortionist." Her husband did not seem to share her deep concerns. He continued to pepper his letters with requests for information about Jefferson's treatment. "How I should like to know all about Dr. Togno and our darling Jefferson up to this moment!" wrote Nicholas. A few weeks later he confronted his wife with her silence: "You say nothing of Dr. Togno." He insisted that her next letter to him must answer his questions.[34]

Virginia tried again to explain her concern to her husband. "Dr. Togno is thought nothing of here," she wrote, "and his advertisements are said to be falsehood from beginning to end." She repeated that family friends, among them trained physicians, advised her against working with Togno and "spoke disapprovingly of him."[35]

Despite his wife's distrust, Nicholas felt that exploring Togno's claims once more was in order. He advised Virginia to consult Dr. Thomas Harris regarding Togno's expertise and reputation. Although Dr. Harris was "one of those cautious persons who never advises you *decidedly* one way or the other," Virginia thought, he nevertheless offered his negative views, "plainly enough stated," of Togno. She reported to her husband that Dr. Harris "discourages my putting the child into his hands" because he felt Togno to be "the greatest 'humbug' (his own expressions) that ever had been known before in Philadelphia." He told Virginia that "in four years he had never heard of Dr. T's doing good in a single case." Dr. Harris further explained his disregard by telling of a young man treated by Togno. Although Togno counted him as one of his complete successes, the young man himself "said he had not been benefited in the smallest degree by Dr. T." Harris went on to say that he "had never known instance of the operation on the Eustachy-on [*sic*] tube giving relief in any degree."[36]

Virginia defended her own views: she felt they were "justified by [Harris's] opinions and the many *warnings* against Dr. T's practice which I received from persons noways interested one way or the other." She knew her husband would be more upset than she was: "*You* will feel disappointed because you had hopes; *I* never felt *any* hope myself." Virginia concluded that if Nicholas were to "disapprove of my decision," he could act otherwise to Togno when he next returned to Philadelphia. But by the time he arrived in Philadelphia, Jefferson had made great headway in his studies at the school, and deafness no longer seemed such an enormous tragedy to the Trists. Finally, Nicholas heeded Virginia's advice to abandon Dr. Togno's promises.[37]

Unlike the Tillinghasts, Lawrences, and Trists, the account of the Martins of New Orleans comes from the letters of the Deaf child herself, giving historians a chance to understand Deaf children's own ideas about deafness and parental attempts at cure. In 1836, when Ellen Martin began to attend the Pennsylvania school for the Deaf in Pennsylvania, her mother took Ellen to Dr. Togno, the same physician the Trists consulted. He attempted to, as Ellen wrote her cousin, "restore me to my hearing, but all in vain." Her mother agreed to pay the doctor six hundred dollars "if he was so fortunate as to cure my deafness." In addition to curing her, the doctor agreed to "superintend my oral instruction as long as he should think it needful." Although Ellen was born hearing and lost the ability from a childhood illness, she had not acquired significant speech before losing her hearing, and therefore would require intense speech training if she were to have any chance of speaking clearly. The doctor promised that "if he should, after a long trial, not obtain this desired result," Ellen's mother "would have to pay him only one hundred dollars after his trial was ended, for his services."[38]

The desire to cure her deafness, even after she had begun an education in sign language, was shared by her father. Ellen wrote to her cousin, "Father was so anxious that I might be restored to my hearing" that he "said that he would never regret any expense or pains it might cost to achieve as desirable result."[39]

Ellen was skeptical of the doctor's abilities. She wrote, "It was said in the city of Philadelphia that he was a quack." Although the doctor claimed he had cured a young girl of her deafness, Ellen knew better: because she had attended the American Asylum for the Deaf in Connecticut with the girl, Ellen knew "it was not so. . . . She is quite deaf and cannot hear the least sound."[40]

Ellen doubted that the doctor could cure her, but she also felt no need to find a cure. She was content with her deafness: "I assure you that I never regret being deprived of my hearing in my life, as I trust that God knows what was best, and that I am as happy as you would wish." She explained to her cousin that "if you ever visit one of the schools for the education of the Deaf and Dumb, you will find this unfortunate class of your fellow beings so happy as to make you forget that they are objects of pity." Ellen knew that pity meant that the hearing world was looking down on her: "I hate pity because it shows a want of good manners."[41]

Ellen, however, felt obliged to do what her parents wanted. "I consider it my duty to submit to my parents' will." She wrote to her cousin, "I would feel bad when I see my parents are unhappy about my being unable to hear." Perhaps because she wanted to reassure her parents, Ellen tried to find more information about other reported cures. When her cousin reported that she had heard news of a successful cure, Ellen asked for more details: "Do not forget or fail to tell me the story of that little boy whose deafness was marvelously cured when you write next." Ellen may have been interested in the information for herself. On the other hand, perhaps her request for information was only so she could better refute the claim.[42]

In order to make her parents happy, Ellen was willing to be subjected to unusual treatments by mesmerists. When a man claiming to be a former Harvard professor came to New Orleans to give demonstrations, the Martins sought advice about how to treat their daughter's deafness. The doctor, wrote Ellen, "told Father that if it was only a polypus of the Nerve of the Ear, he could cause me to hear by mesmerism." The family procured his services, and he came to their home "four times and tried to mesmerize me, but could not put me in magnetic sleep. He looked disappointed." The doctor, however, claimed to be optimistic: "He said that he thought it very likely that he would succeed when I should be tried again and that he would come in again as soon as he gained so much strength as I required." Ellen suspected that the doctor knew he would not succeed. As she said, "He has not yet come in to try me again; perhaps he concluded to forget his engagement."[43]

Ellen knew that people's hopes and fears were being manipulated. She wrote, "I do not believe in this so-called mysterious science, notwithstanding the astonishing experiments I have both witnessed and heard of. There can be no doubt that those who deliver lectures and perform wonderful experiments in illustration of mesmerism are nothing but impostors." She knew that her parents were so desperate to have her cured of her deafness that they could be easily convinced: "Even well disposed persons (among whom are my parents) have sincerely believed it." Ellen wrote to experts for more information. She asked one noted gentleman about a practitioner "who, papers say, has restored the Deaf mutes to their hearing in several instances." What she found out only confirmed her skepticism: the gentleman did not believe that magnetism could cure deafness.[44]

Perhaps Ellen's parents continued to seek a cure even after she was older and educated because she was female. The Martins may have been concerned that Ellen's primary means of maintaining her elite lifestyle—marriage into another wealthy family—was impossible. A privileged hearing man, they may have thought, would never choose a Deaf wife. She might always be dependent upon her parents and friends. On the other hand, most parents thought that Deaf males would be able to support themselves as adults through manual labor, even if they could not maintain an elite lifestyle.[45]

e⌒

Many elite southerners were disturbed about the condition of their Deaf children. Because few had exposure to Deaf adults, most hearing parents accepted the widespread assumption that Deaf people were defective, morally underdeveloped, or even childlike. The parents were afraid their children would face a life of dependence. In addition, they knew that communication with their children would be difficult, if not impossible. Because of their families' fears, and the "credulity of tender-hearted parents," Deaf children were dragged to doctors and others who claimed they could cure deafness for experimentation. Parents were not ready to learn sign language themselves or provide education for their children in their formative years. In the long run, this search for a cure often served to further alienate Deaf children from their families.[46]

CHAPTER 3

ℰ Glad Tidings of Release to the Prisoners of Silence

The belief by antebellum medical thinkers that most deafness was the result of a physical obstruction had a cultural analogy. Parents and other hearing members of society were fearful that their children would be closed off from the world—not only physically but socially, religiously, and academically. Most antebellum parents eventually gave up their attempts to find a medical cure for their Deaf children, but they continued to worry about the social and intellectual effects of deafness on their children.

Families continued to believe that deafness was "a great privation." But they also believed that their children's deafness had been determined by God, no matter how mysterious or even illogical the decision might sometimes seem to humans. Robina Norwood, for example, suspected that God had deafened her grandson so he would not have to hear the "wickedness and folly in the world" and all the talk that was "both painful and dangerous to hear." Perhaps she found solace in a Bible story. When God tells Moses to share God's word with the Israelites, Moses protests, saying that he is unable to do it because he is "slow of speech" and "of slow tongue"— that he has a speech defect. God responds to Moses, "Who hath made man's mouth? or who maketh the dumb, or deaf, or the seeing, or the blind? Have not I the Lord?" God chooses Moses with his flawed body to be a holy representative. Although Robina did not know God's reasons, she knew that "God has given to all His creatures what He knows to be best for them." With that belief, parents began to accept that their children's deafness was permanent.[1]

Hearing parents of Deaf children quickly realized that the major difficulty they faced with their children was effective communication. As one advocate for Deaf people wrote, "It is not easy to persuade ourselves that thousands grow to manhood by our firesides in as total ignorance of the language which is spoken there, as that of which is spoken around the hearthstone of the Chinese." Hearing parents could not use spoken language with their Deaf children. But, as the earliest book on deafness published in the United States said, "nature . . . has not proved herself such a cruel stepmother as to throw these children of misfortune upon the world without a language." Deaf people had the language of signs. Deaf author John Burnet felt that Deaf people used sign language "not because deaf and dumb children were born, more than others, with any peculiar facility for making signs." The language of signs, he claimed, was "a universal language" that all people who "observed nature and her operations" could use. Burnet believed that hearing people, "having acquired and exclusively used, in speech, a more perfect and convenient language," had "forgotten this natural language."[2]

Burnet argued that hearing parents, especially mothers, knew the language of signs, whether or not they realized it. He felt that mothers knew "*two* languages, one for the *ear,* and the other for the *eye.*" A mother could "talk with her eyes" by "looks and gestures" that both Deaf and hearing children could understand. Through her natural behavior, Burnet claimed, mothers "daily and hourly, held intelligible conversation" with their children.[3]

Burnet believed that mothers bore the responsibility for advanced communication with their Deaf children. Although both men and women had access to the language of signs, Burnet expected women to learn to use it well. Mothers usually took primary responsibility for the daily welfare of young children, and they had more time to devote to the skill. They were also, he believed, less tied to the world of abstraction than men. Women were, "if any are," more "capable of becoming *ears to the deaf and a tongue to the dumb.*"[4]

In order to improve their communication with Deaf children, Burnet suggested that the mothers "endeavor . . . to forget *words* and think only of *things*, become for the time dumb." When they could not use words, they would be forced to turn to the physical language of the body—of facial expressions, gestures, and mimicry—to communicate. Precise imitation would require close observation of the "spontaneous expressions of the feelings and passions in the countenance" and "those gestures which nature prompts us to make." In addition, mothers should look for "clear and well defined ideas of the forms, qualities, and uses" of household objects and "the characteristic circumstances" of actions so they could "cultivate the faculty of *imitation*" in their signs. Said one teacher of the Deaf, "It is no difficult thing to invent a sign for visible objects and actions." Other advocates of parental sign suggested specific signs for basic concepts. HARD, for example, was signed "by striking the knuckles of the clenched fist on the back of the left hand, with the suitable and natural expression of countenance accompanying the action." After the family initiated the use of a sign, the child would learn its meaning quickly. Authorities promised that after a few repetitions, the child would adopt those signs.[5]

The "home sign" used by families was often initiated not by mothers but by Deaf children themselves as they tried to express basic needs to their parents. A few advocates for Deaf people recognized the children's abilities: although "the natural language of the deaf and dumb" might be very limited in uneducated Deaf children, their knowledge was "sufficient to enable them to make known their wants." For example, if the child was thirsty, he or she might imitate the action of drinking from a cup. When hungry, the child might move his mouth as if chewing. As the child became more aware of the world and its processes, the signs could become more elaborate. For example, when the child saw a cow being milked, or water being drawn from a well, perhaps he or she might mime those actions to distinguish between milk and water.[6]

Signs to represent specific family members and friends were also quickly developed. When Fanny Lawrence showed her Deaf son Robert a handkerchief belonging to his aunt, he immediately made his sign for her. Having name signs for family members connected Deaf children, at least to a degree, to their parents and siblings. The name signs were usually determined by the child by physical characteristics of the individual. Often the chosen characteristic was a birthmark, a scar, a dimple, or some other physical marker. The sign might refer to unusual clothing, typical behavior, and so on. Even when the concrete reference no longer applied (for example, when a funny hat was removed), name signs already established by the child generally remained. Thomas Tillinghast, for example, designated his uncle Paris "by the sign of puffing out smoke from a pipe or segar [cigar]." To represent another gentleman, the boy stood up very straight and held out his chin, "which was very characteristic of that gentleman." By pointing to his fingers and ears, Thomas signified "some lady . . . by her wearing rings etc. etc."[7]

The universal language that children were supposedly born knowing— like the "spontaneous expression of sentiment" of "the savage of America or Africa" to which it was compared—was not American Sign Language. The communication between hearing parents and Deaf children was, in fact, not a true language but a collection of gestures, mimicry, and a few agreed-upon signs to describe basic ideas. Home sign was not "that beautiful, expressive, and figurative language, which, in a community of intelligent mutes, fully supplies the place of speech."[8]

Home sign had significant limits. Deaf children alone in a hearing family used "only a rude, confused, and most imperfect method of expressing their ideas." Parents typically had more difficulty conveying information than their Deaf children did. They often could not easily explain abstract thoughts or unexpected events to their Deaf children. Using home sign, children found it difficult to understand "every thing beyond their immediate vision" and were often unable to perceive "the causes of phenomena of much that they see and feel" because their parents could not explain them. For example, when Jefferson Trist's father traveled away from home, the boy was confused. When his father's "cup was taken out at breakfast for Sister Ellen," young Jefferson "made signs" insisting that it was not her cup, explaining that his father always "drank . . . coffee out of it," by repeatedly pointing to his father's usual breakfast seat. He had witnessed his father's departure, and gave an account of the departure to his family "very clearly by his signs." Jefferson walked to the window and pointed "to the river, moving his fingers along in the direction the boat went." His mother wrote to his father that when the family still could not explain what had happened, he "gave the account of your going away to us again," starting with "your going out the front door and getting into the carriage." Jefferson was frustrated, and "expressed much feeling on the subject." But his family could not explain to him why his father had left them and that he would later return.[9]

When Jefferson's mother suspected that the salt massages she applied to his head every evening, believed to be a cure for deafness, might be causing her son to develop blisters and scabs, she could not explain to Jefferson why she was discontinuing them. Her son "was very much distressed at the omission" and "made signs to have it done, and expressed discontent at my persisting in putting him to bed without it." He believed that his mother was simply forgetting his bedtime ritual. Their difficulties communicating with each other were similar to the difficulties faced by most Deaf children and hearing parents. Hearing parents and Deaf children often felt frustrated with each other, especially as the children matured and could not share their complex thoughts with their parents.[10]

Advocates for Deaf education extended a promise to the parents of Deaf children—and to state legislatures. Education offered a remedy for the social and intellectual blockage that medicine could not provide. Schooling offered a "priceless benefit" for Deaf children in their future lives. It promised to "unfold and enlighten the darkened and dormant intellect of the deaf mute." Advocates for Deaf people suggested a variety of reasons why families should make arrangements to educate their children.[11]

In the evangelical atmosphere of the South, the rhetoric of redemption was often used to describe the promise of education for Deaf children. Hearing southerners said that Deaf children could be "redeemed from the burden of ignorance" and "have light shed into their minds, receiving the blessings of education." This "light of knowledge" allowed the transition of Deaf people from a spiritual darkness into immortality. Learning encouraged Deaf students to grow just "as a plant in the dark stretches its branches to the solitary opening which lets in the light of heaven."[12]

Educators, argued hearing observers, had the job of "raising [Deaf people] up from their degradation, and placing within their reach the aims and hopes of rational and immortal beings." With education, they could be redeemed and regenerated. A Deaf person could "rise to the majestic contemplation of the character and attributes of the Supreme Head of the universe" and even become a "fit being to bear the likeness of his God."[13]

The education of Deaf people and their religious redemption were linked because these hearing southerners assumed that an understanding of Christianity was not exclusively experiential or merely inspired; it must be taught to rational beings. Only the ability to read the Bible and learn "its blessed teachings" could provide Deaf people with "a knowledge of the truths of Christianity and of the glorious plan of redemption." This textual education in Christianity would, according to hearing observers, allow a Deaf person to "fit himself for a higher and holier existence." Because this kind of education "renovates and elevates their whole being," Deaf people would "understand their duties . . . to God who made them, and the Savior who redeemed them."[14]

Hearing southerners painted a frightening picture of uneducated Deaf people. Without education, wrote one, "prison bolts may be broken, and dungeon bars be rent asunder, and the demon in human form is free to hold his remorseless orgies over the mutilated remains of the hapless victim of his passions." But when teachers gave a Deaf person education, they would "train the heart to feel" and create "a being impersonating the image of his Maker." Education would provide Deaf people with moral principles to keep the monster in check. As one observer wrote, "there is no prison bolt so strong nor dungeon bar so restraining" as education.[15]

Using the same metaphor, hearing southerners described the education of Deaf people with the rhetoric of release from imprisonment. Their minds were bound by "shackles which nature had imposed on mind and body," but through education, "their fetters can be unloosed." Through education, they were "not hopelessly imprisoned" in the dark prisons of deafness imagined by the hearing. The experience of learning would leave "their minds unchained" and the students rescued from enslavement.[16]

Hearing southerners genuinely believed that Deaf people had minds "as blank as a sheet of paper" and felt that only through the help of parents and teachers could Deaf children become full human beings. Hearing people often felt God commanded them to "discharge a duty to these unfortunates," the duty of teaching. Hearing people's sense of duty was based on their pity for Deaf people. Said one hearing observer: "Surely, if any individuals deserve our warmest sympathy and most strenuous efforts in their behalf, they do." Proponents of education for Deaf children suggested that it was incumbent upon hearing people to alleviate deprivation. Nevertheless, hearing observers felt that those people "bereaved of the usual inlet to mental light and activity" were so quickly "sinking into dormant inertness" that it was "always difficult, and sometimes almost impossible, to arouse them." At the beginning of the quest for learning, said hearing proponents, "the pupil is entirely dependent . . . for every idea." Only years of training could put a Deaf person on the road to independence.[17]

Many southern educators argued that education would enable Deaf children to be useful. Without training, a Deaf boy was "an encumbrance and a mere consumer of the fruit of other's industry." Uneducated Deaf people, claimed most advocates, could never be "*producers* in the body politic." And because they could not support themselves, they were a burden to the public. Of course, acknowledged proponents of the education of the Deaf, a good education "increases the usefulness of every class of men"—but with Deaf people it was far more true. "The usefulness of the deaf" was "*created* by education." With adequate instruction, Deaf children could provide for themselves instead of rely on state coffers.[18]

One professional educator advised parents to "let the mute be brought up like his [hearing] brothers and sisters to activity, self-reliance and effort." They would grow up to be "independent and self reliant" and "begging alms from nobody." But even greater than the lesson of independence was the lesson of interdependence. Through education, these children could become members of society and would begin to understand the relations and "responsibilities which man sustains to his fellow man." In short, these long-pitied children could, with education, be recast into citizens.[19]

Southerners also used the rhetoric of equality when they discussed the opportunities that education offered Deaf people. "Give them the advantages of a course of instruction," said one petitioner for Deaf education, "and they are placed nearly on an equality with others." Children labeled as unfortunate could be "elevated to the scale of social and intellectual being" by receiving instruction. Even "the most ignorant mute," said one advocate of Deaf education, could through education be "transformed into an intelligent, interesting companion." Such training could "raise the . . . deaf to the level of other men" and then they could "be permitted to walk forth as companions with the most gifted of our race." In short, a Deaf man, provided with education, could "stand proudly up, a peer among his fellow men, feeling himself A MAN." The entire demeanor of this educated mute could be transformed into that of a southern gentleman: he could "be pleasing and ever fascinating by elegance of manner, by the beauty and grace of his gestures, by the intelligent expression of his countenance, by the cultivated quickness of his perceptive faculties, by the skillful use of the pen, and even by the elegance and beauty of his language."[20]

According to advocates, education also promised happiness to Deaf children and their families. Hearing southerners' fears of the "moody and sullen dispositions" of uneducated Deaf people could be relieved by providing them with instruction. Deaf people, said educators, could be "rendered contented and cheerful." They would enter "into a new and joyful world." Even a few months of teaching, promised one writer, "imparts a new aspect of cheerfulness and intelligence to the countenance." For Deaf students, "a thousand new sources of happiness opened up." They could "revel in the boundless charms which nature yields to her votaries" to which the uneducated Deaf person had no access. Hearing advocates of Deaf education promised parents of Deaf children to ameliorate their "unfortunate condition until half its bitterness is forgotten." Much of that bitterness was felt by hearing parents, not by the Deaf children themselves. Advocates acknowledged that fact directly. In addition to allowing the child "grow up . . . happy," education "carr[ied] joy to many a fire-side circle." In short, "the degree of consolation and delight with education . . . imparts to the family . . . is great, and not to be estimated in dollars and cents."[21]

Marianne Jewell Memorial Library
Baker College of Muskegon
Muskegon, Michigan 49442

CHAPTER 4

ᏋᏉ Guide His Hand

WHEN SAMUEL AND JANE TILLINGHAST realized that they would not find a medical cure for their three-year-old son Thomas, they began to research a variety of educational options. Uncle J. H. Norwood, on his trip to New York, began his investigations at the New York school for the Deaf. As he wrote Samuel, "I visited the Deaf and Dumb Asylum and had much conversation with the principal." He forwarded three pamphlets, "all the information . . . which can be imparted upon the subject." Principal Harvey Peet and other administrators and teachers at the New York school told Norwood that it was "not absolutely necessary" to send Deaf children "to such institutions before 14 or 15" years of age, "but that where the friends can afford the expense, the child is best off in a good institution at 8 or 10." Although administrators recognized that "much must depend upon the chance he has at home," they claimed that no matter how extensive his opportunities, "he can't be so well off as at a good institution." They argued that "his intellectual, moral, and physical education" could be undertaken there and that Thomas would have more opportunities for conversation in sign language with other Deaf youngsters.[1]

One of the pamphlets suggested methods of educating a Deaf child at home prior to formal schooling. "They advise that he be taught as soon as possible to write," Norwood told Thomas's parents. "The mode of doing this is obvious—make him imitate and sometimes guide his hand." By using the picture books he forwarded from the school, the parents could point to the picture—or an object in the room—then to its printed English name. "In this way he may be able to point out the name of an object without knowing a letter," claimed Norwood. Memorizing the alphabet would "require time," but learning to recognize a series of shapes could happen more quickly.[2]

According to Norwood's sources, Thomas's education at home should include a wide variety of subjects. "You must show him everything that you can," especially visually oriented skills such as art: "He should have pictures and be taught in good time to draw." Although knowledge of some abstract ideas might be confusing to Thomas, "give him time to examine and understand them," recommended Uncle Norwood, and "indeed there is nothing that is useful or ornamental or curious that may not with advantage be submitted to his examination." He ended his list of suggestions for Thomas's home education with an admonition that the boy "should be much concerned with."[3]

From the principal of the New York school for the Deaf, Uncle Norwood learned that Thomas was capable of receiving the same level of education that his brothers were expected to receive, albeit by a different method. He also began to understand that the expectations of Thomas's parents with regard to Thomas should be only slightly different from their expectations of his siblings. Although "in the management of the child he is to be like any other child, and made to submit on all occasions," Norwood stated that it was vitally important that "great care" should be used to explain parental demands by the use of mime, pictures, and facial expressions so Thomas could understand "what is wanted with him," or why he was being punished.[4]

Uncle Norwood initially forwarded the school's pamphlets to Tom's grandmother Robina Norwood. "I send them to Ma," he said, "because I know she will like to look over them and will be sure to forward them." Indeed, Robina played a significant role in the education of her Deaf grandson. She continually asked for updates on decisions affecting Tom's education: "What shall be the conclusion about dear little Tom?" She also pressured her daughter and son-in-law to provide him with an education. Uncle Norwood even proposed that "Tom ought to be committed to her charge" because she would have more time to study Deaf educational methods and begin to teach Tom. Jane and Samuel, however, do not appear to have responded to this suggestion.[5]

Following the first advice received from Uncle Norwood, the Tillinghasts considered sending Thomas to the New York school when the boy neared the age of eight. Jane told her husband that relatives, especially her mother Robina, were pressuring her to send the boy to school as quickly as possible. "Every one that sees him here thinks that he is old enough to [go to school]" and that remaining at home in North Carolina "would be an injury to him" because the family would be unable to communicate well with their son or provide him with education.[6]

The New York school apparently refused to accept Tom because of his young age. Robina Norwood read an account of the Virginia state school in Staunton, which agreed with the policy of accepting only older students: "They are not to receive pupils under ten years of age." However, the Virginia school occasionally made exceptions: "In peculiar cases the rule may be dispensed with at the discretion of the Directors." Robina kept her hopes high and considered the possibility of having Tom enrolled at the Virginia school instead. She wrote to Thomas's mother that "from the regulations I have seen of the Institution at Staunton," she believed that the directors of the school had "a discretionary power as to receiving pupils in particular instances under or over the ages prescribed by the rule" and promised that it could "easily be ascertained if you and Mr. T. wish to send him there."[7]

Although the Tillinghasts tried several times to enroll their son in the New York school, their efforts always failed. Thomas's grandmother Robina Norwood told her daughter that she felt "truly sorry to find you are *again* disappointed in sending poor Tom." Because she knew that Tom's parents—with responsibilities for their large family, a farm, and Sam's business—did not have the "power to pay him half the necessary attention," she concluded that education away from home was a necessity for the child. "I am clearly of opinion that some further effort should be made to have him placed in a situation where he may not only be taught the ordinary branches of education," she said, "but his mind and temper disciplined." A few months later, Robina Norwood expressed her frustration that her family's attempts to enroll Tom in school had repeatedly failed. "I understood you were to try to make interest to have Tom received at NY—how did that turn out?" she questioned her son-in-law. She continued, "As I heard nothing of him going I presume the application was unsuccessful." Her frustration with the process led her to even more concern about her grandson's state: "I feel quite uneasy about him."[8]

Robina Norwood pointedly told her daughter that if Tom were not going to be sent to school, he needed serious instruction at home by someone more devoted to his education than Jane seemed to be. She was convinced that "a boy of [Tom's] capacity who had anyone to attend to him, who felt sufficient interest in him to devote themselves to his instruction &c., could easily be taught a great deal at home, and if could be so governed and instructed, there would be no loss of time. . . . I cannot bear the idea of his remaining in his present state for such a length of time."[9]

Robina Norwood once again firmly suggested that if his parents could not (or would not) "devote themselves" to Tom's education, he should be sent to a state residential school, even if it was not the prestigious New York school. "I know it is the opinion of every one of your friends here that he ought to be sent to some institution as soon as possible," she reminded the Tillinghasts. "Perhaps taking everything into consideration," she counseled, "since you are disappointed in sending him to New York," the family should explore the Virginia school. She told her daughter that she should "write or I will do it." Robina wanted to "ascertain all necessary particulars" of admission to the school, "and especially if any provision is made for boys of his age etc. as they would require more particular attention than older ones." Robina realized that the additional dependency of youngsters was "the only reason why they don't like them so young." Nevertheless, she felt, it was a great defect in the school, because "a child of that age, who is deprived by his peculiar infirmity of the common means of acquiring knowledge, has more need of instruction than others and, one supposes, should begin earlier." But once again, Thomas did not begin at a state school, either because of the school's policies or because of his parents' preferences.[10]

By the end of 1841, the Tillinghasts began to consider educational opportunities for Tom other than state residential schools. Family friends approached the Ivey family of Newbern, North Carolina, and asked them to "undertake the tuition" of young Thomas, "at least so as to enable him to make signs and spell with his fingers." He would not necessarily be taught to read and write English, at least not at the beginning of his instruction. Miss Eunice, the Deaf daughter of the Ivey family, "readily and most willingly consented" to the arrangement. Eunice Ann Ivey had been educated at the New York school a few years earlier.[11]

When asked about the payment she would require from the Tillinghasts, Miss Eunice apparently deferred: according to a family friend, it was "a delicate subject with Miss E., who, I am satisfied, if governed alone by her feelings and wishes would never consent to receive any compensation for her services." However, Eunice Ivey and her mother lived alone, and "though once amongst our most respectable families," the women were now "yet poor," and relied upon children's instruction for a livelihood." Therefore Miss Eunice admitted that she wanted compensation "as may be deemed adequate to the undertaking." She would be unable to determine the exact figure she would charge to teach Tom until she was "acquainted with his habits and disposition." Another Tillinghast friend approached Eunice and again asked her price. In response, Eunice wrote on a slate that "she would talk to his Father about prices, and said she hoped she would not get disappointed for she was very anxious to see him, indeed."[12]

Eunice's mother volunteered to provide board for the youngster. "Mrs. I. boards several other children, and your son would be as much taken care of as if at home with his mother," claimed a family friend. Boarding with the Iveys would allow many more opportunities for Tom "to receive instruction every minute of the day, at the table, and on all other occasions." Eunice Ivey said that "it would be more beneficial to Thomas to be with her all the time than to go only in the day," and promised that "if she had him with her all the time" she would be able to "instruct him a great deal more."[13]

Although a family friend living in Newbern offered to take Tom in while he was in the city—saying that her family was "willing to take the dear little creature and do all that lay in our power for him"—the Tillinghasts were persuaded by the Iveys' argument that if he received education from the women, he should board with them as well. His parents inquired about her

price to board Tom during the period of his lessons. Mrs. Ivey boarded "ordinary children" for a charge of "8 to 10 dollars per month," and she promised that she would expect the same rate for the care of little Thomas if his
"habits and disposition" should be "no more than ordinary trouble." She
promised that "if Mr. Tillinghast places his son with me, I shall feel it both
a duty and a pleasure to treat the poor little *unfortunate* as my own son."[14]

Miss Eunice argued that Tom "would feel more at home . . . having a
deaf-mute for his constant companion." With Miss Eunice, Tom would always have another person with whom he could use an exclusively visual
language. She could understand the complex position that Deaf children
occupied in hearing families. And, of course, she would be the first person
to introduce Tom to the unique pleasures of Deaf society, a connection he
would feel for the rest of his life. Eunice Ivey told the Tillinghast parents
that she would be "very happy to teach your deaf mute son," because he
would also provide her with the company of another Deaf person. She
promised to "love him as her dear little brother—and be careful of and
kind to him, and be his friend." When another family friend approached
her, Miss Eunice confirmed her excitement. The friend wrote to the Tillinghasts, "I conversed with her on her slate for some time. I first asked her if
she would like to have a companion. She said yes, very much indeed and
seemed delighted at it." Eunice Ivey "did not like the idea of his not staying
there; if he came she wanted him with her."[15]

Robina Norwood was relieved that her grandson might soon receive an
education. She wrote to Jane, "I am much pleased to learn that you have
met with so good an opportunity of having dear Tommy instructed." The
position at the Iveys would be "better than, I presume, it is possible for him
to be with you, unless either of you could devote your whole attention to
him," which the Tillinghasts were still unable or unwilling to do. Robina
Norwood tried to persuade her daughter to send Tom: "I do think such an
opening ought not to be neglected. He may gain a great deal in the few
months you could allow him to stay at Newbern." Robina suggested that
Tom's mother could travel to Newbern and "get acquainted with the Lady"
that would teach him. Leaving the Deaf youngster alone away from his
family did not concern the grandmother very much, as family friends
could "take some account of him" while he was in Newbern. And the visit

that Robina proposed for Jane would allow her to see some of her relatives and friends in Newbern, allowing her to "be able to make some interest for him." Robina suspected, however, that her daughter would not go: "I suppose you could not leave home."[16]

Although it is not entirely clear from the family's letters if Tom went to the Iveys, he probably spent a few months with the mother and daughter before the Tillinghasts finally arranged to enroll him in a residential state school. In May of 1842, Tom began his years at the Virginia school.[17]

Like the Tillinghast family, the Trists of Virginia sought advice from Harvey Peet, principal of the New York school for the Deaf, about how they should treat their young son Jefferson. In 1834 Virginia Trist wrote to her husband, then in Cuba, that a family friend "went to visit the Institution for the Deaf and Dumb, which is at the distance of 4 miles from the City, on a commanding and healthy situation" to inquire how Deaf youngsters could best be educated.[18]

Harvey Peet suggested that Jefferson begin learning to read and write. The principal explained that "there were no elementary books adapted to beginners" in existence yet. He forwarded a "symbolical primer" and recommend its use, but also suggested that "at the same time that the child is learning with the Primer 'the combinations' of letters . . . he should be taught the order in which they follow in the alphabet." Virginia Trist felt that it would not be confusing to Jefferson since "the sound of the letter" was the same in the alphabet and "when combined in words." Jefferson's mother did not yet comprehend that her son's understanding of the alphabet and written language could never be based on the sound of the letters. Instead, he would depend on the look of the letters—on the page, on the hands, and occasionally on the lips. Although Virginia Trist did not yet understand much about the learning styles of Deaf children, she did show that she was aware of some pedagogical theory and was eager to learn more. She asked her friend in New York to try to obtain "the works of Sicard and the other father of the system" of sign language, but the gentleman told her the books were "not to be got" in the city.[19]

The Trist family began their son's education at home along with his hearing siblings. "Seeing all the other children learning," said Virginia Trist, "has inspired him with a desire to learn also." But she warned her husband that she was unsure how effective the plan would be: "it remains to be seen whether this will be easily directed." Although she had "made several attempts with Jefferson and his book," she could not yet "judge what the difficulties are to be."[20]

Virginia thought that Jefferson could "soon learn to read some of the words I have shown him under the pictures" in the book sent from New York. Reading, she believed, could only follow learning the printed letters of the alphabet, and Jefferson was "very fond of making the two or three letters he has learnt." He was also "eager to make others whenever he sees the alphabet." Virginia Trist knew that Jefferson (along with his hearing siblings) could confuse letters printed in books with the hand-printed variety. She determined to teach him from the school's book until Jefferson had "learnt pretty well what the printed meant" before she taught him to write himself.[21]

Jefferson was also beginning to learn the manual alphabet (fingerspelling)—handshapes used to represent English letters. Because the Trist family was probably unfamiliar with the manual alphabet before receiving information from Harvey Peet, they were unable to reinforce his lessons in fingerspelling to the same degree they could reinforce written English.[22]

Occasionally Virginia Trist became frustrated with her son's progress. She wrote to her husband, "Our dear little Jeffie has not made much progress in learning." While she was convinced that Jefferson was "very intent on learning at times," she felt that it was "difficult to confine his attention to the one little picture and the letters belonging to it." Although she thought he was "aware that the letters printed in the book express the same thing with the picture" and suspected he knew "the letters can be represented by signs made with his fingers," the boy had "forgotten the two or three letters he could make on his fingers, and never learnt the corresponding ones in the book," his mother lamented. Jefferson was sometimes difficult to control, his mother felt. He had "ideas of his own" that frequently kept him from sitting still and learning what she wished to teach. He was "so animated in his endeavors to make us follow his own method" that he frequently gave "great trouble" to the other members of his learning group.[23]

Although Jefferson knew "one or two words" after a few months of training, he was "apt to misplace the letters in them." Learning English spelling was easier for Jefferson's hearing siblings since they could rely on sounding out the words, utilizing their understanding of phonetics to determine the accurate spelling of words. But for Jefferson, learning English spelling depended to a much larger degree on rote memorization of the order of the letters.[24]

Virginia Trist assured her husband that once their son "gets fairly under way, I think he will learn quickly." Although "the task will be difficult enough" and "the progress slow" enough to try her patience, Virginia hoped that "the beginning is the hardest part," and as he progressed it would become easier to teach him. In less than a month, she reported to her husband that hard work had led to some successes: "We are getting Jeffie slowly through the first difficulties, and I think after he is a little more advanced he will learn quickly; the difficulties certainly are sensibly diminished." After two weeks, she wrote with even more optimism, "I have rather more encouraging accounts to give you of dear Jeffie's education now than I have had before." She was charmed with the boy's efforts and told his absent father that Jefferson's "little hands look so sweet making the letters" of the manual alphabet.[25]

Virginia Trist taught her son to spell by pointing out "the word under the picture, shewing [sic] him at the same time the object it represents." After he learned to associate the words with their meaning, she then made "him spell the same words arranged in little columns without the pictures." Typically she required him to fingerspell the word. Jefferson often responded with enthusiasm to the lessons using sign language: "he forms the letters with his little fingers as fast as I can point to them." However, Virginia noticed that Jefferson's understanding often required concrete connections between the words and objects. For example, when Jefferson came across "the word 'Fly' in his lessons," Virginia and her other children had to wait, she said, as "he runs and catches a fly and holds it out in his left hand while he spells the word with his right." Although sometimes exasperated with his antics, Virginia was also amused, as when Jefferson "caught a gnat and brought it to me and spelt fly; I suppose he thought it was a very small fly."[26]

Because Jefferson's mother recognized how effective visual and concrete education was for the boy, she began to explore new educational methods and tried to adapt them to his needs. She felt that object analysis could "give him a habit of observing things with attention" as well as "be some employment for Jefferson." For example, when she held up a piece of glass before his eyes, then held "an opake [opaque] body up," her son would have learned that glass is transparent. Likewise, when she touched it to his cheek, then rubbed "some rough thing" against him, he would understand that the glass was smooth. He would know it was hard "by shewing that we cannot scratch on it with a pin" but that "we can scratch other things." Virginia argued that this kind of close observation would assist Jefferson in his efforts to learn to read. By the time Jefferson Trist faced his sixth birthday, he began to insist that he was ready to attend a real school. Virginia had reached the limits of what she felt confident teaching the boy, and he was hungering for more rigorous pursuits than the family could provide him.[27]

℮⁀

In her attempts to educate her son, Virginia Trist was following the advice of many educators. Advocates for Deaf people asked hearing parents not to ignore their Deaf children. Asked one, "Why should mothers spend hours and days in teaching their little prattlers to speak . . . while their little silent one sits by curious to learn, but without the least instruction?"[28]

Although many parents assumed their Deaf children to be "unfortunate outcasts from society, incapable of improvement," advocates tried to convince them of the possibilities—indeed, the necessity—of educating the youngsters. Argued one advocate, "every parent might do much to prepare his child for future admission" to a state school for the Deaf and for his or her future life. Because of the immense possibilities of education for the Deaf child, educators were insistent in their pleas to parents. "We earnestly appeal to parents," begged advocates, "to make an effort for their training, both mental and moral."[29]

In efforts to instill a moral character in their Deaf children, advised advocates, parents first needed to ensure that the youngsters could become part of the family. Deaf children needed to learn responsibility and duty to their family. Parents were counseled not to pity or coddle them. Instead, advised one educator of Deaf children, "let them keep employed, in carrying

away articles, or bringing them when pointed at, errands to a neighbor, etc."
As one advocate summarized, "They should be brought up to habits of industry and self-denial, and the fond disposition of the parents to undue indulgence and excessive sympathy should be restrained, and prevented from
being a source of injury to their children."[30]

Next, educators of the Deaf suggested, parents must exercise "proper
parental control" and attend to their Deaf children's understanding of
good and bad behavior. They assured parents that they could communicate
with their children and suggested ways to teach moral actions through visual means. "Express abhorrence of wrong doing by an appropriate frown
of the countenance, and gesticulation of the hands," wrote one educator,
"and turning away with disappointment from that which is wrong, and by
discipline if necessary." In addition to "reproof for the bad," parents also
needed to give their child "the commendation appropriate to good conduct," perhaps with a smile and a nod or a hug.[31]

In addition to moral training, advocates for Deaf people encouraged
parents to teach their children elementary academics. Educators of the
Deaf acknowledged that parental instruction of their Deaf children was
not an easy task. "Mutes cannot be taught," wrote one, "as children usually
are, by giving to the pupils a book and leaving them to their own cogni-
tions." Instead, "the ideas communicated must be illustrated and explained
in a great variety of ways, so as to communicate something of which the
Mute has not, from any source, received the slightest conception." Among
the variety of ways were reading, writing, fingerspelling, and signing. Summarized one educator of the Deaf, "The parents might easily teach the
manual alphabet, a legible hand-writing, a large vocabulary of words,
names of sensible objects, actions and qualities, and the earlier lessons of
words combined into sentences."[32]

Many educators provided copies of the manual alphabet to the parents
of Deaf children and suggested that they be taught to use it at an early age.
One educator tried to explain the process of teaching youngsters to spell in
English on their hands: "In the Manual Alphabet it will be seen that the different positions of the hand represent different letters," the author began.
"There is no more difficulty in teaching to a Deaf Mute child the import of
the letter 'A' from a certain and constant position of the hand, than there is

in teaching a child who can hear, the import of the same letter from a certain and constant sound emitted from the throat." The educator insisted that parents recognize the similarity: "The mental process with the two children is this: the former associates the letter and the *position of the hand together;* the latter associates the letters and the *sound* together. The idea will be as clear in the mind of the one as in that of the other, although different mental associations are formed." Another advocate for Deaf education echoed the argument: "there is no mystery about instructing the children of silence. It is just as easy to teach a child to know the letters by the position of the hand, as to know them by their names and sounds." In short, claimed one writer, "with the Deaf Mute the sense of sight is made to take the place of the sense of hearing."[33]

In addition to the use of fingerspelling, many educators suggested that parents teach their Deaf children the rudiments of writing. One instructor advised parents to show an object such as a pin to the Deaf child, then "write the letters P-I-N slowly on a slate" and "let the child imitate them till he can do it well." Some educators suggested using fingerspelling to cement the lesson in the child's mind: "By means of the manual alphabet, the mute learns to distinguish the written letters from each other. . . . Present the object—say a *hat*—to the mute, write its name on the slate, let him spell it on his fingers till the order of the letters is fixed in his memory, and also to learn to write it."[34]

Many advocates of education for Deaf people believed that "half the difficulty" of education could be erased by parents' efforts to "familiarize the mind of the deaf and dumb child with the idea and use of written language." In fact, several argued that it was enough for Deaf children to learn to write only by rote memorization of the movements. "Should they not be able to perceive the significancy of these names" of objects, explained one educator, "to be capable of writing them mechanically will be an excellent preparatory work." The practice of writing, whether with understanding or not, would help the child learn penmanship. "If not taught to write when young," warned one educator, "he will never write an easy or legible hand."[35]

Some educators suggested that parents begin to use signs—visual vocabulary—in the "training [of] the young mind while under the parental roof." Parents "should cultivate the language of signs, and encourage the child in the use of them at as early an age as possible, that his mental powers may be invigorated and strengthened by the exercise." Fingerspelling was a representation of English upon the hands, but signing was a different matter, totally separate from English. Usually the signs used in home education were "insignificant signs"—that is, obvious gestures that hearing family members could initiate themselves without formal training in American Sign Language. This method was simply a more elaborate version of the home sign used by most families.[36]

A few advocates for home education of Deaf children provided parents with practical descriptions of common American Sign Language vocabulary to use at home. Parents were advised to kiss their fists in order to sign GOOD, and to "take the hand from the lips and with the palm down, push if from you" in order to sign BAD. The list went on: "For GLAD, pat the heart cheerfully; for SORRY, rub the closed hand on the heart with a sad countenance; for RED, touch the lip with the finger; for BLACK, draw the finger along the eyebrow; for LOVE, press the heart with clasped arms; for HATE, push the hands out with an averted face; for TRUTH, point the forefinger in a straight line forward from the mouth." As opposed to the concrete objects for which parents and children could invent home signs, much of the vocabulary on these lists involved abstract concepts to which Deaf children had probably not yet been introduced.[37]

After the youngster had mastered a number of basic signs, parents could introduce adjectives such as colors or sizes. By contrasting two objects, such as a white hat and a black hat, or animals of different sizes, the youngster could learn the meaning of different "qualities." Next, the parent could teach the child verbs. "Actions," said one educator, "may be taught, as WALK by moving the hands slowly to imitate walking." Afterwards, the parent could combine the movement with "some agent" to make a short sentence: "'a man walks,' 'a boy walks,' 'a cat walks,' etc." Again, the proposed signs were from American Sign Language.[38]

These signs were neither complete nor graphic enough to be simple mimicry. Although they were all to some degree connected with their meanings and therefore easy for both parents and children to learn, these signs were not simply the agreed-upon gestures of home sign. This list of signs began to introduce Deaf children to the formal language of the Deaf community. Not only did it teach Deaf children the beginnings of a shared language, but it helped shape their future gestures and their invented signs into the rules and traditions of American Sign Language. After exposure to beginning ASL, youngsters were less likely to break the rules of ASL by gesturing with their feet, with linguistically unacceptable handshapes, or with movements outside traditional ASL sign space.[39]

This process of learning both rudimentary English and ASL was not an easy one: "the mountain of labor is there, and it can be neither tunneled or avoided—there is emphatically no sure road to knowledge for the mute." But the effort, explained advocates of Deaf education, was clearly worthwhile. "The advantage is manifestly so great, that we presume no parent who is made acquainted with the process, will decline making the attempt. . . . Experience has shown, that a deaf mute child who has been so trained will outstrip one of equal natural advantages, who has not." Educators' belief in the possibilities of education were so profound that they began to minimize their estimation of its difficulties: "These elementary steps are simple and may be taught by any parent who will make the attempt."[40]

℮ᕲ

During the 1850s, the Lawrence family of Louisiana had to decide how to educate their five Deaf children. Henry and Fanny were unsure what to do. Finally, Henry's sister exclaimed, "Have they no instructor! Would it not be well to try to get a teacher for them?" His sisters Lydia and Hannah were eager to participate in the decision and began to explore the options available to the children. Hannah consulted a cousin about what should be done. Because of the cousin's knowledge of Deaf education—he was on the board of directors of the school for the Deaf in New York—she felt he would be able to inform the family best. He told Hannah that "they take children as young as Walter," their eldest Deaf child, and later would accept "the others as they grow old enough." She was sure Henry would listen to her advice: "I suppose in another year Henry will bring him on and place him there."[41]

In a letter to her sister-in-law nearly a year later, Fanny announced that she appreciated the work that Hannah had done, including the sending of a brochure from the New York school, but that the Lawrences were considering another choice. Although not as prestigious, Fanny was "under the impression that we should send them to Baton Rouge where we can have them near to us." They had not yet made the final decision to send the children to the Louisiana state residential school, but Fanny knew that "should we determine on the Northern school," she would have to leave her home and "go with them of course."[42]

Six months later, the Lawrences were still undecided about the appropriate action for their Deaf children. Henry's sister Lydia inquired of a teacher of the Deaf "what he thought the best way to manage and educate young children." He responded that "decidedly the best course" was to hire a young woman to tutor them at home until they were eleven or twelve years old. With the tutelage of a live-in teacher, the boys would "learn more and better" than in any other way. She could "get the children on in their studies much faster" than in a residential school, where "the younger ones are generally overlooked for the older and more advanced ones."[43]

Although the Lawrence family probably did not yet know it, the addition of a young Deaf woman would expose the children to American Sign Language, which would connect them to Deaf society. She would share more than just a language with the children. She, like the children, understood how the hearing society around them treated Deaf people. In addition to sharing the disadvantages of being Deaf in a society constructed for the hearing, the young tutor could show the children the possibilities for advanced education, self-sufficiency, and community development with other Deaf people.

At the school near Lydia's home, "there are very many excellent young women" who were completing their education at the school and "would be very glad to get a good home" with a family such as the Lawrences. Unmarried Deaf women did not have many employment alternatives after graduation—and the financial support, intellectual challenge, and emotional connection with Deaf children that went along with home tutorship probably made the job quite sought after. There were also disadvantages of the job, however: working in a particular family's home would remove the girls from the community they had enjoyed at the school for the Deaf.[44]

Lydia told her sister-in-law that the teacher she consulted was a "most worthy man" who had turned down the superintendency of the Louisiana School to remain a teacher in her state, so "his opinion is really entitled to great weight" since he was "most highly esteemed." The teacher promised to "take particular pains" to obtain a tutor "in every way suitable for bringing up little ones." He informed the Lawrences that the chosen tutor "would go for $150 or $200 a year"—less than one child's tuition at many residential schools. Lydia also volunteered to "do all in my power," if Fanny agreed to the plan, "to get a suitable person to go to you" and the children. In addition to educating the children in "something that may be useful to them in after-life," Lydia thought that having the children taught could be "such a relief" for Fanny. She hoped that the educated Deaf children could become "a source of comfort to their parents" rather than giving their mother "a life of trial." It is unclear whether the family chose at that point to hire a young Deaf woman as a tutor.[45]

The following year, Walter and two of his younger brothers, Townsend and Robert, enrolled at the Louisiana school for the Deaf. When the school closed several years later due to the Civil War, the family hired a young Deaf woman to teach the boys and their two younger Deaf siblings: "Miss Robinson is here teaching the children. All are home and learning well." Not only was a Deaf adult in the Lawrence family home with the young Deaf children, but the older children, already exposed to the language and culture of the state school, were in the home with their younger Deaf siblings. The youngsters grew up with a large number of people with whom to communicate easily. Deafness in the Lawrence family began to seem like a normal way of life.[46]

ℰ⌢

Like the younger of the Lawrence children, David Tillinghast grew up with his brother Tom to introduce him to the world of Deaf people. Although Tom was away at the residential school in Virginia during David's earliest years, he came home for a few summers and then lived at home for a couple of years after his graduation from the Virginia school and before David's formal education was begun.

Initially the Tillinghasts considered sending little David to the Virginia school while Tom was still enrolled. Jane and Samuel wrote to the principal, Joseph Tyler, asking his advice about their young son's education. Tyler told them that he would "gladly receive your other little boy as a pupil" but advised not sending him until he was a bit older. Although he felt that "a child had better be at school than not, even at a very tender age" in those cases where "money is no object," he felt that keeping the boy at home would not be very detrimental because "these very little folks will waste their valuable time in play." The expense of the education, "paid for with extreme difficulty by parents," might be "half wasted" because of the "giddiness of the baby pupils." Instead, he suggested that the Tillinghasts wait until the boy was ten or twelve, "a better age" to send Deaf children, since, Tyler argued, "the *minds* of the deaf do not grow with their bodies."[47]

Principal Joseph Tyler suggested that when Thomas went home for the summer and, more extensively, after graduation, he could "give little David lessons and greatly benefit him till he is twelve years old." The longer Thomas stayed at the Virginia school, suggested Tyler, the better educated and the more prepared to teach David he would become. In other words, "by keeping Thomas longer at school, you may profit both boys." He argued that it made financial sense as well: because of the head start that David might gain from Tom's teaching, it might be "unnecessary to keep David in school so long" and therefore "benefit yourself in a pecuniary way." Another reason to have Thomas teach David would be to reemphasize the academic lessons he himself had learned in school: it would "be of the very greatest advantage to Thomas himself." The knowledge that Tom could teach young David, however, did not completely ease Principal Tyler's fear that "Tom should *deteriorate* by ceasing to be a learner at so early an age."[48]

Thomas quickly agreed to participate in his brother's education. He wrote to his father, "When I go home, I shall be glad to stay with him. . . . I shall often teach him till he is old enough to go to school." He was excited to forge a deeper relationship with his Deaf brother and wrote that he hoped that David would "always be glad when I am at home." When he returned home, Thomas started to teach his brother to use the manual alphabet. David seemed "to be tolerably willing" to learn to spell on his hands, pleasing Thomas enough to brag in a letter to a hearing brother away at school.[49]

Upon receiving word about David's home education, cousin Amelia wrote to Thomas to tell him that he must "find it pleasant to teach your brother David many things that you have learned while away from home." She must have guessed that the relationship could also soften the loneliness

Tom felt leaving the Virginia school: "I know you must miss your companions at school very much." Family members recognized that Tom and David were beginning to have a special relationship. Elder brother William wrote brother John that David and Tom were "quite fond of being together." They used "a language of their own" that, as William said, was more difficult for him to translate than Latin. Within a few months the relationship between the two Deaf brothers had deepened: "David as ever is [Tom's] almost constant companion." And a few months later, William reported that David was beginning "to look up to Tom as one superior to other persons." As David recalled when he was almost ninety years old, "We became inseparable companions."[50]

The language that the two Deaf brothers used was not, as his hearing brother thought, "a language of their own." It was instead what Tom had learned at the Virginia school for the Deaf: American Sign Language. Looking back, David did not understand how he had learned ASL so quickly. "I do not remember how I learned the language from him. I seemed to understand his signs instinctively." He theorized that "since from infancy I had been accustomed to think in pictures of things and the activities of home life," he made an easy transition between his pictures of real life and pictorial signs. As David said, "As signs are imitations of [real objects], I easily recognized them and consequently learned them with wonderful rapidity."[51]

In addition to learning a language far more developed than the home sign used by his family with their Deaf sons, David was exposed to a new world of the intellect. Tom, working as a bookbinder while tutoring his brother, had been asked by customers to bind their copies of *Harper's Monthly* and *Harper's Weekly* illustrated magazines. As David later recalled, "I had the privilege of looking at the wonderful pictures in them. . . . The natural consequence was that I asked numberless questions, and the answers expanded my mind greatly beyond the previous horizon of my childhood."[52]

After two years of home education, David's parents began to consider more formal alternatives. In March of 1852, Samuel Tillinghast stated that the New York school for the Deaf was a prestigious school, "superior to the Virginia" school where Thomas was educated. Although physically closer to their home in Fayetteville, North Carolina, the Virginia school was not easy to get to, despite the many Norwood relatives near the school. Samuel felt that the New York school would be "quite as convenient" for the immediate family.[53]

Samuel was not yet ready to make a final decision about the choice of residential schools. As brother William said, "Pa" had not yet "concluded upon sending him to any particular school." As the months passed and no further action was taken on behalf of David, William told his brother that although his father was "undecided about him," he felt that "David ought to be at school." Although William said that he might "think and hope" that David would probably end up in New York, he was not at all pleased that the new state school in North Carolina, "our own institution," was not under serious consideration. Robina Norwood, David's grandmother, thought it would "be so much more convenient" to send him to North Carolina. But she knew that the quality of the fledgling academic program was "not such as to induce Mr. T. to place [David] there." In addition to the strong academic reputation of the New York school compared with southern schools, Samuel thought that it was a "cheaper institution" than the school established in North Carolina.[54]

In the middle of August 1853, Samuel traveled to New York City with his two Deaf sons. Unlike Thomas, David would begin his formal training at the New York school. Thomas traveled to New York as well, in order to "learn something more of his craft" of bookbindery. Very soon, however, he enrolled in the advanced class at the New York school. While at the school, Tom looked after his younger brother. Their time together, so far away from their parents and siblings, further cemented their deep bond, as brother William predicted: "Tom and David will be very happy together."[55]

Families turned to a variety of options for the early education of their Deaf children. Thomas Tillinghast was sent to a young Deaf woman who tutored him in her home, his younger brother David was taught at home when Thomas returned from residential school, Jefferson Trist learned along with his hearing siblings under the instruction of their mother, and the Lawrence family hired a live-in tutor. Eventually, however, all of these families decided that their children needed more extensive educational opportunities. They found those opportunities at state residential schools for the Deaf.

Part II. The Early Years of Deaf Education

Early in the nineteenth century, formal education for Deaf children began in the United States. As the first public Deaf school, the American Asylum for the Deaf in Connecticut inspired states throughout the nation to open their own schools. The new schools used sign-language-based pedagogy modeled on the New England school's methods. By 1860 almost every southern state had built a residential institution to educate white Deaf children.

When parents brought their Deaf children to residential school for the first time, the children often did not understand their parents' intentions. Hearing families could not tell their children about the dramatic changes in store for them. Many Deaf children were terror-stricken when left alone by their families at large and imposing buildings. But thanks to the ease of communication with other students at the state schools, children often quickly developed a deep sense of belonging.

Educators realized that the main difficulty they faced in the instruction of Deaf pupils was the struggle to teach English. Hearing children seemed to learn basic English spontaneously, but in truth they absorbed aurally the spoken English of their parents. Deaf children, on the other hand, could not hear the language being spoken around them. They could only be taught the vocabulary and grammar of English once they were old enough to read and write. Teachers disagreed about the most appropriate way to teach English. Some educators advocated the use of American Sign Language, a language with a grammar distinct from English, as the language of instruction. They taught written English as a second language.

Other instructors used a pidgin combination of ASL and English. Still other teachers emphasized writing and fingerspelling. Very occasionally
schools taught spoken English to pupils deemed either semi-deaf (hard of
hearing) or semi-mute (losing their hearing after acquiring speech). The
fierce debates among supporters of oral education, ASL proponents, supporters of signed English, and those who preferred to use only fingerspelling were very real, but the vast majority of teachers shared the same
ultimate goal—teaching Deaf children to share the language and culture
of the hearing.

Despite the fact that Deaf people were constantly aware that hearing
administrators and teachers did not see them as equals, the experience of
school life offered a place where a Deaf community could emerge. No
matter what language was taught in the classroom, American Sign Language was almost certainly the language of the dormitory and the playground. Although students worked with their instructors to perfect their
English skills, they spent much more time with their peers. They shared
dormitory rooms, studied together, ate together in the dining halls, always
conversing in American Sign Language. Sign was passed on from Deaf
staff to pupils, from older pupils to younger, and from pupils who grew up
in homes where ASL was used to pupils who were the only Deaf people in
their families. ASL and a Deaf community, both available at residential
schools, offered an escape from the difficulties these students faced in
hearing America.

In 1817 in Connecticut, the first successful American school for the Deaf
was founded by a hearing New Englander and a French Deaf man. Religious benevolence rooted in New England Protestantism had inspired
Thomas Hopkins Gallaudet, a graduate of Yale College and the Andover
Theological Seminary, to travel to Europe to learn methods of educating
Deaf people. He received a warm welcome in France and spent the next
months learning the pedagogical techniques of the Royal Institution for

the Deaf and Dumb at Paris. He invited Laurent Clerc, a distinguished graduate of the school, back with him to Hartford, Connecticut, to open a new school for American Deaf pupils. Clerc brought to the school both a model of sign-language-based education and the specific sign language of France.[1]

The new school, the American Asylum for the Deaf, was financed in its earliest years not only by private charity and pupil tuition but also by the state governments of Connecticut, Massachusetts, New Hampshire, and Vermont, as well as by a donation of public land by the federal government. Gallaudet and Clerc traveled to other large American cities outside of New England to raise more funds for the Hartford school and ignite public interest in the education of Deaf people.[2]

Cities with large populations of Deaf children soon considered opening their own schools. The New York school opened its doors in 1818, and the Pennsylvania school for the Deaf started in Philadelphia two years later. The Hartford school's system of manual pedagogy spread from New England throughout the nation. As other states formed schools for the Deaf, many new institutions hired either teachers or graduates of the American Asylum to be their first principals and teachers. Other schools sent local teachers to Hartford to be trained by Gallaudet and Clerc.[3]

In 1823 the Kentucky Asylum for the Tuition of the Deaf and Dumb, the first school for the Deaf in a slave state and the fourth school in the nation, opened its doors. By 1824 there were nineteen students but no satisfactory teacher. A hearing eighteen-year-old college student, John Adamson Jacobs, was hired. Because he was inexperienced in the instruction of Deaf pupils, the school sent Jacobs to the American Asylum to learn sign language and the method of instruction used there. He studied under Laurent Clerc for thirteen months before returning to Kentucky, where he assumed the principalship. Traveling throughout the South accompanied by one of his pupils, Jacobs gave exhibitions to state legislatures. Word spread of the performances by the Deaf child. Soon, students from every southern state and several northern ones were enrolled at the Kentucky school.[4]

In the coming years, other institutions were built, both in the South and throughout the nation. Fifteen years after the opening of the Kentucky school, a school was opened in Virginia. The school employed as principal Joseph Tyler, a Yale-educated Episcopal minister and an experienced teacher from the American school for the Deaf. Tyler brought with him Job Turner, a Deaf pupil from the American Asylum, to be the institution's first teacher. Virginia's first pupil was registered on November 30, 1839.[5]

Within the next ten years, Tennessee, North Carolina, Georgia, and South Carolina all opened their own state schools for the Deaf. During the 1850s, Arkansas, Missouri, Louisiana, Mississippi, Texas, and Alabama started Deaf schools. Like Kentucky and Virginia, these new schools hired teachers who had trained either at the American Asylum or with teachers who had studied there.[6]

Antebellum southern schools for the Deaf seem to have differed little from northern schools. Perhaps the most obvious reason was that so many of the founders were either northern by birth or had received training at northern schools for the Deaf. On top of that, the South did not have a well-developed tradition of state or region-level charity, instead relying on a system of more localized benevolent activities. But education of the Deaf called for a more integrated system. Only a small proportion of the population was Deaf, so providing cost-effective education necessitated forming alliances beyond the immediate community. Because the North had established models of state and regional benevolence and education, southern leaders of Deaf education did not have to create a new system out of whole cloth but could imitate northern developments.[7]

Rather than having a primary motivation of religious benevolence like that expressed by Thomas Hopkins Gallaudet, southern educators typically argued that an expensive building and good teachers would boost the reputation of their state. Honor and pride were at the heart of their concerns. Institutions for the Deaf were, in the words of the 1852 governor of Mississippi, "noble charities so characteristic of southern generosity."[8]

Because the number of Deaf children attending the state school might not be large enough to make the school financially feasible for the state, many southern states decided to add another population to the schools: the blind. The two groups of children did not intrinsically belong together since they generally could not communicate with each other, much less be educated in the same classrooms. But many southern states saw both deaf children and blind children as having an "intimate connection"—as children with sensory disabilities excluded from the community. Perhaps more important, educating both Deaf and blind children at the same institution was cost-effective: it was a way, as one state official said, of "lessening the expense to the state without detriment to either."[9]

Southern schools for the Deaf respected the cardinal rule of the white leaders of the region: that white be privileged and black deprived. No antebellum school for the Deaf located in the South even discussed the possibility of admitting African American students. Differences of opinion between teachers raised in the North and legislators and parents living in the South were an undercurrent rarely addressed. An institutional history of the Virginia school pointed out that principal Joseph Tyler was "an open and avowed abolitionist." But despite the violent conflict between his views and the views of the people who paid his salary, Tyler's private beliefs were tolerated by his antebellum southern institution.[10]

Southern schools admitted white pupils from all economic classes. The state supplied tuition for families who could not pay. This practice encouraged a kind of interaction among people of different classes that was not usually allowed in the antebellum South. Young elites who felt isolated because of the difficulties of communication with their families at home could form strong bonds with signing lower-class pupils living at the same residential school. The pupils often found their life partners at school, a fact that allowed the possibility of interclass marriage. All the pupils studied together, worshipped together, and learned in gender-specific vocational classes that transcended class barriers. The poorest Deaf students gained both literacy and job skills that were almost certainly not available to their hearing siblings. But for the wealthiest pupils, their education was not as advanced as what their hearing peers might have received. Instead of learning classical languages and advanced science, Deaf elites were trained along with their classmates of all social classes to be independent skilled laborers.[11]

Elite southerners did not always attend the schools for the Deaf located in their own states. Some families chose to send their Deaf children to one of the three most prominent institutions for the Deaf in the United States: the American school in Hartford, the New York school, or the Pennsylvania school. When parents chose to send their children to a highly respected northern school, the children in no way avoided exposure to children from a variety of backgrounds. They might even attend class or live in a dormitory with an African American pupil. Additionally, while attending these established and prestigious schools, southern students were more likely to form attachments to places and people unconnected to the South.

$\mathcal{C}\sim$ An Education of the Lips at the Expense of the Mind

THE MAJORITY OF SOUTHERN TEACHERS of the Deaf did not rely on spoken English to educate their pupils. Most principals would have seconded the head of the Georgia school, who wrote in 1850 that "very little effort . . . to teach 'labial reading'" had been made at the state-run school. Many European schools for the Deaf—especially those in Germany and England—taught articulation in the classroom, but American educators routinely dismissed the practice. For Americans, claimed Colonel Robert H. Chapman in the Alabama school's annual address, the "triumphant success" of sign language "decided the contest in favor of De l'Eppee," one of the leaders of the French manual system.[1]

Despite their commitment to instruction in sign language, educators sometimes faced opposition to the system of manual instruction from general society. Much of this opposition was based not on true pedagogical debate but on parental desire to have "normal" speaking children. As word spread throughout America about the pedagogical system designed to teach Deaf people to speak in many European countries, southern parents' hopes for their Deaf children rose. As the principal of the Deaf school in South Carolina stated, the subject of oral education would never have been mentioned in the school's annual report were it not for the "well-known eagerness of parents of deaf and dumb children, to lay hold of every means which can, in any wise, benefit these children." The principal continued, "And if, in any way, they could be so far misled as to believe that American schools are at fault, many would cast reflections on themselves because they had not availed themselves of all known advantages." Hearing parents hoped to have children who communicated as they did, and therefore they latched on to the rhetoric of oral education circulating in American newspapers and journals. This information was, as far as many educators of Deaf children were concerned, a bother: they were "called upon to meet influences calculated to produce unnecessary restlessness in the public mind."[2]

Hearing parents were especially concerned that their semi-mute children often lost the ability to speak when they enrolled in an institute for the Deaf. The loss of articulation skills happened in as little as one year if the pupils were not required to continue speech training. "It would be a serious drawback to the benefits she would receive," one educator paraphrased a parent's concern about his daughter's loss of speech, "if she were to lose the means of communicating with persons who do not understand sign language."[3]

Most teachers of Deaf children recognized that not only parents but the majority of hearing society viewed the ability to speak and speechread as the ultimate skill for Deaf people. It was "an art of the greatest refinement and delicacy" that took many years of "patient toil" on the part of student and teacher alike. But despite their long effort, the writer claimed, as soon as the pupil graduated and stopped practicing daily, the skill of articulation was quickly lost.[4]

A handful of educators agreed with the general society. Even if they believed oral education would be an inappropriate means of pedagogy, they felt that spoken languages were naturally far superior to signed ones. Speech was, as one Kentuckian wrote, "the result of original divine endowment, modified and refined by the best efforts and skill of man through many generations." The spoken voice, he thought, was the "most powerful of all educators." The signs invented and acquired by a young Deaf child were merely "rude" communication, thought the teacher, which would corrupt his or her intellectual development. These signs were but a "weak echo" of the child's "own incorrect and untrained ideas." Unlike speech, which would be a "powerful trainer and educator" of the mind, sign language would "only serve to set and harden the crude and bad intellectual habits" of the savage.[5]

Most southern educators, however, did not hold to such ideas. They openly criticized teachers for their belief in the "absurd" and "fallacious" concept that thought and the spoken word were inextricably connected. They rejected the European oralist claim that natural sign language would not encourage human thinking—and the belief that its pedagogical use would leave Deaf students in what supporters of articulation training perceived as an animal state. They rejected attempts to teach speech as "unnatural" and "unphilosophical," as well as "painful" and "inefficient." One southern teacher claimed that all American instructors without exception rejected the teaching of speech. This claim was only a small overstatement.[6]

Teachers of the Deaf often objected to the impractical nature of articulation training. There was no "*practical* good," stated one educator from the state school in Georgia, of teaching speech or speechreading to Deaf children, whether they were deafened congenitally or accidentally. One reason for the impracticality of oral education for Deaf people was its high cost. Rather than classrooms with twenty pupils sitting in a horseshoe in order to see the signs made by the teacher and each other, oral education required much smaller classes, a great deal of one-on-one training, and consequently many more teachers. Teachers would spend long "wearisome hours" teaching the mechanics of speech and arranging and then repositioning the vocal organs. For the large expense of both time and wages, "very inadequate compensations" were seen.[7]

Teaching Deaf children to speak, thought Virginia educators, was fruitless and a waste of the pupils' time. Rather than the key to higher thought, speech would merely retard pupils' true learning. They would learn only a rote skill, not a language of ideas, the "more appropriate work of intellectual and moral improvement." Deaf pupils who were taught to articulate, claimed many educators, were trained to "speak many words to which they often attach no meaning." Learning to manipulate one's vocal cords and the mouth itself taught no knowledge at all: it was "mere mechanical articulation" that left Deaf children "as ignorant and unenlightened" as they were before their oral education. Speech would mean nothing to them, explained teachers, because English was still an enigma for these Deaf students. One educator compared the teaching of articulation to teaching a hearing person a foreign language "unaccompanied by a verbal translation into his native tongue." Oral language was "wholly artificial and unmeaning" for Deaf pupils. Time spent teaching speech was "just so much subtracted from their advancement in intellectual knowledge and the use of written language." In short, articulation was "an education of the *lips* at the expense of the *mind*—a sacrifice of sense to sound."[8]

Some educators realized that relying on speech exclusively would be detrimental to a "community of deaf mutes." Teachers were aware that the use of speech by a Deaf person trying to communicate with other Deaf people would be "utterly futile." Therefore, when used alone, articulation training would be both useless and cruel. As one South Carolina teacher wrote, "The Sign-Language is the most natural and efficient vehicle of communication." As the Deaf pupils moved their bodies as they signed, claimed the educator, the physical activity would not only cement the Deaf community but excite the mind and inspire a "zeal" or "fervency of the soul." If a common sign language were not taught in schools, one Deaf person would not necessarily use the same signs as another. Without knowledge of a complex sign language learned both in the classroom and in the dormitory, Deaf people would be isolated. As one principal claimed, without signs congenitally Deaf students would be "left at home in their 'animal' condition."[9]

In addition to the belief that articulation training would be unsuccessful for Deaf pupils, religious beliefs also influenced a few teachers of the Deaf. According to one southern educator, only the "miraculous touch of Christ" could teach Deaf people to speak. Even after years of training, explained educators, Deaf people's voices were "necessarily harsh and unnatural," proving that God did not intend for them to speak. Therefore teachers had the responsibility to use sign language when communicating with their pupils.[10]

Political ideals also motivated many teachers of the Deaf to oppose oral training. They were fascinated by Jacksonian rhetoric of the common. Like France, America had fought a revolution and declared itself a democracy. By the early nineteenth century, ideals of universal participation were even

more popular in America. Such rhetoric even affected southern slaveholders. Educators noted that at the Berlin school for the education of the Deaf,
only students who could already "articulate words" were admitted. Deaf
students who could not speak were simply never educated: "If the poor
deaf mute, be none more intelligent, cannot furnish abundant proof of his
ability to enunciate clearly and distinctly," wrote an American proponent
of the manual system of sign language, "he must wend his way through life
untaught." Many Americans ridiculed the German school's policy and saw
it as contrary to American political beliefs. "Such a course may do very well
where royalty reigns," one critic wrote sarcastically. An exclusively oral education required careful selection of pupils and was, claimed one educator,
"assuredly uncompatible [*sic*] with the genius and spirit of republicanism."
Articulation, as another said, was effective for "the few not the many" and
therefore was "certainly a very anti-republican system."[11]

Despite the fact that American educators resisted the use of speech as the
primary language of the classroom, several southern antebellum schools
began offering supplementary articulation classes for a small number of
their pupils. The head of the Kentucky school for the Deaf recognized as
early as 1843 that a few students might be able to profit from training in articulation. He was quick to point out that experiments in oral education
were overwhelming failures: for the vast majority of Deaf students, especially those with profound and prelingual hearing loss, oral training was
not only "inefficient" but "painful." Nevertheless, the principal felt compelled to admit "that success may have attended this attempt in a few favor-
able cases," however rare these success stories were. Within a year of the
principal's statement, the Kentucky school offered articulation to a limited
number of hard of hearing (or "semi-deaf") and later-deafened (or "semi-
mute") students. Although education in "new ideas" and "significant new
words" continued in American Sign Language, the instructors tried to bring
these students' vocal expressions of English "to a considerable degree of
perfection." The classes proved successful for a small number of qualified
students. Only for the few pupils "thought deserving of it" could the expense and effort to teach speech be justified.[12]

Often students who were enrolled in articulation classes were already
adept at speech. These "semi-mutes" did not have enough residual hearing

to be admitted to common schools for hearing students, but their parents often resisted the idea of educating their children with profoundly Deaf peers. "Children of this description are sometimes not sent to the Institution," wrote the head of the Kentucky school for the Deaf, because parents feared their children would "disuse their speech" and lose their ability to articulate. Education in written English would automatically increase their powers of speech, claimed the principal. He promised that the school would make special efforts to maintain or even improve the vocal abilities of hard of hearing students.[13]

Explained one educator, "Where a child has from birth partial hearing, partial speech will follow." Similarly, "if the child once heard, and while hearing, learned to talk, but subsequently lost hearing, the speech, too, will be lost, in proportion to the age of the child when the hearing was lost." He suggested that children who lost their hearing before the age of four had little likelihood of learning new speech. "All that may be hoped," he stated, "is to retain the use of such words as have been learned by the child." He agreed with other specialists in the field of Deaf education that children born without hearing would probably never learn to speak, since "no knowledge of sound can be communicated." The principal of the Missouri school agreed. Using spoken language as the language of instruction was, he claimed, "entirely abortive" with the majority of Deaf pupils. Only "the most gifted of those who could once hear" had any hope of acquiring even limited fluency in spoken English.[14]

The Virginia school established an oral class in the 1850s. Although established initially in "a private and almost incidental manner," the class soon became a formal part of the school's curriculum. It had, claimed the principal, produced many "happy results." The principal recommended training in articulation to supplement the regular sign-based curriculum only for students who had both "acquired some knowledge of language by means of the ear" and "retained their hearing sufficiently to understand loud conversation." Any speech absorbed by the ear would allow Deaf students to learn to articulate much more easily. Students born without hearing could not learn to articulate successfully because they had "no knowledge of sound." The Virginia school opposed articulation for all students born without hearing. For them, thought a school official, oral education was "only the subjecting of them to a painful ordeal without profit."[15]

The Virginia school for the Deaf was more restrictive than many other southern schools when choosing students for its newly established articulation class. At the South Carolina school, for example, articulation classes also included "a very few of the highest order of mind of congenitally deaf children". Although the great majority of pupils born without hearing required the use of sign training and would be "hopelessly left at home in their 'animal' condition" without the manual system of education, a few of these students "particularly gifted in perception and imitation" could be taught limited speech. Most of these pupils were restricted to "certain irregular sounds expressive of certain meanings." They could also be taught to analyze visually many of the small movements of speech on the mouths of friends and family. Other educators thought teaching articulation to exceptional pupils was a waste of time: "Even with them, half the time and labor spent," wrote one proponent of Deaf education, "would lead to results of a more valuable and satisfactory character" if sign language were used instead.[16]

Although hearing family members might view efforts in articulation as quite different from use of the manual system, teachers of the Deaf recognized that spoken words and lip movements were simply visual signs to Deaf pupils. Another educator admitted that for Deaf people, learning spoken English was merely another kind of sign language: a sign language of lip movements. Unlike the large and easily visible signs made by hands, however, tiny differences in speech were much harder to teach and learn. While limited oral communication abilities might be of practical use in everyday situations within a nonsigning, hearing family, educators believed that such minimal communication could never be the basis for true instruction between teacher and pupil.[17]

A few educators believed that almost all Deaf people should learn to pronounce a few useful phrases. Although their speech might not be intelligible to outsiders, family members and friends could learn to understand the words. And almost all Deaf pupils could also be trained to recognize a few "strongly marked words on the lips." Even if these skills were "imperfectly possessed," wrote one educator, they would be valuable, especially to hearing parents.[18]

Principals occasionally gave examples of successful instances of oral education. With training in articulation combined with teaching in sign language, one female pupil at the Kentucky school was learning to "read vocally with ease." A few years later a few other students followed in her footsteps. The young female pupil performed at a pageant, reading aloud "fluently and distinctly" a portion of the Bible. By 1861 at the Georgia school, the principal taught speech to a class of six and claimed the results were "highly gratifying."[19]

Other principals were not as optimistic about the possibilities of vocal training for Deaf pupils. One even presented a Deaf student's negative attitudes about articulation. One little girl from the Missouri school, previously "under the vocalizing process . . . for three years," often told the principal how grateful she was for "the expressive language of pantomime" that she had been taught at the school. Sign language was "beautiful and magnificent" for this girl and for the other students at the school. Speech training made the process of education "an irksome task" for both student and teacher, rather than an exciting adventure.[20]

Claimed one educator, all "well-informed and judicious persons" had made up their minds about articulation: they were "completely settled against the utility." But educators acknowledged that there was a problem. "Spoken language is an *open sesame* whose magic power causes the door of [the house of knowledge] to fly asunder," admitted John Burnet in *Tales of the Deaf and Dumb* in 1835. Since such a power was inaccessible for most Deaf people, "a passage must be cut through the wall itself." Educators recognized that one way was to depend on written English.[21]

CHAPTER 6

ᘓ✦ *Think in Words*

As Jefferson Trist approached his sixth birthday, he began to express interest in attending school. One day he accompanied a cousin on his walk to school, and when he arrived, he saw the young pupils practicing writing. He recognized that both reading and writing, as visual modes of communication, would be accessible to him. His mother, Virginia, wrote to her husband a few months later, "Jefferson is worrying me at the moment to send him to school to learn to write."[1]

Virginia Trist wanted to satisfy her Deaf son's desire for education. She considered sending him to various prestigious schools for the Deaf, including European schools or the American Asylum for the Deaf in Hartford, Connecticut. Finally she decided to try to teach him herself when her many relatives left the household in June and she had more time.[2]

In December 1835, six months after the writing lessons were to begin, Virginia Trist took her son to an exhibition at the school for the Deaf in Philadelphia while they were visiting the city. She herself was "much gratified with the exhibition," as it demonstrated the possibilities for learning that existed for her son. For Jefferson, the exhibition was the first glimpse into a new world of people with whom he could easily communicate. His mother wrote, "Jefferson became quite animated" while watching the signing students: "When a little girl arose and gave an account by signs of the whole process of making bread, beginning with the ploughman rising in the morning to go to his work, Jefferson laughed aloud at some of her signs." He was delighted to find others who communicated by visual means. Jefferson "appeared to understand much of what she related," possibly because of his own inventive use of gesture and home sign.[3]

The purpose of the visit to the Pennsylvania school's exhibition was not only for Virginia to learn more about the education of Deaf children. The Trists were considering enrolling their son at the school and wanted to introduce young Jefferson to the setting before they made their final decision. After the exhibition, Virginia walked with her son to the doors of the school. At first, Jefferson was both shy and obstinate: "Jefferson hung back and refused to enter." Virginia could not explain to her son that they were only there to visit. Jefferson may have feared that he was about to be abandoned by his mother and left alone at the large institution. But despite his fears, soon the boy "became interested in what was going on" at the school. He was "much pleased" with his interactions with the many young signing pupils.[4]

When Jefferson's mother saw that her son responded positively to the Pennsylvania school, she decided to enroll him a week later. She planned to dine with a family who lived near the school, then "leave the poor dear little boy" there. Virginia told her husband, Nicholas, that it would "almost break my heart to part with him"—"troublesome as he is." Many of the difficulties that arose from the lack of communication, she hoped, would be alleviated. After learning to read and write, Jefferson would be able to communicate with his hearing relatives through written English.[5]

On the last day of December 1835, Virginia began to leave Jefferson at the school for short periods. She was accompanied by a family friend and by her hearing daughter Martha. Once again, Jefferson did not want to enter the school: "Jefferson appeared to ascend the steps leading to the portico of the asylum very unwillingly, and refused to pull off his cape and cloak." After a short struggle, though, Jefferson began to play with the other children. "As soon as he was engaged in the room with the other children," she reported to her husband, Jefferson was "so perfectly happy and content . . . all day that he did not appear to miss me." Because of the earlier struggle to get Jefferson to stay, Virginia had decided that Jefferson would return that evening to her quarters in the city. She reported that "when he returned in the afternoon he expressed his wish to go again the next day." In the morning, he "was quite impatient to be off." Again, Virginia decided that Jefferson should return to her at night to help him adjust slowly to life at school. When family friends went to pick him up that evening, "he showed no desire to accompany them home." The Matron of the school realized that Jefferson was ready to spend the night there. She forwarded a message to Virginia "proposing that he should remain when I sent him next." The next morning when she "proposed to him that he should stay there all night" by showing him his night clothes, he "readily agreed" and "departed as gay as a lark."[6]

On Sunday after dinner, Virginia decided to go to the school and ask "if he had kept up his spirits during the night." If he had, she said, "I would not see him lest I should put the wish to return with me into his head by the meeting." As she entered the doors of the school, "his sweet, cooing voice" convinced her that he was playing happily in the adjoining room. When she asked the Matron for confirmation of his happiness, she replied that "he had not drooped a moment." He spent the night "in a bed by her side" and slept soundly. When he awoke, he "raised up his little head and 'made his little good humored noise' then laid it on the pillow again and waited very patiently to be dressed." Virginia told her husband that Jefferson was "so happy there that I cannot pine as I should have done in *weaning from my baby* if I had imagined him sad and homesick. Then my heart would have almost broken, but now I bear it well."[7]

After Jefferson was enrolled at the Pennsylvania school for the Deaf, Virginia read "a very interesting little book," *Tales of the Deaf and Dumb* by John Burnet, "written by a young man who lost his hearing at eight years old, after having learned to read however." The book convinced Virginia "so thoroughly of the importance of beginning the education of the deaf early, that I rejoiced in every page I read that our precious boy was placed where he would have the advantage of early education."[8]

Although Virginia was confident that the school for the Deaf was the best place for Jefferson, leaving the boy was not always easy. Although the family generally believed he was very happy at the school, occasionally his actions made his mother question his satisfaction there. Once, for example, when his mother visited him at the school, Jefferson "insisted on returning home" to the family's Philadelphia house. Later in the day, two pupils came to collect him, but Jefferson "made them signs that he wished to sleep with me, and that they must return without him." A houseguest suggested to Virginia that she attempt to bribe the boy to return to his dormitory. "By way of an experiment" she complied, offering the boy a coin if he accompanied the two girls to the school. "He consented at once," she reported to her husband, "and made a sign that he should get candy with the money."[9]

After a long summer vacation with his family, Virginia feared the boy would again not want to stay at his dormitory. As they left him at the school, Jefferson "made signs that we must come again to see him," she reported. Her fears were relieved: he "did not express a wish to accompany us."[10]

After Jefferson's second summer away from his fellow pupils, Virginia did not return to Philadelphia with her son. At first, he "made some objection" to leaving his family. Soon, though, the memory of the pupils and teachers—and the memory of the residential school's culture and language—made Jefferson eager to return. Virginia told her mother that Jefferson "was soon reconciled to the idea on being told that he should soon return (and being ignorant of the length of time that would probably elapse first)." He began to pack away the "little treasures" he had collected over the summer. As Virginia explained, Jefferson "describes the scene he anticipates in displaying them on a large table around which he says the children will assemble to see them." Despite his growing anticipation of the beginning of the school term, his mother confessed that she dreaded the "parting moment" which would "have its agony" for both mother and son.[11]

When the moment came, "he behaved like a man" according to his mother, although he did not eat the day of his departure. As he boarded the ship with his family members, "his little heart never failed" until the launch that took guests back to shore carried his family away. At that point young Jefferson "broke out into fits of crying and sobbing as if his heart would break." Father Nicholas returned to the ship to comfort his son and stayed all night, leaving only when the ship was ready to set sail the next day. "He bore the second parting better," reported his mother. "He sat by during the packing of his trunk and basket, and watched all the arrangements with great interest and intelligence." Although even this second leave-taking "pained" and "distressed" Jeff, the difficult departure did not shake Virginia's belief that sending her son off to the school for the Deaf was wise: "I feel convinced that he is better at the asylum than with us."[12]

e⌒

By the spring of Jefferson Trist's first year at the Pennsylvania school, his mother wrote to her husband about their son's first attempts at written English. One Sunday, Virginia walked to the school with her other two children, both hearing, to see the boy. He brought out his slate and "wrote several little words on it" such as *cat, dog, ear, eye, lip,* and *key*. As he tried to spell the last word, young Jefferson paused after the first two letters and "put his finger to his forehead in token of forgetfulness of the last letter." His mother recognized that her son's sign was "a very significant sign . . . taught to them to express forgetfulness." When she took the chalk and completed the word, Jefferson immediately "made with his fingers" his own *y*. Virginia wrote to her husband that after such a visit she was "more pleased with his situation" at the school. Now that she could get to know her child, she was also "more convinced what a fine boy" he was. Jefferson assured her of that fact again in June when he began to write his own name.[13]

David Tillinghast remembered his own efforts to learn English. He noted that upon entering the New York school for the Deaf, he "began a life of trying to master word language." He believed that American Sign Language was easy for him to acquire because it was pictorial and imitative of the physical world around him. Written English, on the other hand, presented David and his peers the challenge of a foreign language. They mastered vocabulary to which they had never been exposed. They memorized spellings, learning them without the help of sound-based phonics. They also painstakingly practiced grammar that differed from the grammar of ASL. English was the key, at least in the eyes of hearing Americans, to the world around them.[14]

e⌒

In 1834 J. A. Jacobs, the superintendent of the Kentucky school for the Deaf, constructed a textbook for use with his southern pupils. When the volume was first published, Jacobs intended it to be used exclusively at the Kentucky school. Quickly it became apparent that educators at schools throughout the South were seeking such a volume as well. As the director of the South Carolina school explained, "*Locality* has much to do in the development of the deaf mute mind, and must necessarily enter, largely, into any system of books prepared for their use." Needed were books "prepared expressly for the South" upon which teachers could rely, as opposed to books reflecting the ideology of the North.[15]

In staking out a position different from both manualist and oralist pedagogy, superintendent Jacobs argued that signing Deaf people could not think in English words: "The Deaf and Dumb can no more think in words than a blind man can conceive of colors," wrote Jacobs. He published a revised version of his textbook in 1860. Designed to teach English vocabulary and usage, the book deemphasized the use of sign in the classroom. Illustrations graced most pages. The book included these illustrations so that pupils could "understand it without any signing whatever." He did not advocate the banishment of signs altogether. Jacobs felt that when the illustrations were not enough, teachers should resort to "signs following the order of the words only," not the "colloquial signs" with ASL grammar. Preferably, signs would be used only to translate single English words. "When the combination and the order of words are to be taught, [signs] should be dispensed with, as far as possible." Their use would be "antagonistical [*sic*]" to the goal of learning standard English. Students should be encouraged to "disuse, as far as it is possible to lead them to do, the order and method of thought natural to them." Most lessons should be conveyed by spelling on the fingers (dactylology) or by what Jacobs called "language itself," that is, written English.[16]

In the 1860 edition, the author repeated his 1834 assertion that natural signing was damaging to students' efforts to learn English. He acknowledged that while ASL "in skillful hands" was "a perspicuous and powerful instrument for the communication of facts and ideas," he again argued that American Sign Language had no place in the English classroom. Natural signing when used as the means to teach written English simply placed "a great obstacle" before the Deaf.[17]

Why was rejection of American Sign Language so important to Jacobs? The language, he explained, was "different from, and opposite to, that of the English language." ASL was merely a "natural pantomime" that was "destitute of connective particles, and of grammatical inflections, concord, and government." In short, American Sign Language was, according to Jacobs and his supporters, "mere jargon" and "a chaotic mess."[18]

Jacobs's textbook tried to teach not only English grammar but lessons in life as well. For each exercise in the book, the author presented a set of sentences demonstrating a grammatical principal. As Jacobs acknowledged, "every sentence taught, should, as far as practicable, be made the vehicle of some useful information—some truth, fact, principle, or event in religion, science, philosophy, or history." Race and gender ideologies were embedded in the practice sentences. While teaching about English usage of the word *must,* for example, Jacobs presented instructional lessons as well, shown in the following sentences:

> You must be obedient to your father and mother. . . .
> We must love and obey God.
> We must be careful of fire.
> You must rise early.
> You must learn your lesson well.
> You must be silent in school.
> We must not eat too much.

To demonstrate the concept of opposition and difference, the textbook used sentences expressing acceptable gender roles:

> Are little boys fond of dolls? No.
> Little boys are fond of hammers,
> or sticks to ride on, or marbles.
> They care nothing for dolls.

and

> Little boys and girls are unlike—
> men and women are unlike.
> Men plough, cut wood, make ships, &c.
> Women sew, knit, and keep house.

And when teaching about subjects and objects, Jacobs attempted to convey his Christian religious beliefs to pupils: "God made us. We are made by God," students were to write. "The Jews crucified Jesus. Jesus was crucified by the Jews."[19]

Primary Lessons for Deaf-Mutes often used the experiences of Deaf pupils to help them connect to the lessons. Students were instructed to copy the sentence "You can not talk," so they would learn the word *can*, or they would be given a sentence with blanks to fill in: "_____ can hear a little. _____ can hear with one ear. (Fill in with appropriate names.)" To learn more about present-tense verbs, students copied the sentences "The teacher whips a bad boy. He does not whip a good boy," and "_____ signs awkwardly. Mr. _____ signs gracefully." Such sentences described not only the actual experiences of pupils in the residential schools. They also clearly portrayed the author's perspectives. People addressed as "Mr.," that is, hearing "professors" in Jacobs's school who learned sign at brief teacher training programs at schools for the Deaf, were deemed graceful signers. People who were not given titles, such as the students and Deaf teachers who had learned sign at a young age and relied on signing for most of their communication, were supposedly awkward. This assumption was the opposite of what was most likely true.[20]

Jacobs offered sentences about the agricultural life of the South: "In the South a great deal of cotton is raised," students practiced writing. "Where is cotton raised? In the South. Where is sugar raised? In the South." Students also rehearsed sentences about hog production in Kentucky and the growth of tobacco in Virginia.[21]

Interestingly, the practice sentences also contained reference after reference to people with disabilities other than deafness. "I saw a man who had no arms," one page said. Another paragraph lamented the difficulty of blindness: "See the poor blind boy! He cannot see the blue sky, or the green grass, or the faces of men. His dog is leading him home." The author continued, "Oh! How sad it is to be blind. I am glad I can see the bright sun, and the green grass, and the flowers of spring, and the snows of winter. The poor blind boy lives in perpetual darkness." Another sample sentence tried to explain why many people with retardation shared the lack of speech with the Deaf: "Some idiots can hear but can not speak, because they have not sense enough." Even Deaf pupils should look with pity on others, taught the author.[22]

Jacobs's textbook encouraged students to practice English by writing letters to their friends and family. Students were urged to begin by copying sample letters provided in the textbook:

> I am well. I am trying to learn to read and write. I can write a little. I can answer some questions. Mr. _____ is my teacher. He is kind to me. I love to learn. I have a pretty book, full of pretty pictures.

and

> I am happy to be able to write you a letter. I know you will be happy to receive a letter from your little deaf-mute girl. When I was at home, I could not talk to you by writing. I knew nothing. I was as ignorant as the horses and cows. But now I am beginning to know many things.[23]

Written English allowed Deaf children to correspond with their families. The letters between pupils and their parents were often class assignments, or at least the fulfillment of teachers' expectations for the students. These letters were considered to be opportunities to practice English skills and, thus, were often joint productions of pupils and teachers. As one student wrote, "The teachers tell them they must write letters to their parents and friends. Their parents and friends hear from them. Their parents and friends wonder that the Mutes improve so fast."[24]

When students could not understand letters from their families, educators chided that the problem stemmed not from poorly educated Deaf youngsters but from their ignorant hearing relatives who misspelled words and had bad handwriting. Because Deaf students depended upon the visual presentation of the writing and could therefore not sound out misspelled words, "uncouth spelling" meant the pupils had as much difficulty understanding the writing as they would trying to "recognize . . . their most familiar friend in a mask." Wrote one teacher, "They write, in general, better letters than they receive from their parents and friends." When the correspondence was poorly understood, "the fault is wholly with those who are communicating with them" and their "imperfect knowledge of the simplest rudiments of orthography and composition."[25]

Faculty and staff encouraged, or even required, students to write to their families in part because such letters helped make up for their children's absence from home. Contact and communication through letters also encouraged families to continue the children's education at the school. Since most of the pupils knew no written English before their formal schooling and many hearing parents knew no formal sign, letters allowed communication at a level higher than most parents had ever had with their Deaf children. But at the same time, mediated as the letter writing was by familial outsiders and carried out in a language still not typically comfortable for the Deaf pupils, these indirect efforts at communication highlighted the developing pattern of separation between hearing and Deaf family members.

Like Jefferson Trist, young Thomas Tillinghast of North Carolina was separated from his family when he entered school. And he too was drawn in quickly to this new world. In the middle of May in 1842, Robina Norwood took her grandson to the school for the Deaf in Staunton, Virginia. She and the eight-year-old boy were accompanied by family friends and carried a letter from William Norwood, Thomas's uncle and Robina's son, to give to the principal of the Virginia school. The letter contained "every thing relating to Tom's interests," and Robina knew that William's letter would assure that the "reception will be properly attended to as if he were present." She was concerned that if an older woman presented a child to a professional, the child might be overlooked, but with a letter from a powerful male relative from Virginia, the child would be assured of respectful, and perhaps even preferential, treatment.[26]

Robina was pleasantly surprised at Tom's maturity on the journey. She wrote her daughter that "Tom was much less trouble than I expected." Because he was so well behaved, she suspected that he was ready to be a student at the boarding school and could be "very easily managed" there. Robina enjoyed seeing the boy's excitement during the trip: "He has been greatly delighted with everything and found constant amusement all the way." She herself was delighted with "the Beautiful and often grand and sublime scenery" of the Virginia mountains that they passed through as they approached the school.[27]

When Robina and Thomas arrived in Staunton at the school for the Deaf, Robina filled out the paperwork to enroll her grandson. Although she hoped to have Thomas show off the skills he learned at home and at the Iveys, the boy refused. When Robina wrote Tom's mother and wanted him to sign his name to the letter, "some whim or other took hold of him and I could not get him to do it."[28]

After the formal admissions process, Thomas and Robina were introduced to the staff of the school, including the principal and several teachers. She was especially anxious to meet Margaret Eskridge, "the Lady who conducts the Domestic Establishment." Robina wanted to make sure the woman would take care of her grandson. Upon meeting her, she was reassured: Eskridge was a "sensible plain Motherly Woman" who would "take as much care of Tom as if he were her own son." Robina was also pleased with the relationship she seemed to have with the young pupils. The matron invited Tom to sleep in her own room with her young sons (presumably hearing) instead of in the large dormitory rooms with the older male (and not elite) pupils. To Tom, newly removed from his home and likely not sure why, the invitation was probably reassuring. Robina noted that it "pleased him very much."[29]

In addition to meeting the staff, Robina and Thomas met a few of the school's pupils. Although the great majority of pupils were older or even grown, Tom was "greatly delighted" when he found "a little boy of his own size and age" named Silas Long, commonly called Oliver Twist. Young "Oliver" was "still more pleased with Tom," presumably because he was eager to have another young boy at the school. There were also "two little girls from 9 to 10 years old" at the school, and Robina found them not only "very smart and intelligent" but "as happy as any children" she had ever met.[30]

Although Robina Norwood was impressed by what she saw at the school, she noted that "the only thing that distracted from my satisfaction" was the pain of parting. Robina was sad to leave her grandson, but even more, she was aware of the "distress . . . it would be to Poor Tom." In

Robina's few days at the school, Tom had "learnt the way" from his sleeping quarters to her room, and "he came several times every day" to see her, checking that his grandmother had not yet left him. Robina noted that the eventual parting was "a very painful business." On the other hand, she felt that Mrs. Eskridge "seemed to know so well how to manage" such family disruptions that Tom would be "soon reconciled" to his new situation at the Virginia school.[31]

After Thomas's grandmother Robina returned home, she sat down to write her daughter Jane a complete account of Tom's admission to the Virginia school. Although she knew "how anxious" Jane would be to find out about her "dear boy," Robina had not written earlier from Staunton because she was "in such a whirl that I could not find time or collect my thoughts sufficiently to say what I wished." After describing some of the particulars of her journey, she assured Tom's mother that she was "greatly pleased with everything I saw relating to the Institution" and that she thought "our dear little boy" was "very happily situated" at the school.[32]

Although Tom, Jefferson, and other Deaf youngsters may not have understood why they were being taken away from their homes and then left by their families at the schools, they were probably pleased with their new situation, where they could communicate easily with their peers in sign language, as opposed to using halting home sign with their families. Tom Tillinghast's grandmother noted that the boy's style of communication was readily understood by the other pupils: "His signs appeared to be perfectly intelligible to them." Perhaps this is confirmation that Tom had received tutoring from Eunice Ivey, who would have learned American Sign Language at the New York school. But the other students might have understood him even if he came to school using only home signs. The Deaf pupils' ability to understand the mime and gesture of a new student would surely have been extensive. They had learned how to understand without knowing precisely what was said because of their experience with their own families.[33]

Within a month of Thomas Tillinghast's enrollment at the Virginia school, principal Joseph Tyler wrote to the boy's father that Thomas was "happy as the day is long." Already he showed "a great aptness at acquiring knowledge" and had, in fact, already learned several words of written English. The principal assured Samuel Tillinghast that his son "manifest[ed] a daily increasing desire to learn." Samuel eagerly awaited the time when the family could begin to exchange letters with their boy: "I look forward with great pleasure to the time when we can communicate with him." Already, members of the family wrote letters to Thomas which the boy's teachers translated into sign language.[34]

School was dismissed for the summer holidays only a month after Thomas enrolled at the Virginia school. The young pupil boarded at the school over the summer, as did a number of more advanced students. The results of his "vacation instruction" by his peers was that by autumn, Thomas could "write a slate full of the words in most [common] use instantly upon the sign being made."

Letter writing was a valued art in the antebellum South. By November, the boy sent home his first letter: "I am well. I am fat now. I hope that you are well. I love my mother and father. I wish to see my mother and father. I like to learn." He finished the effort with his full signature. The letter was enclosed in a missive from the school's principal assuring the Tillinghasts that their son was "acquiring habits of study which will carry him rapidly onward." This letter, like most of the letters that followed, was presented to the principal to read, correct, then forward to his parents. Perhaps his teachers helped him construct the letter, or perhaps he copied the note from models provided in his textbooks. Requiring students to write letters to their families assured that parents were receiving the kinds of reports that teachers and the school would approve of. By the end of December, principal Tyler prefaced one of the boy's letters by adding, "The above [letter from Thomas] are his thoughts, but he was aided in putting them into the English language. The whole was suggested by him, and I hope that by [February] he will need no aid at all in speaking his mind to you." The letter follows the basic outline of the textbook models: "I am well. I hope that you are well. I like to learn very much. The deaf and dumb are all well. I often think about you and my grandmother. I love you very much. I wish to see you. My teachers are kind to me. I pray to God every day."[35]

A letter penned in March 1843 revealed to the Tillinghasts the limits of Thomas's literacy in English. "I am well. I love you," began the young pupil. "I hope to see my father and mother often. I learn my books. I wish deaf and dumb are well. Father glad letter. I think good Mr. Tyler teaches know. I love Susan W. Harwood [a Deaf teacher at the Virginia school]. Fayetteville man school learn boys. I love Mr. Eskridge, keep good. I love mother." Thomas then continued with a phrase he learned from the textbook models: "You are, I hope, well." As usual, the letter was enclosed in a package from Joseph Tyler. This time the principal asked for understanding of the boy's limited writing skills: "You must not by any means mistake his knowledge of our language for the measure of his attainments. He knows much which he cannot communicate to you yet in the English language." Afraid the Tillinghasts would blame the Virginia school for the pupil's grammar failings, the principal was quick to defend the school. Instead of focusing exclusively on written English, he pointed out, the school taught a variety of subjects by means of a language more readily accessible to the pupils: a signed one. "By the sign language [Thomas] has been made acquainted with an endless variety of things of which he knew nothing before, including much bible history and precept." He also stated that a well-developed signed language would facilitate indirect communication between Thomas and his parents: "By signs also I can easily and distinctly make anything you wish to write to him known to him," explained principal Tyler. He continued to send Thomas's "uncorrected lines written by himself" because he believed the letters, however ungrammatical by hearing society's standards, would "no doubt be welcome" to the Tillinghasts. He also continued to "hope he [would] by and by write more and better."[36]

During Thomas's second year at the Virginia school, he began to send home letters asking about his southern family's welfare. "How are the crops in your neighborhood?" asked this elite southern boy. By his third year, in addition to his occupation with agriculture ("God created the rain and the soil is fertile"), Thomas began to express political opinions. In October he wrote to his father, "I am against Polk Dallas and Texas." A few months later he stated, "Whigs are greater than democrats. Perhaps. Democrats are not very wise. Henry Clay is very wise." These statements were contained in letters approved by Principal Tyler and received no response whatsoever from Thomas's family, who may or may not have agreed with his comments. Almost certainly Thomas could not have acquired his political understanding from discussions with his immediate family since no letters exist chronicling such a discussion and since he and his family were unable to communicate face-to-face at such a sophisticated level.[37]

𝑒

Although the practice of letter writing did assist Deaf pupils in the learning of written English, J. A. Jacobs's proposed method of relying for the most part on writing to teach Deaf pupils seemed to be a failure, according to Jacobs himself. He insisted that, since written English was for hearing people simply symbols of spoken words, Deaf people should be able to use English written words to be "written signs [symbols] of their own language." Writing was no more a translation for the Deaf than it was for the hearing. Somewhere though, Jacobs acknowledged, there was a flaw in the system. Jacobs publicly admitted defeat: "It is not pretended that by th[is] mode of instruction . . . anything like general accuracy has been secured, either in single sentences or connected composition, with a majority of deaf mutes. Whatever methods I have tried, I have to confess with the bitterest regret, not to say shame and mortification, have failed of such an attainment. I fear that I have fallen short of the success which others have obtained by different, and, as it seems to me, inferior methods." Despite his admission, Jacobs felt certain that his methods, "in more skillful hands," offered great potential in Deaf education, "not in conveying a greater amount of knowledge to the mind of the pupil, but in enabling him to express better his knowledge and thoughts in the order of written or spoken language."[38]

The majority of southern educators of the Deaf recognized that neither articulation nor written English were panaceas. Instead teachers turned to sign language as the primary method of teaching Deaf pupils. They felt that instruction through sign allowed students to learn rapidly about a wide range of subjects, including science, arithmetic, and religion. Despite their interest in developing the minds of their Deaf pupils, however, instructors never lost sight of their primary goal: to teach the Deaf written English. As the principal of the Texas school for the Deaf observed, "The objective point in the American System is to communicate to the deaf mute a knowledge of written language which becomes for him a substitute for speech in his intercourse with those around him, and a means of becoming familiar with the printed knowledge expressed in printed books."[39]

CHAPTER 7

$\mathcal{C}$ ⌒ *With the Eyes to Hear and the Hands to Speak*

WHEN DEAF PUPILS FIRST ENTERED THE CLASSROOM, the majority of southern schools for the Deaf immediately began to offer lessons in elementary sign language. Students themselves had already fashioned rudimentary sign skills by combining home sign with their experiences in the dorm with other pupils. Teachers quickly tried to intervene. Many instructors believed that although signed language was created by Deaf people, educated hearing people could improve upon it. It was expected that the "limited and imperfect" sign of Deaf people would be "improved" by hearing instructors who could inject some of the complexities of an oral language. Through hearing input, instructors believed, signed language would enter into a "highly cultivated and improved state."[1]

Using American Sign Language extensively to facilitate lessons, teachers introduced written English by trying to connect a physical object or concept, its ASL sign, and its written representation. A teacher would hold up an object such as a hat or pen and present its sign. Depending on the level of the pupils' sign literacy, the teacher might then ask the pupils to explain the object's uses in "the pantomime language." Next, the teacher might write the name of the object upon a slate, encouraging students to see a connection between the concrete object and "the particular combination of letters composing the name of the object." As soon as students understood the concept of written language (in other words, that "speaking and

92

hearing people have a written language by which they can recall to the mind of another the same idea which occupies the mind of the writer"), the teacher might begin to teach many other nouns by the same process. Eventually, students would be exposed to the entire alphabet through the variety of written words.[2]

After students learned how to express a handful of nouns in both ASL and written English, the teacher could introduce adjectives by focusing on the color, size, or shape—"the most obvious qualities"—of the object. The students would begin to learn phrases (in both ASL and English) such as the "black hat" or the "red bird." Colors were often the first adjectives taught because they could be "readily brought before the eye" and presented "such a marked difference in contrast." Later, "less obvious attributes" could be taught through the use of example. For example, one teacher explained that "if we wish to teach the quality of 'hardness,' we select a stone or some other substance possessing that quality, and present it to the pupil, with the desire that he impress it with his fingers. It of course will resist pressure. He is then directed to strike it with his knuckles. It hurts them." The author continued, "He is directed to bite or cut it. He makes the attempt but fails to make any impression. He is directed to throw it on the floor or table and it makes an impression instead of receiving one." The experiments continued: the teacher would hammer the stone until it became powder, without the "resisting power" of stone. When the teacher asked a student to compare a new stone with the leftover stone particles, he or she would discern that the main difference was the power of resistance. "He would then be told that '*hard*' is the name of the resisting power," said the teacher. At that point, other hard objects such as a key or nail could be offered to the pupils so they could expand their understanding.[3]

After the students mastered lists of adjectives, the teacher would begin to present verbs. Educators recognized that the verb "presents more difficulties to the deaf mute teacher than any other part of speech," partly because ASL and English were so different structurally. One teacher advised introducing verbs by teaching their imperative form, that is, directing the pupils to stand or sit, or carry one of the concrete nouns they had learned earlier. The proposal was made because "this form of verb . . . represents the conceptions of the deaf mute's mind more nearly than any other form of the verb." Next would be the introduction of the present participle "because it is next removed from the imperative in its capacity to represent the suggestions of the pantomime language." The real difficulties in teaching English verbs began to surface when pupils were introduced to verb tenses. American Sign Language sentences did, of course, have a sense of tense, but tense was expressed through the context and spacing of the sentence rather than through conjugated verbs. Deaf pupils, therefore, had no recourse to direct translation when they were learning English conjugation. Instead, teachers contrasted present and past, or present and future, verbs: "A boy has bought and is eating an apple" or "A boy is picking and will eat some berries." Such examples may have helped the students grasp the English tense system but, as the author of the teaching guide admitted, "not however without great labor."[4]

In addition to teaching students to write the English language, the teachers taught the manual alphabet. After the letter *A* was written on a slate, the teacher would then "place his hand in the position representing it" and the students were instructed to imitate the teacher. After the pupils had learned the signed alphabet, the class would begin fingerspelling the same short words they were learning to write. Soon, students would be able to fingerspell at roughly the same speed as they could read written English. Fingerspelling, since it mediated between ASL and English, was not usually as comfortable for Deaf people as American Sign Language. Although they could generally sign at the same speed their hearing counterparts could speak, fingerspelling was a slower process. Nevertheless, fingerspelling allowed schools for the Deaf to teach written English via a form of sign language in a visual classroom. The manual alphabet also allowed people to inject sign language with English words with no direct sign equivalent.[5]

Despite the fact that almost all instructors of Deaf people agreed that manual pedagogy was most effective, argument over which method was the best continued. A major debate raged during the nineteenth century about what kind of signed language should be used in the classroom.

Because relatively few of the teachers in schools for the Deaf grew up knowing American Sign Language, teachers were often not fluent in the language and could not communicate all of what they wanted to say while using only the signs they knew. Their limited fluency was only part of the problem. Because ASL was not a codified language in the nineteenth century, it almost certainly varied widely from place to place. Because the pupils themselves rarely learned the language via familial transmission, very early ASL may have lacked some of the richness that languages acquire over time and across generations. Because of all these limitations, instructors often invented new signs and added them to the vocabulary of the classroom.[6]

One type of sign was what instructors called "significant." A significant sign immediately conveyed what it represented: it "represents an idea so clearly that it needs no explanation." In other words, clear gestures that could be understood by the rudimentary signer were considered significant. Signs such as HAT, made with the palm patting the top of the head, were deemed significant. Although less obvious, the sign DANCE was also significant. It was made by shaking the inverted V of the first and second fingers over the palm of the other hand. Human beings performing an action were so frequently symbolized by the inverted V hand miming the action that even a new signer would have understood the majority of such signs. Many significant signs were part of the already established vocabulary of the Deaf community, and when instructors wished to add new vocabulary to ASL, they tried to create significant signs.[7]

Another class of vocabulary was made up of "conventional" signs. A conventional sign was "one that has been agreed upon, which has some resemblance to the idea to be conveyed" but which was not immediately understood if one had not been introduced to the sign. For example, the sign GIRL "would not be understood by even an educated deaf mute, if he had not seen it." The sign was made by tracing the jawbone with the thumb, supposedly to indicate the ties of a bonnet. The sign WOMAN was a compound sign, beginning with the sign GIRL but followed by holding the palm at the general height of women. After being told how the signs were derived, the Deaf person would "at once see the fitness." A conventional sign was not a transparent gesture, but nevertheless the roots of the sign could be traced (accurately or not) to a concrete object. According to educators, this kind of signing was the most common in schools across the South.[8]

Signs could also be "arbitrary." An arbitrary sign was "one that has no resemblance to the idea being conveyed." Abstract words were by necessity signified by arbitrary signs. For example, when a signer wanted to sign SIZE, he or she would position her palms facing each other about twelve inches apart, then open them roughly another four inches. Sometimes concrete words such as the metal LEAD, made by tapping the back of the hand against the chin, also had arbitrary signs.[9]

Sometimes arbitrary signs were attacked as "stupid abuse" of the manual method of education. When a teacher chose to sign ROASTED CHESTNUTS with the sign ROAST used for a roasted animal (cranking a spit), the sign was not only arbitrary but it actually worked at cross purposes to the concrete. If an instructor wanted to sign BURN UP but for BURN "he signed as if plucking his hand from contact with a hot stove," and for UP the teacher signed the direction, students would not necessarily understand that the teacher meant CONSUME. Most instructors argued that the fact that arbitrary signs could be abused was no reason to dismiss all of them: "As well might a fork be pronounced a useless instrument, because some simpleton was detected eating soup with it."[10]

Some teachers wanted to make an explicit link between signs and written English words. One way to remind students of the connection was to use an initialized sign. An initialized sign incorporated the handshape for the first letter of the sign's English equivalent into the performance of the ASL sign. Instructors felt that such transformation of the sign would give "aid in giving distinctiveness and perspicuity to the idea: as C for color and W for weather." Instructors were constantly trying to infuse ASL with the vocabulary of English and references to written English.[11]

Disagreement about the appropriate grammar for classroom sign language was more heated than discussions about proper signing of individual vocabulary. Teachers debated whether they should teach pupils to sign in the "natural" grammar of American Sign Language or whether pupils should use ASL vocabulary arranged in English word order.[12]

Kentucky principal J. A. Jacobs, despite his suggestion in some of his texts that American Sign Language be "dispensed with" in favor of written English, was an outspoken advocate of "methodical sign." Methodical sign, as Jacobs wrote, referred to the "the natural signs of deaf mutes, extended, systematized, and conformed to the arrangement and idioms of written language." Using the signed vocabulary of American Sign Language but following the order of written English, methodical sign, by Jacobs's designation, would also include signs for grammatical symbols and even parts of speech. The application of English grammar to the vocabulary of American Sign Language—that is, "the use of a sign for every word"—was, according to Jacobs, "not only convenient, but necessary." After all, the goal of education for Jacobs was to teach the Deaf students to put words "in their proper order—that is, in our [hearing people's] order." His goal was that of "inducing the mute to discontinue, by degrees, his powerful, picturesque, and impressive, but disconnected and unscientific pantomime." If students were not taught to think in English word order, they would continue to express themselves in a language that Jacobs felt was "destitute of connection and logical principles, and grammatical inflections, concord and government." American Sign Language's effect on the learning of English was "mischievous." If Deaf people continued to "retain and cherish their natural language," they would be condemned to confusion and "logical poverty."[13]

One hearing educator on a crusade to eradicate English-ordered sign language compared it to "teaching Latin and Greek by arranging the words in the order in which they would be translated into English." To him, using the grammar of English in order to communicate in other languages was not only disrespectful to the other language but pure lunacy.[14]

"Natural sign language" was not a pedagogical form of communication but rather the method of communication that Deaf people themselves routinely used when talking with each other. It was, according to advocates, "a language by itself, based upon nature, perfected by philosophy and art, tending toward greater beauty, force, scope, and perspicuity" than did constructed sign systems. Natural sign language, or to be more accurate, early American Sign Language, was for Deaf people "a substitute for oral language." The signs were developed within the Deaf community rather than by hearing teachers. As one educator stated, natural sign was the "mother tongue" of Deaf people.[15]

While some educators saw natural sign language as "utterly devoid of law or system," many hearing advocates for Deaf people recognized the

complex grammar of ASL. Speech, stated one writer, was an artificial creation based upon human construction. Natural sign language was, he
claimed, much more akin to art. Sculpture, like ASL, was a language
"founded on natural principles." So were the classical languages. Although
hearing Americans assumed "from habit" that English grammar was "the
most natural and expressive form of the language," anyone with knowledge
of other languages knew that other people expressed their ideas in a different order. The author gave an example to his readers: The English sentence
"The Christian worships God," would be written in Latin, "Christianus
Deum adorat." The phrase would be conveyed in American Sign Language
following the Latin order. Like Latin, claimed the author, sign language was
"in accordance with natural principles." To follow the most natural se-
quence, "we must consider first the *Christian*, second the *object*, and last *the
act of worship*. We do this because an analysis of the mental process by
which a knowledge of the act is arrived at, will show us that the *worshipper*
first attracts our attention and the *object* of the worship, and both occupy
the mind *antecedent* to the act of worshipping."[16]

Translating the sentence "I am going to Richmond tomorrow," another
advocate of Deaf education pointed out that the sentence would start with
a tense marker: "The thumb (the fingers being closed) resting on the cheek,
is passed upward and outward, with a slight curve, until the arm is extended": TOMORROW. Next, a perpendicular wave of an R handshape would
represent Richmond. Finally, the signer would point to the signer's own
chest then the pointing fingers would revolve around each other toward
where the shaken R was signed. "Thus we have, TOMORROW, RICHMOND
I GO." Another ASL analyzer stated that the object of the sentence was always listed first in a sentence, just as "nature prompts": "'THE WOODS I
WENT, AND SQUIRRELS KILLED FIVE'—'MAN SAW I, HORSE FALL
FROM, AND LEG HIS BROKE.'" While an English speaker might say,
"Yesterday a small boy caught a rabbit," an ASL signer would order the sentence "RABBIT BOY SMALL CAUGHT YESTERDAY."[17]

To explain "the minor elements in a logical classification of a sentence,"
such as adverbs and adjectives, one could expand the exemplary religious
sentence: "'The humble Christian devoutly worships the omnipotent
God.'" In sign language, the adjectives and adverbs would generally follow

the noun or verb they modified. In other words, the "greater elements" of the sentence would be stated, and only following them, when the recipient already knew the topic, would the words be modified. One would sign "'THE CHRISTIAN HUMBLE, GOD OMNIPOTENT, WORSHIPS DE-VOUTLY.'" As in the Richmond example, the signer probably located the nouns in the sign space in front of him or her, acknowledging the locations (essentially using them as pronouns) to make the order of action clear to the recipient. The linguistic use of space was perhaps the biggest difference between English-order pidgin sign and American Sign Language.[18]

Although the authors disagreed about the specific constructions that ASL required (all of which were likely valid), the authors recognized that applying English syntax to American Sign Language destroyed its linguistic integrity and made the pidgin sign difficult for non-English speakers to understand. They agreed that attempting to teach "the illogical unnatural hearing way" to Deaf pupils was "a task of immense labor" since even "the educated mute" continued to formulate thoughts in natural sign language.[19]

ASL's linguistic use of space, coupled with the grammatical use of dramatic facial expression, often upset hearing people for reasons other than concern about learning English. The physical language of ASL attracted other people's attention and was sometimes seen as source of embarrassment for Deaf children's hearing companions. For example, despite her newfound pride in her son, Virginia Trist was not entirely comfortable with what she sometimes saw as the spectacle of Jefferson's life in the Deaf community. When she ran into a group of pupils including her son on a field trip to the Masonic Hall to see a hydro-oxygen microscope, she was immediately happy to see them. But when they exited the Hall into the streets of Philadelphia with "many . . . waves of hands from the band of mutes," she was relieved that it was "not a fashionable hour or I should have felt rather awkward heading this procession attracting the notice of the passerbys."[20]

ᘒᔕ

Despite the frequently patronizing attitudes of hearing advocates of state schools for the Deaf, the young pupils and the adult Deaf staff quickly formed a community that did not always share the goals of hearing educators. No matter what language was taught in the classroom, whether it was speech or writing or English-order sign, American Sign Language was almost certainly the language of the dormitory and the playground. Although pupils spent long hours in the classrooms trying to perfect their written English skills, they spent many more hours—after class, on weekends, during summers—with their peers. They shared rooms in the dormitories, studied together in the evenings, ate together in the dining halls—all without the limiting classroom rule to use some form of English. American Sign Language was "the vernacular of the deaf and dumb": it allowed them "the full measure of social enjoyment." Sign was shared from Deaf staff to pupils, from older pupils to younger, and from pupils who grew up in homes where ASL was used to pupils who were the only Deaf people in their families.[21]

Exclusive reliance on signed communication could have the effect of marginalizing the Deaf community. Educators and hearing parents wanted their Deaf children to learn English sufficiently so they could work within the hearing world, passing notes with their hearing peers. A knowledge of English would prepare Deaf people "for transacting business with all their countrymen" in the "vernacular language of their country." Educators also wanted to facilitate "social intercourse" with hearing people. The use of American Sign Language, many hearing people believed, simply meant that Deaf people were wasting their time and perhaps even doing damage: they were learning to think in a language other than English. On top of that, American Sign Language facilitated social intercourse with other Deaf people, not with the hearing world. Hearing families feared that American Sign Language would remove their Deaf children from the family circle. Instead of identifying with hearing people with whom they could not easily communicate, Deaf people formed more significant bonds with people unrelated to them by blood: other Deaf people, whether or not they were from families of the same social classes, the same political perspectives, or even the same region of the country.[22]

American Sign Language encouraged the development of a separate culture for American Deaf people. Members of the culture did not feel that English was their native language. It was a language forced upon them by an often oppressive educational system. Deaf people usually struggled to master it, while their hearing counterparts easily absorbed its basics. ASL did not present these difficulties. It was a language wholly accessible to Deaf people. It was the language of the Deaf community throughout the United States. Camaraderie with other people using a signed language offered Deaf people an escape from the struggles their deafness caused in hearing America. American Sign Language was the grammar of liberation.

Part III. Self-Reliance and a
Sense of Community

Children who attended state residential schools for the Deaf
gave one another an understanding of deafness that was often at odds with
what it meant to their hearing families and to the southern community at
large. Although nineteenth-century schools were not free from discrimination against Deaf people, they fostered a sense of self-reliance among
their pupils and showed them the value of a strong Deaf community.
Membership in a community of people who understood deafness in similar ways and communicated with American Sign Language allowed Deaf
individuals to experience a taste of equality. But once outside the walls of a
school, Deaf people faced the negative assumptions of, and often direct
discrimination by, hearing society. Deaf southerners who never attended
residential schools, as well as those who had left or graduated, struggled to
find their place in a world not constructed for them.

John Jacobus Flournoy, a later-deafened man from Georgia, tried to
build his life in the world of the hearing, the world in which he had come
of age. Hearing society's negative assumptions about deafness meant that
Flournoy had to fight for the respect of the southern community. He
failed to achieve it. Flournoy's feelings of isolation, not merely his hearing
loss, led him to identify himself as Deaf. Perhaps it also encouraged his
turn away from the politics of his region and class. At a time of increasing
division between the North and the South, Flournoy saw the potential for
the transregional Deaf community to come together to control their own

lives. While few Deaf people embraced his actual proposal, the concept of
independence that underlay Flournoy's plan resonated deeply among Deaf
southerners.

Discussion of Flournoy's proposal fizzled out as sectional conflict
loomed on the horizon. The Civil War changed the face of southern education for the Deaf. Beginning at the time of secession, southern schools
began to differentiate themselves more and more from northern models.
Northern teachers and administrators were threatened with removal from
southern schools when legislators doubted their loyalties to the Confederate cause. The traditional northern association between abolitionist
thought and reform efforts for the Deaf became increasingly disturbing to
white southerners. The vagaries of the Confederate economy threatened
schools with cutbacks or closures. Many hearing male teachers and administrators left their academic positions to join the war effort. Several
schools were in the direct line of battle. As the war progressed, many of
the buildings not burned to the ground became either Confederate or
Union hospitals for wounded soldiers or jails for prisoners of war.

During the Civil War era, hearing southerners were concerned that
young white Deaf southerners could be more easily swayed toward northern ways of thinking than would their hearing counterparts, regularly surrounded by southern philosophies. Deaf individuals often did not have
well-developed bonds with their families. They had not necessarily absorbed a strong proslavery southern identity at their families' hearths. Instead they had grown up at state schools, learning a language separate
from that used by their neighbors and kin. Deaf people were set apart
from the hearing South. When loyalty to the white South was considered
the height of virtue in the late antebellum period, Deaf individuals ran the
risk of treason in the eyes of their hearing friends and families.

Sometimes hearing southerners' fears were realized. When war threatened the running of southern schools and many Deaf pupils transferred to
northern schools, the antagonisms between North and South and the

ramifications of that conflict encouraged at least one southern student, David Tillinghast, to reconsider his identity. Sent to a northern school for the Deaf to complete his education during the war years, David began to assert himself in ways often surprising and disappointing to his hearing family. The separation from his family allowed him to take a teaching job that made him self-sufficient. As the war devastated the finances of his hearing family members, David was able to use his salary to assist them. Although during the antebellum years David and his Deaf brother Thomas were not expected to be heads of the Tillinghast clan, the tumultuous social and economic changes of the postwar period allowed them to become exactly that.

$\mathcal{e}\frown$ The Dignity and Honor of Human Nature

IN 1808 JOHN JACOBUS FLOURNOY was born into an elite southern family. His father, Robert Flournoy, was from Savannah, Georgia, where he owned several cotton plantations and two hundred slaves. When he died in 1825, Robert was worth more than a hundred thousand dollars, and his estate was divided among his seven children. With his share of the inheritance in hand, John Jacobus Flournoy began his adulthood. In 1830 he was admitted to the freshman class at the University of Georgia.[1]

After only a few months in college, Flournoy began to experience a dramatic decrease in his ability to hear. He wrote that he was becoming as "deaf as a white oak post," and he lost the ability to modulate his voice. Soon his hearing classmates had difficulty understanding Flournoy's speech. Isolated and frightened, the young man fled from his quarters at the university.[2]

Deafness was not something unknown to Flournoy. One of his older brothers, Marcus, had been diagnosed with deafness as a young child. It is possible that John Jacobus Flournoy grew up in a household that used some sort of signed communication, at least a home sign that the family could use to communicate with their Deaf relative. In the years between Marcus's education and Flournoy's adult-onset deafness, the first school for the Deaf was established in the United States: the American Asylum for the Education and Instruction of the Deaf in Hartford, Connecticut.

Perhaps because of his brother's deafness, Flournoy was familiar with the school and decided immediately upon his hearing loss to go there in order to reconcile himself to what he termed later "the universal wreck of soul and body." After packing his belongings, he left Georgia for Hartford.[3]

The American Asylum for the Deaf was not designed for students of Flournoy's age or academic level. It was a place for the education of Deaf children, especially those who were Deaf before they learned English. Pupils learned to read and write, practiced mathematics, and prepared for careers, many in vocational fields. Classes were not appropriate for a college-level student.

But Hartford did offer something to John Jacobus Flournoy: it provided the model of a community of people who could communicate with each other easily. The American Asylum for the Deaf showed Flournoy a new way to define deafness, one that was quite different from the exclusion he had experienced at the University of Georgia. Refusing to accept the assumptions of hearing Americans both northern and southern, the Deaf students and teachers at Hartford knew they were competent individuals and the equals of hearing people. This vision of community and the equality of Deaf people affected Flournoy profoundly.[4]

When Flournoy realized that the American Asylum could not offer him appropriate instruction or even a large number of Deaf peers his age, he searched for another place of refuge. Still reeling from the diagnosis of permanent deafness and experiencing a few other physical and psychological symptoms, Flournoy decided to check himself into the Lunatic Asylum in South Carolina. When he first arrived, Flournoy suffered a series of fits of "terrible strength." In order to end the seizures, the Asylum physician "dashed [the patient's] head with Pitchers of cold water. [The fits] instantly ceased." The following day, the physician instructed the staff to shave his head. Flournoy was diagnosed as epileptic and bled by the asylum physician as therapy. Soon he withdrew himself from the South Carolina Lunatic Asylum and went back home to Georgia, asserting that he was *"not crazy."*[5]

Flournoy then decided that he had made a mistake in going to the Lunatic Asylum and that instead he should have gone to Pennsylvania Hospital. Rather than packing his bags yet again, the young man turned to the medicines he found on the carts touring the countryside and the remedies advertised on broadsheets. He became interested in phrenology, "as sublime a science as ever was made known." Later in his life he even developed "Flournoy's Medical Head Bands." He claimed that by using "Animal Magnetism, Mesmerism, Electricity, Magic, and the manifestations of the Spirit, together with impulses from the Aurora Borealis," the headbands would cure the common cold (as long as it was not a summer cold) and assure a lifespan of one hundred and twenty years.[6]

What might have been the correct diagnosis of Flournoy's condition? He was certainly Deaf, but was he "crazy"? Did he have epilepsy? Flournoy himself acknowledged that he had seizures. He wrote that he was "periodically afflicted with mysterious convulsions, proceeding from the mind, medically and commonly known as spasmodic, operating upon and violently exercising [*sic*] the body, by spasmodic influences." Others acknowledged that he had, as his obituary put it, "some peculiar freaks of mind." Throughout his life, Flournoy was very conscious that people thought he was crazy or at least eccentric. And he was—at least the latter. According to legend, Flournoy rode a small donkey around town, wore his rubber overcoat in sunny weather, and never cut his beard or hair, the latter perhaps in response to the South Carolina Asylum's involuntary shaving of his head. Flournoy said he knew others looked at him as if he were "some nonedescript [*sic*] specimen of Zoology." Flournoy even claimed that parents invoked his name in order to scare their children into obedience, saying he was a "wild man who would kill and devour them in less than no time!"[7]

After his initial failed attempts to find a place where he belonged, Flournoy, as he said, finally "obtained relief" in prayer and in "a voluntary exertion of the mind to turn itself away from gloomy anticipations." As his biographer stated more expansively, Flournoy "determined to find an outlet for his pent-up ambitions: he would become a great reformer and moral teacher, not only for Georgia but for the United States, and, perhaps, for the world."[8]

Flournoy set out to give speeches to spread his "great reforms" and "moral teachings." Here, his deafness got in the way. His audiences "would not listen to him. They reviled him and made fun of him." People could not understand his voice. As Flournoy's biographer said, his "speech-making performances always left his audience confused or threw them into a riot of laughter and rowdiness."[9]

Flournoy was undeterred in his efforts to spread his wisdom and do good for his fellow white male citizens. In addition to publishing a large number of editorials and pamphlets, Flournoy put his name on the ballot for the lower house of the legislature in 1835. He listed his name on the ballots for both the Union party and States Rights party on the grounds that he would represent all the people. He received ten votes, less than one half of one percent. He ran twice more for the legislature, eventually upping his vote tally to twenty-one.[10]

By this point, Flournoy was livid. His personal crisis had turned into anger. He was tired of people blasting him, as he said, "as the mildew." Although he knew that Deaf people were capable of becoming political representatives and should be given the chance to do so, the voters of Georgia rejected him. Flournoy was sure it was his deafness that caused his fellow citizens to discriminate against him. In what was perhaps his first oppositional stance, Flournoy began signing his pamphlets, "J. J. Flournoy, The Deaf and Dumb." In a place where he could have hidden his deafness, he chose to flaunt it.[11]

As early as 1833, Flournoy publicly discussed the position of Georgia's Deaf people. He urged the state legislature to open a school for, as he said, "Southern Deaf." The state legislature did begin to pay for Georgia's Deaf children to attend the American Asylum for the Deaf, but they did not institute a school of their own for more than a decade, by which time the issue of states' rights was being discussed at every turn. By the time the Georgia school opened, Flournoy's vision of a regional school for southern Deaf was no longer feasible. Southern states decided to meet their educational responsibility as individual states, not as a region. Virginia, North Carolina, and Tennessee had already opened state schools, and other southern states were passing legislation that would lead to opening their own.[12]

Flournoy was rankled by an 1840 Georgia law that allowed the state to appoint a legal guardian to a Deaf person if he or she were "incapable of managing his or her estate, or his, or her, or themselves." In actuality the state rarely applied the law, and when they did, they required extensive documentation that the person was unable to oversee his or her own estate. But Flournoy railed publicly against any law that classified Deaf people as incompetent. Perhaps the young man, deafened for ten years when the law was passed, took the law personally. Years before, he had seen his own father unsuccessfully attempt to disinherit his Deaf brother Marcus. The gentleman stated in his will only that Marcus was too rebellious, but perhaps the family knew or suspected that the father viewed Marcus as irresponsible or incompetent because of his deafness.[13]

J. J. Flournoy's two statements about deafness did not garner much attention. Neither did a request to revise the United States Constitution in order to make more explicit the nation's gratitude to God. Flournoy was perhaps best known for his 1835 pamphlet on race and slavery entitled "An Essay on the Origins, Habits, &c. of the African Race: incidental to the propriety of having nothing to do with NEGROES." He angered proslavery southerners and abolitionists alike with his extreme proposal for the "EFFICIENT INSTANTANEOUS EXPULSION . . . of every Negro and Mulatto from this Country, back to their own Africa." Flournoy was not opposed to slavery in general, but he felt American slavery was a moral evil because it had brought Africans to this land. He called himself the "Sarah of America," seeing a parallel between his own efforts to rid his home of blacks with Sarah's efforts in Genesis to rid her home of Hagar.[14]

Africans were, in Flournoy's radical rhetoric, "a direct agent of Satan." He argued that Africans were black "in accordance to the will of God respecting Ham." After the monumental flood in Genesis, Noah's son Ham had looked on his father's nakedness. As punishment, God had cursed Ham and all his descendents, whom Flournoy believed were the Africans. He believed that "the sin of Ham was foul and abominable, and . . . the Savior has not accepted of his progeny. *They are, I believe, predestined and preordained to death, before the arrival of the Millennium.*" And as long as enslaved Africans and African Americans remained in the states, whites were doomed—and with them, the American nation.[15]

The crisis that Flournoy imagined was twofold. First, he was seriously concerned about the "amalgamation" of whites and blacks. "Who can suppose Christ to have intended a state of things so appalling, a scene of society

so unseeming, an admixture of races so repulsive, and a confusion so inevitable?" he wrote. Slaves were "whoremongers" and slaveholders could not
resist their temptations. Nonsexual intimacy was also of concern: How
could whites in the South keep their families from "deep-laid depravity" if
"brutish and obscene negro girls are entrusted with the nursery of children!" Flournoy believed that the connections between blacks and whites
would remain unacceptably intimate as long as Africans remained enslaved
or even in close proximity.[16]

Flournoy was also sure that the "peculiar institution" of slavery effec-
tively enslaved nonelite white southerners. Black slaves, he argued, could
"poison your heart against your neighbour [sic]; [they] can infuse into
your veins a fell and Cainish spirit." From this spirit had come southern
policies such as primogeniture which degraded poor whites. The South, argued Flournoy, could never be a true land of liberty until the "magical
virtues" of "oligarchic birth, connexions [sic] and emotions" were discarded. Flournoy "publicly admitted that he used every opportunity to stir up
the poor against the rich." His goal was a society where "the white man will
be living in God's happiness, etc." as "one mighty band of peaceful American brothers" rather than as a family split apart by class.[17]

Like many other southerners who voiced concern about slavery, Flournoy was an elite who owned slaves himself. After giving away much of his
property to his immediate family (that is, his wife and children), he continued to own roughly a dozen slaves on a six-hundred-acre plantation on
St. Helena. His critique of slavery was not dissimilar to Hinton Rowan
Helper's argument that appeared in print almost a third of a century after
Flournoy's. What made Flournoy react with such revulsion to both slavery
and slaves? And what made him interested in the welfare of nonelite white
southerners?[18]

Clearly, his interpretation of Christian religion was central: perhaps due
to his struggles in his society, Flournoy needed a world of strict truths and
rules. And perhaps he was by nature adversarial and eager to alienate his
community. Or perhaps his disabilities gave him insight into the class
struggles of his region. His disabilities, "which made him an object of mer-
riment, prevented his reception socially by the well-to-do and the planter

aristocrats," theorized his biographer. "Being relegated to the position of the other half, he found it natural to take up the cudgel for their side."[19]

Over all his years of writing controversial pamphlets and newspaper articles, Flournoy's desire to serve in the government did not disappear. He felt that his moral vision of a country with neither Africans nor slavery required him to render his services to the leadership of the country. Certain that attempts to run for office would be met with discrimination by the masses of southerners he defined as backwards, Flournoy decided to seek appointed office. In 1850 he first approached his relative Howell Cobb, then Speaker of the U.S. House of Representatives. Cobb laughed at Flournoy, gave him money, and sent him home. Three years later, Flournoy went to Attorney General Caleb Cushing and asked for a post. Flournoy stated that he did not care what post he was given, as he only wanted the opportunity to serve. Again he was dismissed. Finally, following further dismissals, he wrote directly to President Buchanan in 1857, asking to be appointed "Ambassador to the Mormons." Buchanan ignored him, so Flournoy wrote to the assistant secretary of state suggesting that he would be an excellent candidate for emissary to Brigham Young.[20]

What was John Jacobus Flournoy's connection with the Mormons? He adamantly claimed he was not a follower. But about the time he was campaigning for political appointment as emissary, Flournoy released two pamphlets that shed light on his fascination with the exiled religious group.

In 1858 Flournoy proposed what he termed "trigamy," suggesting that all men should have three wives. Upon reading this novel proposal, Oliver Wendell Holmes summarized that it was so men could be "solaced at once by the companionship of the wisdom of maturity, and of those less perfected, but hardly less engaging, qualities which are found at an earlier period of life." Flournoy's motivation for his proposal was partially personal: his own marriage was in a shambles and apparently he viewed his sex life in even less charitable terms. (He himself tried bigamy: while his wife was still living, he married a thirteen-year-old girl.)[21]

There were also political motivations for Flournoy's proposal. Deeply concerned about white men engaging in sexual practices with African

American women, Flournoy argued that trigamy would destroy all brothels and stop "race amalgamation." When one wife refused a husband sex, he could simply ask another one of his wives rather than seek alternatives outside of marriage—alternatives that could lead to racial impurity. Although many people laughed at his proposal, its author continued to discuss trigamy because, as he said, due to the threat of amalgamation, it would *"destroy the State for me to pause!"*[22]

Flournoy was insistent that it was not the Mormons who inspired his proposal: "I was for my peculiar *'reformation'* before I ever heard of Joseph Smith." It was his interest in trigamy that drew him to the Mormons.

℮

In 1855 Flournoy showed another link to the Mormons: his interest in establishing a new utopian community in the West. A land with neither slaves nor free African Americans was, in his view, the "only vigour [*sic*] and hope of the poor white man—his real independence." The community he proposed, however, was not to be for all non-slaveholding white men but specifically for those who could not hear. Flournoy suggested that he and his Deaf peers create their own state in the western territories: a "Deaf-Mute Republic." As he wrote, "It is a political independence, a STATE SOVEREIGNTY, at which I aim, for the benefit of an unfortunate downtrodden class." Only by this measure could Deaf people "attain the dignity and honor of Human Nature." He concluded that a separate state was the "manifest destiny of our people."[23]

In such a state, Deaf people could manage their own affairs, elect their own leaders, and live in a state that embraced American Sign Language as its primary language: "We will have a small republic of our own, under our own sovereignty, and independent of all hearing interference." Deaf people, Flournoy wrote, would not have to "encounter insurmountable prejudice where we would assert equality" or have "hearing arrogance . . . shove aside" Deaf competence. "We are capable of many [things] of which the prejudice, and sometime even malignance of our hearing brethren deprive us!" Discrimination by hearing people vexed him deeply and seemed to be a deliberate conspiracy: "The auricular are not satisfied with hearing, nor with the usual mutual sympathies of their own class, but are banded and combined together in associations, open, and societies, secret, until they form a compact moral mechanism, that fairly by their majority, puts us in the shade." Flournoy responded viscerally, "We are not beasts, for all our deafness! We are MEN!" He could imagine no other way to avoid the emphatic dismissal that he daily experienced than to secede from his homeland. At least in the South, Flournoy claimed, Deaf people were "condemned, spurned, degraded, and abhorred, and I see no redemption but in forming a powerful oligarchy of our own to control a State at the West."[24]

The leadership of the Deaf republic would be totally in the hands of Deaf men. As Flournoy stated, "We would . . . allow no hearing man to have any lucrative office. This is all I care about. Its Legislature, Judiciary, &c., all mutes." He repeated, "This is what we want and for what we may emigrate: *The government of a piece of Territory.* Nothing more or less. . . . *This Government is to be sacred to the Deaf alone.*" He did acknowledge that hearing people would be allowed to come into the Deaf territory, and even that "the auricular" would be allowed to vote within the territory. Suffrage for the hearing would be necessary to maintain a sufficient population to become a state. The quest for voting citizens convinced Flournoy to extend the right to vote to almost any group: As he said dismissively, *"We would give women that right."*[25]

Flournoy believed the leadership of Deaf people in a Deaf state might be superior to the leadership of hearing individuals: "Many of us [Deaf people] have hearts, of an integrity superior to the *mad* hearing partisans that go to Congress and to legislatures, and fill presidential and gubernatorial seats." Hearing men, after all, were "often our inferiors in every thing but hearing." He continued, "I spurn . . . thousands of my hearing *inferiors*—who give the fatness of power and office to their own class—and keep me, like Lazarus, out at the gate of splendid and munificent patronage without sending me a solitary crumb." Flournoy argued that if the citizens of his Deaf state would elect him to office, "my intelligence and judgement may prove better and superior to the hearing majority." And unlike the hierarchical American nation, Flournoy's proposed state would be a model where "brotherly and sisterly love shall continue without invidious distinction."[26]

Flournoy's proposal was discussed at length in the *American Annals of the Deaf and Dumb.* Although Flournoy had the support of many Deaf southerners and a few others, most northern leaders were opposed, primarily on two grounds. First, many people, both hearing and Deaf, denied that Deaf people faced discrimination. "Mr. Flournoy takes too disconsolate a view" of the condition Deaf people face, said one of his Deaf critics, Edmund Booth. "I am acquainted with at least one thousand and I have not perceived that they are much more unhappy than, or held inferior to, the masses around them." Booth did concede that Deaf people rarely held political office, and he did acknowledge that they could not "enjoy life in its fullness as do their hearing associates." But the reason for this exclusion was not discrimination but, in Booth's words, "a part of the punishment inflicted for violation of nature's laws, which violation . . . results in deafness."[27]

Hearing people involved in Deaf education came down hard on Flournoy's claim that Deaf people were treated unfairly by hearing people. What about paternal and maternal love for Deaf children? Legislative funding for Deaf education? The contributions of hearing teachers and administrators? The hearing editor of the Deaf journal, Samuel Porter, made a note that the claim that Deaf people were despised by hearing people had "no foundation . . . in fact." And the hearing son of the hearing founder of the American Asylum for the Deaf complained about Flournoy's "morbid state of feeling, a dislike to the society of hearing men."[28]

The second critique was a practical one: how exactly would the community remain all Deaf? Even if hearing people did not move into the new territory in order to buy inexpensive land, the community would face one major hurdle: approximately 90 percent of the children of Deaf parents are hearing. Within one generation, the territory would become primarily hearing. And if hearing people did have the vote, as Flournoy proposed, they would change the law stating that only Deaf men could lead. And would the community allow estates to pass to hearing children? Flournoy stated his answer: "If our children hear, let them go to other States." But critic after critic complained that Flournoy would "consent to a separation for so utopian a whim." They stated that "sundering the ties of parent and child" would be a violation of "the laws of nature." Questioned another, "Drive to the neighboring states our hearing children whom we love so well? I reckon Mr. Flournoy has no little prattlers of his own to cheer the solitude of his plantation." One critic even joked that perhaps parents could "stop their [hearing children's] ears with wax.

They would then have no advantage over deaf-mutes in public meetings and conversation at least, which is all that can be reasonably required."[29]

Readers raised other practical questions about Flournoy's utopian proposal. Where exactly should it be located? In Indian territory? In Arkansas or Maine? Iowa? Nebraska or Minnesota? Oregon? Perhaps Kansas? Should it be a United States territory or state? All in all, summarized one critic, "the obstacles to [the plan's] ultimate success are truly formidable. . . . Nine-tenths of the whole deaf-mute community in this country can not raise up the wind so as to swell the flapping sails of Mr. Flournoy's scheme; besides, it is a well known fact that the majority of them show little decision of purpose in any enterprise whatever." Another critic explained a little less stridently that Flournoy was a dreamer who, "while tracing out his castle in the air, gives but superficial attention to the nature of the materials with which it is to be built, or the foundation on which it is to be laid."[30]

Some critics responded not to the plan itself but to Flournoy. They attacked what they viewed as his self-serving motivation: Flournoy was unelectable in his state, so why not start a new state where he might have a chance at elected office? John R. Burnet, author of a widely read volume on deafness, suggested facetiously that perhaps instead of a territory, they should build an independent republic, for after all, "Will not *President* Flournoy sound better than *Governor* Flournoy?" Other opponents of his plan noted that Flournoy's racist statements and pamphlets were not in keeping with the reformist nature of northern Deaf activists, many of whom were active in the abolitionist movement.[31]

Flournoy's "new promised land" for Deaf people never came into existence. Too many Deaf leaders were opposed to the idea. Even those who were theoretically in support of the proposal were full of doubts about its feasibility. It is hard to know how average Deaf Americans (who probably faced deeper discrimination) responded to Flournoy's proposal. Away from the eyes and editorial pens of hearing people, perhaps educated Deaf leaders agreed with Flournoy's proposal, or at least its motivations, more strongly than they did in print. Perhaps those who were uneducated and underemployed, or those who were removed from the company of other Deaf people, agreed with his sentiments more.[32]

Despite the proposal's failure, it is interesting how seriously it was debated within the Deaf community. Some people supported him, while many were vociferous in their objections. Flournoy's earlier pamphlets addressed to hearing people, such as his suggestion for immediate removal of African Americans and his advocacy of trigamy, were never addressed seriously. But the Deaf community, even those who disagreed vehemently with his plan, discussed the proposal in depth. Flournoy's call for a Deaf colony tapped into the dreams of Deaf people worldwide. Whether called the land of Gallaudet, Deaf-Mutia, Gesturia, or Eyeth (instead of "EARth"), Deaf people fantasized about what their connections could build. For Flournoy and for other Deaf people, living in the margins might provide more freedom than living in the mainstream. They shared a vision of the world—and a language—that differed from the hearing people who surrounded them. And that connection transcended the regional identities that hearing Americans were feeling so profoundly by the late 1850s. Extraordinarily few elite Deaf people saw the hearing world as so alien that they were willing to make the sacrifices necessary to create a new country or state. But still, this time, Flournoy's "wild and fantastic" proposal hit a deep nerve. Even though his vision came to naught, Flournoy was taken seriously. His ideas were riveting to Deaf Americans.

While the Civil War loomed on the horizon, Flournoy abandoned discussion of a colony in the West for Deaf people. As early as 1838 Flournoy had predicted "the disruption of the American Union, . . . the wars civil to come, if the race of Ham remains here in any light and aspect for a long continuance of time." By the late 1850s, he continued to think war was a terrible choice, but one that was inevitable without drastic action.[33]

He decided to run for president in 1860, saying that he was willing to be nominated as a Democrat in order to save his country from annihilation. Of course, he was not taken seriously. He again picked up his pen with the goal of saving the nation. He wrote to Jefferson Davis detailing what the South needed to do: obey the rules of God. Later he wrote Andrew Johnson a fourteen-page letter outlining how he should go about reconstructing the broken nation, begging him to treat white southerners leniently. In both cases his letters appear to have been ignored.[34]

Although Flournoy was not completely cloistered after the Civil War, he changed profoundly. Primarily, rather than thinking of Deaf people as a cohesive whole united against hearing people, he began to articulate a view of southerners versus northerners. He no longer routinely classified himself as "deaf and dumb" after signing his name to essays. Instead, he noted how radically different the lives of northerners and southerners were due to the large number of freed African Americans living in his region. Suddenly, it seemed that his longstanding concern about the presence of blacks was shared: it was the fear of all elite southerners. Without the economic prosperity that was possible because of slavery, southern elites agreed with Flournoy that, as he said, "the evil has come" and "Confusion reigns!" Occasionally he went further than his peers: blacks serving in the legislature made him wonder if only a monarchy could guarantee justice. But then he backpedaled and agreed with his peers that the most appropriate response would be lynch law. Flournoy no longer differed so greatly from his hearing southern peers. As a result, he all but muted his pen.[35]

Flournoy did not define his deafness by his literal hearing loss. What defined his disability for him was its cultural context. Deafness meant discrimination and isolation. Its medical reality seemed almost irrelevant. The social experience of deafness allowed Flournoy a certain kind of insight. His vision was changed, changed enough that the meaning of his white southernness was shaken. He saw areas of commonality with non-elite white southerners that other slaveholders could not imagine. In addition, he was on common ground with nonsouthern Deaf people in a way that challenged the growing sectionalism of the nation.

For J. J. Flournoy, self-governance was the key to true parity. He was inspired by the Mormon struggle for self-determination in a separate land. And clearly he was inspired by the southern elites and their talk of secession, although he never acknowledged it. What a time for a southerner to be using the rhetoric of independence! The white elite southern world of the 1850s imagined a release from northern tyranny, a release brought about by removing itself from one government (secession) and beginning a new one (the Confederacy). Flournoy, using similar rhetoric of tyranny and release, believed that it was exactly that quest for political independence that would provide him and other Deaf people with true equality.

CHAPTER 9

ℰ⌒ *The Peculiar Institutions*

"It has been a period of prosperity," claimed the Alabama school for the Deaf in its 1861 annual report to the state legislature, notwithstanding the heightened sectionalism in the public mind and predictions of war beginning to percolate throughout the southern states. The school was determined to be better and stronger than ever. The board of directors felt that the heightened antagonism between North and South would encourage many of Alabama's elite, who had previously sent their Deaf children to northern schools, to send their sons and daughters— "from choice as well as necessity"—to schools in the South. The Alabama school, thought school directors, would be their choice. It would be "inferior to none in the South," promised the leaders. The directors were sure that the state legislature, eager to encourage pride in the state following secession, would fund the school liberally. As the war started, the Alabama school for the Deaf had high hopes for the future.[1]

The entire town of Talladega, where the school was located, celebrated Alabama's secession from the Union in January of 1861. Although prior to secession the city was "not unanimous" in their politics, and "debates on the issue had raged for months," when the actual news of withdrawal from the Union reached Talladega's citizenry, all of their disagreements were "suddenly resolved." The white residents of the town broke into celebration. Talladega's two militias, one led by the principal of the school for the Deaf, paraded around the town square in full dress uniform. Town politicians recited patriotic speeches to assembled town residents. The city was, according to one history, "ready that night for a gallant, exciting, and hastily concluded victory" over the Union.[2]

Despite the optimism of the school and the town in which it was located, trouble loomed on the horizon. Printed inside the back cover of the 1861 annual report was a suggestion of the turmoil that would soon overtake southern schools for the Deaf. There the school acknowledged that after the annual report had gone to press, the school principal resigned his post at the school to join the Confederate army. Soon, the school's steward joined him. By the next report, the school was suffering from the "exorbitant prices of every description of supplies" that had meant the school was "hardly . . . able to keep the current expenses of the Institution within the sum of the annual appropriation" made to the school by the state legislature. The report warned that if future appropriations were not increased to match the inflation that racked the Confederacy, the state school for the Deaf would be obliged to close its doors.[3]

Although the Alabama school did face wartime difficulties, the principal's southern identity and Confederate leadership prevented the state school from experiencing the political turmoil that occurred in other states, including Georgia. The board of the Georgia school for the Deaf submitted their 1860 annual report, acknowledging that the year had been of "more than ordinary interest" as sectional tensions built between the North and the South. "The various vicissitudes of prosperity and adversity, of persecution and success," through which the school had survived, "marks an era in its history of no common occurrence." The board was forced to report a story that, as they acknowledged, struck them with sadness. Despite "the preponderance of good over evil, of success over difficulty, of triumph over trials," a major conflict had arisen at the Georgia school for the Deaf.[4]

A "clamorous accusation" had been raised against the recently installed principal of the Georgia school: Principal S. F. Dunlap was accused of being an abolitionist. The man was not, according to a former principal, a true southerner. "It was charged," wrote the head of the board of trustees of the school in December of 1859, that the principal was "not friendly to the institutions of the South"—including the institution of slavery—and "that he had expressed himself" and "tried to instill anti-slavery sentiments into the minds of the pupils in the Institution." The board acknowledged that if Dunlap was, in fact, against the traditions of the white South, he should "be at once discharged" and replaced with a "sound Southern man." They proposed to investigate, saying that "if Mr. Dunlap is found to be unfriendly to Southern institutions, Southern interests, and Southern honor," he would be "forthwith discharged" as principal and his position filled with a "true man."[5]

The governor of Georgia echoed the concerns of the board of trustees. He feared that principal Dunlap could be "instilling into the minds of our youth sentiments of hostility to the South." If the accusations against the man were true, he would deserve "the rebuke and scorn of our people." The governor hoped to defend the state school from attack. He had almost certainly read the recently printed newspaper editorial suggesting that because Dunlap had "spoken his strong anti-slavery sentiments" to the students, the school had become "a disgrace, instead of an honor to the state." Pupils were not only being taught dangerous politics. The writer also charged that "the mutes are badly clothed, badly fed, and many of them covered with vermin and putrefying sores." A true southerner, the author implied, would never allow such treatment to occur at his school.[6]

At the governor's insistence, the school's board of trustees determined to institute a full inquiry into the matter of the principal's politics. To determine Dunlap's "soundness . . . as a Southern man," the accused principal must be given an opportunity to "repel the assaults of his enemies." When asked about his politics, principal Dunlap denied the charge that he was an abolitionist, saying that he was "a *Virginian* by birth and education" and that he was "truly a friend of the South."[7]

After a full investigation into Dunlap's background and careful questioning of his peers, the Georgia school decided there was nothing to the accusations made by the school's former principal. The accuser himself had been removed from office—"for misconduct" and for "a want of veracity"—and had "a jealous heart." He, according to the board of trustees, "could not bear to see any other man succeed in [the school's] management so much better than himself." He "took advantage of the high state of political excitement" occasioned by the John Brown case in Harper's Ferry, to "prejudice the public mind" against the new principal. The board of trustees felt that the man had "really duped many first rate men" in Georgia "who were sound and zealous on all Southern questions" into believing that Dunlap was misusing his power over the young Deaf pupils at the school. The former principal's many followers "join[ed] him in a crusade of persecution" of the new principal and of the school. They tried to "dissuade and prevent" white southerners "from sending their children and wards to the Institution." Although the board acknowledged that if Dunlap had been proven to be an abolitionist, "he should not be countenanced nor supported by the people of Georgia," after investigation they "were unable to procure any evidence in all . . . inquiries, that would in the least degree criminate Mr. Dunlap in the charges made."[8]

Despite the fact that the Georgia board could not find hard evidence of the principal's abolitionism, the board did receive a letter alleging that before coming to Georgia, Dunlap had been dismissed from his post at the Illinois school because of some "impropriety" there. Although the investigators thought at first that the charge was merely "additional slander, intended to annoy and injure Mr. D.," they knew it was their duty to investigate further. They then received "full authentification of the facts from undoubted sources." Because of the evidence of his previous misdeeds, the board felt they must force out the principal: "it would be incompatible with their own sense of honor," reported the chair of the board, "as well as the interests of the Institution, to retain him longer." They passed a resolution of dismissal: "Whereas, the board has recently received official information from the Illinois Deaf and Dumb Institution, that Mr. S. F. Dunlap, our present Principal, was guilty, while connected with that Institution, of improper intimacy with one of the female pupils of his class, in consequence of which he was dismissed," they wrote to the state legislature, "be it therefore, resolved, that . . . we deem it improper and inconsistent with the interest of the Institution to retain him any longer."[9]

With this formal dismissal, the principalship was vacated and soon filled by the former principal of the North Carolina school for the Deaf. The board of trustees felt sure that although the new principal was "born at the North," his thirty-five years' residence in the South and his "intermarriage with a Southern family" had made him into an acceptable choice, as the board said, whose "views of Southern institutions fully accord with our own."[10]

In a time of growing political tensions between North and South, it was no surprise to see charges of abolitionism applied to a state-paid leader. Principal Dunlap's accusation also tapped into a variety of southern concerns and fears about Deaf education.

First, there were fears about teachers. Some writers argued that hearing principals, because of their responsibility for children "greatly inferior to themselves" and therefore "accustomed to enforce subordination without interference or constraint," began to acquire "the most inordinate thirst for power and its unlimited exercise." Their sense of entitlement and authority was only increased by their good salaries (high only because of "the scarcity of those engaged in teaching sign language" and not from any "superior excellence") paid from the state coffers. Hearing administrators could easily become unreasonable autocrats, state officials felt. On top of that, many teachers of the Deaf in the South were themselves northerners, or at least people who trained for their profession in the North, often motivated by various reformist beliefs. Major proponents of Deaf education in the United States, such as Thomas Hopkins Gallaudet and his son Edward Minor Gallaudet, were quite vocal in the abolitionist movement. The traditional link between reform efforts for Deaf people and other reformist activities became increasingly disturbing to white southerners. Southern politicians were aghast that they might be paying the salaries of men with political beliefs in opposition to those of the white South. Teachers were threatened with removal from southern schools if legislators doubted their loyalty to the Confederate cause.[11]

There were also fears about students. Deaf children often experienced a profound sense of separation from their families and communities. Parents sent children to residential schools where the pupils made friends with strangers and learned American Sign Language, a language not shared with their families. Southern leaders were concerned that white Deaf individuals might believe northern rhetoric more readily than would their hearing siblings who grew up surrounded by southern ideology. The inability to share their families' language meant that many Deaf people did not necessarily receive a strong proslavery southern identity as youngsters. Elite Deaf children attended school without personal servants and were often required to care for not only their own clothes and rooms but to attend to the other parts of the school as well. Elites attended class with children born into illiterate poor white families, children who would be their classmates and who might become their close friends or even their spouses. Such interaction between rich and poor would not have occurred for hearing siblings and therefore served to intensify existing distinctions between hearing and Deaf family members. Because a Deaf person was "an utter stranger to the language in use all around him," the individual was made "an exile in his own land." When loyalty to the white South grew in importance during the late antebellum period, Deaf educators and Deaf individuals became tainted with danger and treason.[12]

In addition to these political concerns of sectional identity, many southern state schools for the Deaf suffered throughout the Civil War because of the exigencies of the war. "It is by no means the least of [the Civil War's] evil consequences," reported the Kentucky school for the Deaf, that it should have "destroyed these monuments of benevolence and Christian civilization, erected for the relief and restoration to intelligence and usefulness of one of the most deeply afflicted classes of our race. . . . Over few of the numberless objects of devastation which our unhappy country presents, will the spirit of humanity wail more deeply than these desolated schools for deaf mutes."[13]

Like the principal of the Alabama school, faculty members from every school left their posts to join the Confederate cause. Several hearing teachers and administrators from the Virginia school for the Deaf resigned to become soldiers. The Georgia school lost two of their most experienced teachers. In late 1861, the school's board of trustees asked the governor of Georgia to intercede to have one of the two honorably discharged from the army so he could return as principal of the school. When suggested to the teacher, he refused the offer. He told the committee, "'I appreciate your past and present kindness, but I have cast my fortunes with the Confederate Army and I shall abide the result." Instead of spending the end of the war in the principal's chair, the teacher spent it as an inmate in a northern prison.[14]

The financial situation of the straitened Confederacy caused much suffering through the region. The Georgia school for the Deaf struggled through the difficult years of war. The area around Cave Spring, Georgia, where the state school was located, was often labeled "the garden of Georgia." Nevertheless, at the beginning of the Civil War the state was experiencing an "unprecedented drought." Despite the land's usual fertility, many of Georgia's farmers' crops were drying up in the fields. Food prices soared as much as 300 percent because of the drought. At the same time, the northern blockade of southern ports made it nearly impossible to import goods such as clothing and furniture from Europe. The high demand for such scarce articles, and the danger of trying to smuggle them across blockade lines, led to serious inflation of their prices as well. Despite the "ruinous" prices charged for such goods, the Georgia school had to purchase food and clothing for the pupils living there whose families could not afford to bring them home.[15]

Traditionally, the Georgia school (like other schools for the Deaf) had charged tuition to those pupils' families who could pay. Now, many of these families faced economic ruin themselves and were suddenly unable to pay the school to educate their children. The supplemental financial support upon which the school depended eroded. "Some of our patrons who were formerly amply able to pay for the board and tuition of their children, have been so reduced by recent events," lamented the South Carolina school's director in 1866, "as to be compelled to retain them at home, or ask a participation in the bounty of the State."[16]

The South Carolina school also faced high prices and numerous scarcities. Even when the school could afford to pay for improvements, it was impossible to acquire "competent workmen" or "proper material" to rebuild. Instead, both workers and materials were involved in the war effort.[17]

Although the South Carolina school survived the inflation of the early war years, by 1864 the price of food and clothing had risen by several hundred percent. The school had not expected such a dramatic change in their financial responsibilities. The appropriation, they knew, had "fallen considerably short of meeting the wants of the Institution," despite the careful economy practiced by the school's administrators.[18]

By the end of the war, the directors of the South Carolina school realized they would have to close the school's doors. They pleaded for more support from the legislature. "The Institution has successfully struggled through almost four years of the war," they wrote proudly, "and shall it now succumb to the inauspicious darkness of that hour which may be the precursor of the dawn?" In April 1865, the same month that the Confederacy surrendered to the Union army, the South Carolina school for the Deaf suspended activities for a period of eighteen months as the state tried to regain financial capability after the "sudden extinction of Confederate funds."[19]

As the war progressed, many school buildings became hospitals for wounded soldiers, soldiers' bunks, or jails for prisoners of war—sometimes by the Confederacy and sometimes by the Union. The Mississippi school for the Deaf was forced early in the war to surrender its buildings to the Confederacy. The governor of Virginia allowed the Confederate military to turn the state-owned buildings into a military hospital. The Georgia school also became a hospital for wounded soldiers, as did those in Arkansas and Tennessee. Tennessee's buildings were used as a military hospital alternately by the Confederacy and the Union.[20]

During periods of northern occupation of school buildings, state governments had no ability to assist the schools. Instead they were left to their own resources. Female pupils baked cookies, cakes, pies, and breads to sell to neighbors and soldiers. Male students took charge of selling vegetables that they grew in the school's garden. These efforts were rarely enough to keep schools running.[21]

Sometimes schools arrived at compromises with their occupiers without the help of the state government. At the Louisiana school, Union troops occupied all but one wing of the school building as a hospital for wounded and ill soldiers. Upon the request of the board of directors, federal authorities provided the Deaf pupils and their instructors living in the remaining wing with food and fuel.[22]

Several schools were in the direct line of battle. After a struggle to stay open despite the lack of leadership and despite the poor financial situation of the school, the Georgia school for the Deaf was eventually forced to suspend classes for almost five years as the school watched the surrounding town pass from the hands "first of one Army and then the other." Federal troops occupied Staunton, Virginia, the town where the Virginia school was located, and disrupted the exercises of the school. As late as 1881, war trenches could be seen in front of the central school building of the Virginia school for the Deaf. Though the grass had begun to grow, there was still evidence of soldiers' camps. In the school library, students could still read the inscription engraved on a pane of glass by a wounded Confederate soldier with his ring: "The Yankees are expected. They came."[23]

In May of 1863, General Sherman occupied the city of Jackson, Mississippi, where the Mississippi school for the Deaf was located, then burned much of the city to the ground. The Mississippi school was one of the buildings destroyed. After the war, the state did not try to rebuild the school for the Deaf for several years. The principal stated, "The iron heel of War was on the neck of this child of the State, and she lay trampled in the dust." As the legislature explained, the state lacked funds to rebuild the school and simply could not impose high taxes on state residents who were, because of the destruction of their lives by the Civil War, "unable to bear the weight of heavy taxation."[24]

At the end of the war, after Confederate and Union occupiers left, those state school buildings that remained standing were often in a shambles. The wooden buildings of the Texas school, never as fine or extensive as those of other southern schools, were in "a very dilapidated condition and much in need of repair." The Tennessee school also faced destruction: when it was returned by the military to the board of trustees, the school was "in an astonishingly damaged condition" and deemed not suitable for occupancy by Deaf pupils.[25]

Even when the buildings were in adequate condition, the interior appointments were often not. When the Georgia school reopened at the beginning of February 1867, it reported to the state legislature that "the buildings and premises were in a great state of dilapidation." With the exception of a few desks and the large slates in the classrooms, all the school's furniture and "everything movable" from mattresses to tableware had been either destroyed or removed by looters. After Union troops left, the Louisiana building was still habitable, but it was "almost destitute of furniture." The directors petitioned the legislature for funds to buy replacements. Because of the general destruction of the state's economy, the directors did not ask for an appropriation substantial enough to replace the beautiful antebellum furnishings: "We could not ask that the furniture should be on the same magnificent scale as before the war." Then the state of Louisiana "could well afford to be liberal." Now the school must settle for furniture merely serviceable.[26]

No southern state had the ability to rebuild schools to the former grandeur, although some states looked for other ways to overcome their poverty. After several years as a military hospital, the Louisiana school's buildings were returned to its directors at the end of the war. The school prepared to reopen, hoping to augment the small postbellum state appropriations with tuition from out-of-state students. Since the Mississippi school had been burned by Sherman's army, Louisiana saw an opportunity. For $250 per pupil, paid either by individual families or by the state of Mississippi, the Louisiana school agreed to educate Deaf Mississippians. The superintendent suggested that "similar arrangements" be made with other southern states whose buildings had been destroyed or whose school exercises had been otherwise suspended. Although this practice of interstate education never became widespread, the idea of providing education for the entire region rather than just the state differed sharply from antebellum ideology. The crisis of the Civil War and the fiscal disaster that followed it forced southerners to consider regional responses.[27]

Unlike other southern schools for the Deaf, the school in North Carolina claimed that during the Civil War, it was in a more prosperous condition than at any former period in its history. The directors of the North Carolina school for the Deaf greatly strengthened its finances by making the work of the school and its Deaf pupils necessary to the state. Because most of the hearing printers and bookbinders of North Carolina had left their jobs to enlist in the Confederate army, both the state and Confederate government, as well as many private businesses, turned to the Deaf school. Before the war, schools taught printing in order to provide graduates with a marketable skill. As the war progressed, the pupils performed a large amount of work for both North Carolina and the Confederate government, as well as for the railroads and private individuals. Deaf students printed everything from state publications to Confederate scrip. The usefulness of the school's printing press to the state and to the Confederacy could have been limited: the federal blockade of southern ports made it difficult to acquire new machines, paper, and other printing and book-binding supplies. But in 1864 the state governor himself helped smuggle English machines that cut envelopes and assisted in bookbinding—machines that were unavailable in the Confederacy—across the blockade for use at the school. Funding the continuous operation of the school, or at least its vocational wing, became a high priority for the state because of the school's usefulness to the state. The North Carolina school for the Deaf found a novel way through the destruction of war. Instead of relying on the charity model of Deaf education—that is, showing that Deaf people depended on the welfare of the state—the North Carolina school turned the tables and showed the state that the state relied on the work of the Deaf pupils.[28]

CHAPTER 10

This Unnatural and Fratricidal Strife

EVEN THOUGH DAVID TILLINGHAST was a man born to the slave-holding class, because of his deafness his family did not bestow upon him a birthright of mastery. Instead they viewed him as a dependent to be protected. What follows is the story of how David recognized his own competency, struggled against the role of dependency, and fought to gain his family's acceptance of his independence. As long as the girdings of slavery held the system of mastery intact, it seemed impossible for David to be recognized by his family as both self-reliant and southern. The upheaval of the Civil War, which fractured the system of mastery, enabled David to force his society to embrace his position as an independent Deaf man.[1]

Because of the disruptions and uncertainties of education at southern schools for the Deaf at the outbreak of the Civil War, many southerners who could afford it considered sending their Deaf children to northern schools, especially those in New York, Philadelphia, and Connecticut. Although many parents had qualms about sending their young children away from home—and especially to schools across enemy lines—during such a crisis, it was often the children's only chance for education during the war years.

Elite white southern families who sent their children to northern schools risked having their Deaf children challenge the ideology underlying their southern identities. In January 1860, the Tillinghast family of North Carolina began to express their concerns that young David, then a student at the New York school for the Deaf, would be influenced more by the ideology of his northern teachers and friends than by the perspectives of his white southerner family and society. David's hearing sister Sarah Ann wrote to him, "I fear that they will make an abolitionist of you way off so far from your home." The Tillinghasts feared that David's exposure to northern values and perspectives, and perhaps more specifically to the values of his teachers, many of whom were reformers intimately connected to the abolitionist movement, would distance him from his home and his family.[2]

In mid-May of 1861, Sarah Ann wrote a long letter to David telling him she feared for his safety as well as his values. South Carolina and Virginia both had broken off from the Union. North Carolina had not yet seceded, but life in North Carolina was nevertheless disrupted. The family had recently sent several letters to David but had not received a single reply. "We have been anxiously expecting a letter from you for some time," wrote his sister. Although the Tillinghasts thought the boy was "in no particular danger" and "safe from molestation," they could not "help feeling anxious" because of David's "southern birth." Sarah Ann feared, she wrote, the uncontrolled "mob law of New York" which might do anything to her Deaf brother. After expressing her fears, she again exhorted David to send word: "You must write to us very soon now that letters can come through." Sarah Ann knew that David was not fond of sitting down to his correspondence, but she felt it was more important than ever before. The family wanted to be reassured of both his safety and his continuing commitment to the South.[3]

Sarah Ann continued her May 1861 letter by sharing the family's Confederate perspective on the events between the North and the South. She feared that David's exposure to northern newspapers such as the *New York Herald* and the *Boston Courier* might lead David astray. He believed, she feared, that northerners were acting out of goodness and justice. She assured him it was otherwise: "Have the men of the North become transformed into *devils;* have they lost all sense of decency and *honor?*"[4]

Near the end of the long and angry letter to David, Sarah Ann addressed her brother's unacceptable political views. Although surrounding states had already seceded, North Carolina had not yet severed ties with the United States. "We were quite shocked at your idea of North Carolina standing neutral in the great question," wrote Sarah Ann. "Did you think that we would stand and see our brave brothers north and south Virginia and South Carolina suffer in the cause and not fly to their help?" she continued. "Never, never. We will fight with them, bleed with them, die with them ere we submit to a tyrant." Sarah Ann feared that David's northern friends would continue to share their political views with her brother, but hoped that her own viewpoint could be at least as persuasive. She encouraged him to show her letter around the school: "you have my free permission to show this hastily written letter to *any* of *your Republican friends.*" Sarah Ann apologized for its careless quality, but assured David it was "not hasty as to sentiment but only in execution."[5]

David wrote a careful, controlled letter in response to Sarah Ann's outpouring. He chose not to respond to the majority of her claims. He did write assurances to his family: "You were right in supposing I was safe from any molestation on account of being from the South." He told Sarah Ann that even if he "were a secessionist" he would be "safe from physical abuse" since his peers never injured anyone regardless of their politics. Three students at the New York school were southerners, and David assured his sister that all of them would be "taken good care of as long as war prevents them from going home." It was "impossible for any one here to molest me unless," David teasingly added, quoting her words, "he should be 'transformed into a devil.'"[6]

David's hearing brother John agreed with Sarah Ann. "I regret to see that your mind is biased so much by your surrounding association," he stated, "tho' I confess I am little surprised." David's long association with northern reformers and abolitionists had prepared some in the family for David's resistance to white southern ways. John tried to reason with David: "We of the South consider that the US gov't which was framed for our protection, is now to be used to oppress us and make war on us and our institutions." John continued, "We therefore, as did our fathers of the Revolution under like circumstances, have resolved to withdraw and frame a government for ourselves."[7]

After receiving intense letters from several of his family members, David suspected his siblings would be hesitant to allow him to remain at the New York school for the duration of the war, especially after he realized how much "spirit . . . animates the South." In preparation, he asked his sister her opinion on whether he could "continue as a pupil here next session." He suggested that even after graduation, he would like to remain in the North: "I think I can contrive to get a situation at the North and stay in it till the war is over."[8]

John soon wrote David that the family hoped he would stay in New York until the academic session ended. He hoped by then that the situation between the Union and the Confederacy would "take a decided change, for better or worse," and that the Tillinghasts could then decide on the best course for David. The family was committed that David should complete his education "if it can be done." They continued to believe that at the school, David was "perfectly safe," despite the poor influences on his character. Brother Will reiterated the family's belief in David's safety: "I have no fear whatever for your personal safety while you are at the Institution." He did, however, fear that David's return home was impossible for a while: "I should be afraid to have you attempt to come home now while Maryland is filled with troops—many of whom would like nothing better than to maltreat a Carolinian." But the Tillinghasts could not condone David's idea of staying in the North after his graduation. Wrote his sister Eliza, "I reckon that Ma and brother William will want you to come home as soon as the session is out. . . . I think when we get you at home we will soon make a good *Southern rights* man of you."[9]

By December, the family had determined to try to bring David home as soon as possible. They continued to believe that David was safe at the school for the Deaf: "Knowing the kind feelings of the teachers in the Institution toward you, . . . [we] have felt anxious for you only as regards your health and comfort." Nevertheless, the tumult of war experiences convinced the Tillinghasts that David should be home with them. William arranged for his brother to travel back to North Carolina "under the flag of truce." The boy would be able to travel, suggested William, as long as he carried a passport that would, as he told his brother, "shew that you are a mute." If he did not carry such proof of his deafness, Will warned David, he "might be suspected and meet with difficulty" while on his journey. Being Deaf meant David could not, thought many hearing Americans, participate in the war effort in any substantial way.[10]

David did not come home in 1861, although no letters exist to explain why. After his graduation in June of 1862, his family continued to pressure him to return to North Carolina. He applied for a passport, but his request was denied and he "was told that passes were not granted," as he wrote his brother William. David decided he wanted to stay in New York for a least another year. Although he might "visit . . . next winter," he had determined to "not go home till next year." He confessed that he could have returned home "several times" but was always "kept back" for reasons he did not explain in his letter.[11]

In fact, David had just accepted a three-year appointment as instructor at the New York school. He tried to explain the decision to his family: "I think I had better stay where I can be useful and have employment." At the school David felt appreciated and needed: "Providence seems to me to keep me here that I may do some good to the deaf mutes." At home, however, he would not have that opportunity. David dreaded the idea of returning to North Carolina. Although he might help support himself and even assist his family there, as his Deaf brother Thomas was doing, he would be constantly reminded that society did not consider Deaf men equal to hearing men. He and Thomas would be kept at home with his sisters—and barred from serving in the Confederate military with their hearing brothers. By staying in New York at the school for the Deaf, David could live as a respected member of his society. He tried to explain to his family the kind of respect he garnered at the school by telling them of his graduation: "I graduated here under circumstances that would be flattering to your pride if you had seen them. I received a gold medal for excellence in all my studies and exemplary conduct during my whole connection with the school. I was the only person that had such a honor." David did not want to trade that acknowledgment of his talents for the life of a subordinate.[12]

The Tillinghast family members were not willing to acknowledge David's desire to stay in New York. They continued to refer to his decision to stay as a "compelled separation from home and kindred." But brother John did congratulate David that he was in a "situation to gain a comfortable support." John reluctantly admitted that "perhaps it is all for the best" that David had not come home. Perhaps he understood why David wanted to stay, or perhaps John was thinking only of the privations the family faced as the hostilities between North and South escalated. Despite the positive elements John saw in David's situation, the family continued to press David to be loyal to the Confederacy and to encourage him to come home to North Carolina.[13]

As the months passed, the Tillinghasts began to realize that David had deliberately passed up opportunities to come home. After the receipt of yet another letter from David apologizing for not fulfilling the family's wishes, brother William finally confronted David. Apparently David decided not to respond: after the letter, wrote William, "we . . . never heard from you." He was frustrated with his brother and felt the young man was not trying hard enough to return to the family circle. "We cannot imagine why you should have been refused passports," wrote William, "when so many people are constantly crossing." He could not understand why the Union authorities had stopped the Deaf young man. His crossing could be no threat, said William: "As you cannot be a soldier and are not a mechanic I can see no reason on earth why you should not come home." The family continued to hope their brother might not be at fault; the Tillinghasts felt David was being brainwashed and tricked by his northern acquaintances. Said William, "We *do* believe that those with whom you are living used every influence and method to prevent your coming," especially since "other people can come whenever they get ready." With great hope, the family wrote David that they would continue to "trust that you have no part or lot in *their* object." Wrote William, "They want to *use you* (Yankee like) and prevent your coming to those to whom you naturally would yearn to be with." He was sure that if the principal of the New York school had "chosen to interest himself in the matter," David would already be home in North Carolina with the family.[14]

Despite the family's hopes, they were beginning to fear the decision was David's alone. Wrote William, "We fear you have not been so anxious to come as we hoped for." Sister Robina echoed his suspicions: "I hear of truce boats very often; persons are constantly coming, if you would only come we would be so happy." Sarah Ann reiterated her thoughts: "People are constantly coming and going—and we can't see why it is that you can't come too."[15]

In the autumn of 1862, David's mother died. The family was "almost thankful" that she was now in "a better country," no longer suffering "the sorrow and anguish" of the "horrid war" that disrupted her earthly country. John wrote David that because he was "detained" in New York, David was "cut off from the opportunity of meeting our dear mother once more." Guilt, however, did not induce David to come south after his mother's death.[16]

The Tillinghasts then tried to persuade David that his Deaf brother Thomas, living at home in North Carolina, needed his companionship. William told him that Thomas had a great deal of work and professional responsibility in his envelope business, but that he was lonely, with no Deaf companions nearby. "Thomas would be delighted to have you with him," wrote William. "It would be such a comfort to him to have you here." Unlike some of the hearing Tillinghast family members, David of course signed fluently and understood the experiences and perspectives of a Deaf person. The two Deaf brothers had always been close, and the family sought to exploit that closeness and identification to bring David back to North Carolina. The first attempt did not work. Soon, sister Robina intensified the family effort. "Brother Tom is very poorly. He has had several attacks of asthma this winter," she wrote, "one quite lately from which he has not recovered. He looks pale and thin." She begged, "I wish you were here on his account. . . . It would be such a comfort to him to have you with him." A few months later, William supported Robina's claims. "Thomas has had several attacks of asthma within the last year," he wrote. "He often wishes you were here." William added that David could earn much more working with Thomas in the envelope business than he could teaching at the school. David was not convinced. By the middle of 1863, Sarah Ann was more plaintive in her request. "Tom wants you," she wrote. "He needs your company."[17]

The family continued to worry about David's political commitments in addition to his physical location. At first they denied they felt such concerns: "We trust that from your long residence among them [northerners] will not come one shred of sympathy for any of the accursed notions." The family's denials merely proved to David that they did worry. Perhaps the most disturbing of David's attitudes, thought the Tillinghasts, were his pro-abolitionist statements. In letters to the young man, the family vehemently defended the system of slavery and viciously attacked the motives of northern abolitionists and emancipators. William argued that the Emancipation Proclamation was "surely the most ridiculous production of modern times" since Lincoln had no authority in the Confederacy. Further, he argued, freedom would ruin the lives of the slaves themselves. Hundreds of African Americans had left "homes of plenty" and exchanged their lives as slaves for "a life of penury." This exchange had been "entailed upon them" by Union soldiers who encouraged them to leave plantation life. "Poor misguided wretches," William lamented, "who in their ignorance think freedom and Yankeedom better than their homes and friends and plenty to eat and wear, plenty of wood and everything necessary to their comfort!" Slaves, he claimed, worked "not half so hard" as free Blacks, whom he labeled "the most *debased* and degraded of our population." William confronted David, "You know yourself that a free negro is not considered nearly as respectable" as the slave of an elite white family.[18]

Early in the war the Tillinghast family began to experience economic shortages resulting from the Union blockade of the Confederacy. "We now find that many things which were once thought indispensable were mere luxuries and that we can not only do without them," wrote William, "but are really better without them." Without the trade from Europe, the elite of the South had to go from wearing imported high fashion to wearing clothes they could make themselves. Said William, "I think our Girls look prettier in their Homespun dresses than they ever did before."[19] As soon as William told his brother about the deaths and the many shortages, he realized that in order to encourage David to return home, he needed to reassure the young man that the Confederacy was not truly suffering and not giving up hope. "I understand the Northern people think we are almost in a state of starvation here," began William. "They are mistaken."[20]

Sarah Ann reaffirmed to David, "Don't let them persuade you that you will starve here. People look as fat and well as ever and every thing goes on very smoothly in spite of the falsehood that the Yankee papers are constantly publishing to inflame the minds of the populace against the South."

The South would not starve, she assured him, as long as the rich southern soil continued to give to them: "As to our starving there's no danger of that I assure you—we have out of our garden peas, beans, lettuce, turnips, onions, cabbage, and will soon have plenty of potatoes and root vegetables; we try our potatoes today for the first time. . . . Our garden is very fine indeed."[21]

Southerners continued to have faith in the Confederacy's military prowess: "*As a people* we are now *confident* of the success of our cause," wrote William. "Our troops are now all veterans and they have beaten the Yankees so often that they feel perfect confidence in their ability to do so whenever they have any thing approaching to equal terms." Sarah Ann suggested reasons why the Union would fail: "The fact is their *cause* is a bad one, and they *can't fight well* when their *cause* is not one that calls forth every spark of bravery and patriotism existing in their natures." Nevertheless, the Union bragged about their successes. "Great goodness! How the Yankee papers can *lie,*" wrote David's sister. "I think from their abominable lying about everything that they must have given up all hope of conquering us. The very idea of the cowardly wretches conquering us is ridiculous."[22]

Immediately after writing David a vitriolic account of Yankee aggression and degradation, Sarah Ann yet again told David that the she and the family continued to "hope and hope that you will manage to come home this summer. . . . Please do try to come this summer." In addition to missing her brother, Sarah Ann felt the family's honor was at stake, given David's absence and the infrequency of his letters home: "We are tired of telling people how long it is since we heard from you." All were bothered by not only his absence but also his associations. Even Tom's Deaf friend Hart Chamberlayne asked, "What has become of your brother David? Is he still in Lincolndom?"[23]

In early June of 1863, the Tillinghasts received a long-awaited letter from David. "*Everybody* was pleased to hear from you," wrote Sarah Ann. David's Deaf brother Tom agreed: "I was very much relieved by hearing that you were still safe and well. It has been about *8 months* since we heard from you. You can imagine how anxious were we to hear from you." It is unclear if David had not written or if his letters had not been delivered because of the pandemonium of war. Tom told David, "You spoke of having written two letters to us. If they were not the same letters we read last summer, we have never got them."[24]

After upbraiding their brother for not having written more regularly, the Tillinghasts rejoiced that he was finally planning to come home. Everyone in the community, wrote Sarah, was excited to know that her brother would return to them. Tom echoed the family's deep desire to see David again: "Be sure to come home as soon as possible. We cannot endure the idea of you staying away from home any longer." Brother Will, however, was still convinced that somehow David would manage not to come home after all. "I think if you will try in the *right way* you can get a passport to come home," wrote an impatient Will. He gave David explicit instructions: "Write to the Sec'y of War. Tell him you are a deaf mute," counseled Will. "Tell him that you have no trade i.e. you are not a mechanic who can make munitions of war or anything of the kind, and that being a mute you are not capable of being a soldier." He hoped to convince the officer that David could not be a threat because his Deaf status rendered him less than a man. Finally, Will urged David to further manipulate the officer's sense of pity: "Tell him that you have lost both your Father and Mother." William was certain that this portrayal of David's situation, complete with a certification by the New York school's superintendent that the "statements are true," would leave no room for rejection by the secretary of war: "I can see no reason why you should not be permitted to come home." David must have felt uneasy with William's portrayal of his dependent status.[25]

Sarah Ann began to prepare David for his return. She suggested that he bring "plenty of clothes, shirts, coats, pants etc." because all were unavailable in the Confederacy—unless they were smuggled goods, transported illegally across the Northern blockade at "an immense risk" and therefore at "enormous prices." Because of the inaccessibility, the Tillinghasts now wore clothes made from homespun, of which Sarah enclosed a sample. Wearing homespun clothes was a point of Confederate pride, showing that southerners were not dependent upon "Yankee goods and notions." The Tillinghasts were "living in comfort," and despite being deprived of many things,

they "seldom miss[ed] them," according to Will. "So much for having a res-
olute purpose. We are willing to *suffer* if need be" for the sake of the Confederacy.[26]

Inflation had hit the South hard. As Tom confirmed, "I must tell you
that every thing here is very high." He added, "I hope you will come home
safely. . . . I trust God will protect you from all danger and attend to your
safety in coming home." Like his family members, Tom wrote his brother
that he was sick of the war: "O! I wish to Heaven that we had no war. It is a
great calamity that has inflicted upon this country but I trust to God whose
almighty hand will alone stay the progress of the war."[27]

Unlike his hearing sisters and brothers, however, Tom asked David about
his work experiences and shared his own. He wrote David that he was "glad
to hear that you have been doing well in teaching" and that he hoped that
after the public examination of his pupils, David would "receive much cred-
it for it." His own work making envelopes, begun in July of 1862, kept Tom
"busy" and "doing very well." He claimed he was "very fortunate to have
been engaged in such business for it is very profitable." Despite his claims to
love his work, Tom added at the end of his letter that he was considering
"going to the mountains" in order to "refresh" himself as he was "considerably broken down by being engaged in making the envelopes." He then tan-
talized his brother with a promise: "When you come home, I will tell you
about my other business." Tom continued his letter with family news. The
boys' younger brother Walter was still "rather small for his age" and "still re-
tains the looks of a baby." The boy had "improved much in the art of talking
to me in the finger language," said Tom, "though not very rapid[ly]."[28]

In 1863 David wrote his family about his work experiences at the New
York school. Although the school helped give him a sense of himself as
an independent man, examples of discrimination against Deaf people
there were all too frequent. The year before, David had taught a class of
fourth-year students, working "hard to get knowledge into about twenty
heads," and now he had followed his pupils to the fifth level. He noted his
exceptional position: "It is flattering to my vanity to confide such a class to
my care," wrote David, "considering that it has been regarded many years
unsafe and unwise to trust a class more than thrice years old with a deaf

mute teacher." He continued, "I shall try to justify the confidence evinced by the principal in my abilities as a teacher." Although he was flattered that the school recognized his abilities enough to place him in charge of such an advanced class, David was rankled by the usual policy of not hiring Deaf teachers for such jobs.[29]

He was also frustrated with the pay scale at the school: "I confess that I am not satisfied with the compensation for my services," he wrote his brother. "Several teachers who evidently do considerably less good than I do receive a larger salary than me." One new teacher, "a speaking young man," who taught an elementary class, was paid more than one hundred dollars per year more than David. David was irked by such an imbalance: "There is a great disparity between the salaries of deaf mute teachers and those of teachers who hear." The school suggested that the reason for the different pay scales was the ease of recruiting young Deaf teachers and the difficulty obtaining "speaking teachers of education without the inducement of good remuneration." David did not find the "alleged reason" at all convincing. Instead, he found it to be straightforward discrimination. His irritation mounted: "They here pay speaking teachers about thrice more than deaf mutes," he told Robina. He continued fiercely, "I do not intend to sit down tamely under such injustice." David's strong sense of the capabilities of Deaf teachers in the classroom helped develop his righteous anger at the unfair treatment of Deaf people in society at large.[30]

At the same time that David was contemplating such matters, he received a letter from a former classmate who chafed against one of the paternalistic restrictions of the school: "The members of the H[igh] C[lass] were to my recollection, not allowed to take a sail or play with a football, for the reason of the rules of Dr. Peet," the head of the school. Peet feared for their safety, he said. The young man wrote, "I think the restrictions were not right. . . . The members of the HC should have the privilege of enjoying the sailing in the river and kicking the football." David was beginning to feel that teaching was a job requiring more dedication than he sometimes had. "Teaching the deaf mutes is not always pleasant," he explained. "One of the requisites in a teacher of the Deaf and Dumb is an ample stock of patience."[31]

In July of 1863 the Tillinghasts again tried to persuade David to return to his southern home. His brother John, at Will's request, wrote to the United States secretary of war on David's behalf, requesting that the young man be given a pass to come home and that the pass be delivered to David in New York. He told David that when he reached the border of the Confederacy he should hand over the pass and request passage aboard a flag-of-truce boat. Despite his promise and all the efforts of the family, David did not come home in 1863. William told him in August that he had not written recently because he assumed the young man would be traveling home by the time the letter arrived in New York. When David did not arrive in North Carolina, however, Will understood that yet again David's trip was postponed.[32]

What David had failed to do was get certification of his deafness by the head of the New York school for the Deaf to accompany the letter to the secretary of war. William was sure that if the superintendent would assist David in his plans, there would be "no difficulty" in coming home. But David seemed unwilling to go to Dr. Peet. Surely he would not have embraced the idea of showing his employer and mentor, whom he felt discriminated against him, that his family considered him somehow less than a man—mute, unskilled, unable to become a soldier, orphaned. David would not have accepted that his deafness, which he considered a core part of his identity and in no way pitiable, could be used in such a negative way. He rejected his family's view of him as a dependent. His pride, and perhaps even his southern honor, made David refuse to accept the role of helplessness and powerlessness. David implied that the secretary or war had refused him, and told his family that he would not return home at least until the Civil War ended.[33]

Despite his decision, David confessed that he missed his family and his home. He wrote his brother, "It has sometimes saddened me to think that I was absent from home at times when I might be very happy there." His brother suggested that David might make a living at home teaching at a southern school and reminded him that there were many Deaf children in the South whom he could instruct. David replied, "I have thought of it and wished to be in the N[orth] C[arolina] Institution at Raleigh." He further confessed to his family: "Long before the war and when I was at school I had a dream of what I should do when I left school—It was to establish a small school for deaf and dumb sons of rich parents in the south." His plans fell through in the early 1860s when "alas, war came" to his home region. "I am here far from the place where my imagination located my school," he ended his letter. Coming home was in David's plans, if he could have fulfilling and respected employment. But as long as "rich parents" struggled with the financial turmoil of war, no opportunities emerged for David to return on his own terms.[34]

Because of his frustration with his employment at the New York school for the Deaf and his unwillingness to go home to the South, David began to consider other job opportunities. He "decided on a course" for his new life: during the school's summer vacation, he would move upstate to work on a farm. "If I should find it suits my taste and capacity to learn the business of farming," David wrote home, "I shall give up teaching." Farming could pay more than teaching at the school for the Deaf, he believed. David knew that if he could "perfect his knowledge of farming," he could borrow money from "some rich friends" and buy a farm of his own, possibly in New York. After he was installed on his own land, he wrote, he would "devote all my industry to clearing myself of the debt" of the money he had borrowed to buy farmland.[35]

When William received news of David's plan, he wrote him that he "did not approve" of his brother's "scheme." William warned his brother: "You would be considered a laborer and required to *work hard while well* and be expected to care for yourself or be taken care of by your friends if taken sick." He continued that it would "not be likely to find *friends* who would be kind to you and take care of you in case of sickness." William understood that a job on a rural farm would almost certainly isolate David from the Deaf community. But he also felt that David needed the paternalistic care of the hearing administrators of the Deaf school, despite David's age. "I think your farming plan Utopian," he concluded. Perhaps the hearing members of the Tillinghast family were upset by David's plans to establish a small farm because such a position would remove him from both the family's protection and from their social class. If he owned a plot that he farmed himself, he would be abandoning his family's elite status to become a simple yeoman. His family was disturbed that the young man would trade his standing in the community for his personal independence. William strongly encouraged David to remain at the school rather than move to a country farm. "You have abundance for all your personal wants and a pleasant position," counseled William. "That, under the present times, is a great boon." He seemed peeved that his Deaf brother complained about the unfairness of his situation. Perhaps thinking of his own difficult situation in the wartorn Confederacy, William continued, "When you learn to know life and *this world* better you will find that it [unfairness] is as much as it gives any of us."[36]

David understood his family's desire to see him: "I sympathize with you in your wish that I should go home next summer," he told his sister Robina. In June of 1864 David apparently agreed to come for a short visit. Family members asked David to bring goods with him that were hard to procure in the Confederacy. Tom and Eliza requested such goods as linen tape, a comb, and black shoestrings. As they had before, the Tillinghasts warned him of the changes that had occurred in the South and to his family during his absence. They no longer had access to much meat, so they hoped their brother was "fond of vegetables," as they were the family's "principal food." Tom was the family gardener, and he grew the majority of what the family ate. He had, according to Will, "some delicious muskmelons to regale you with." But, Will warned David, he would have to "bid goodbye to beef-mutton and butter." The Tillinghasts had milk and bread, said Will, "and sorghum syrup" which he claimed was "much better than West India Molasses." The losses the family faced were not primarily culinary, however. Will cautioned David that he would see "many sad changes" and "miss many once-familiar faces." Even though the Tillinghast home would look so changed to David, William told him, "I trust you will find it still a happy one and feel that it is really *home*." He was not only thinking about the family land and house; Will was concerned that David did not believe the South was his homeland. Once again, when the time came, David did not visit his family in North Carolina.[37]

One month before Lee's surrender at Appomattox, General Sherman moved through North Carolina and occupied the Tillinghast's hometown. Sarah Ann felt violated and tried to share her fury with David in a letter written the day after the Union army's invasion of their house. After ransacking neighbors' houses and "impressing" all the alcoholic spirits they found there, Sherman's "foraging parties" were wild by the time they reached the Tillinghast's home. The girls were afraid of the drunk soldiers and locked themselves in their room. But when the men threatened to "break the door down," the girls agreed to open it to the soldiers. One of the soldiers opened Sarah's writing desk and began to read one of her letters. The drunk men took control of the family's food supplies, leaving them "entirely dependent" upon the "enemies' commissariat." Sarah Ann begged to retain the family cow so she could prevent the youngest Tillinghasts from starving. The experience of defeat left her feeling broken and vulnerable. The whole family had "excitement and trouble in our hearts." As Sarah stated, "We tried to treat them [the soldiers] politely, but were we to live a million years the 11th of March will be one of the darkest spots in our memories." The Tillinghasts were personally vanquished by Sherman's army. With the ruins of their country all around them, the family was, as Sarah wrote, "dependent upon the *charity* of our enemy." Their provisions for the year were raided by the Union soldiers and they had no money—except "a little Confederate, which is no more than waste paper now."[38]

Despite their defeat, the Tillinghasts remained defiant. In her letter detailing Sherman's invasion of the family home, Sarah Ann continued to refer to southern whites as "the just." That emotion, however, was only the beginning of the anger expressed by her and her sisters. "I tell you as *upon oath*, 'the truth, the whole truth, and nothing but the truth,'" insisted Sarah in a letter to David six weeks after Sherman's army had visited their home: "The South is *not whipped*—it is overwhelmed, and by *brute* force." The Union army had been unfair: "Had the Yankees carried on the war by the rules of warfare, we would have been successful. Our men have *never* been whipped on a *fair field*." The Union army had traveled throughout the Confederacy, tearing down mills and burning farming equipment, explained Sarah Ann. This destruction was "*mean*" and "low." She concluded, "We are not *humiliated* that our army . . . had to surrender." She admitted that the Confederate army had been "completely overwhelmed by an immense army of well-fed, well-equipped men," but reminded David that they had been nobly "resisting, to the bitter end, the aggressions of the tyrant." She continued, "*No, we are as proudly defiant* as ever. We can *hate* them and we will hate them forever. We had *a right* to be governed as we pleased. We only asked to be left alone." The Union, led by "that scab upon humanity, Lincoln," lied constantly about the white South, claimed Sarah Ann. She concluded, "Such a pack of falsehoods are enough to make Satan grin with delight."[39]

Sarah Ann recognized that David might be stunned by her violent rhetoric: "You think I am *needlessly bitter,*" she defended herself, "but, oh my brother, if you knew what we have suffered in the cause of our Precious Country you would not wonder." She continued, "Our beautiful 'sunny land' is ruined. We have lost everything but our homes, and poor North Carolina . . . has almost lost that." She struggled with the connection between the state's great loss and her own identity: "Were it not for the noble blood that has been so freely shed on every battle field I would be ashamed that I was born a North Carolinian." Family and friends had been killed, along with many more countrymen. She could see that a "river of blood" would "flow forever" between the South and its foe. The dead had been "laid upon the altar of our country. *Our country!*" She mourned its death. Sarah vowed never to forgive the North's hateful actions: "Until they cut a canal to the waters of oblivion and deluge our land with Forgetfulness, we can never consider a Yankee anything but an oppressor and an enemy." She continued, "I hate the nation from the bottom of my soul, even as I hate Satan, and all things low, mean, and hateful." Sarah promised David that "the sun [would] rise yet upon the retribution of Heaven upon the Yankee nation." She understood that God was then punishing the South yet also swore that "as there is justice in Heaven, the Yankees will get theirs in due time."[40]

Sarah Ann, in order to prove to David that her anger was "not personal," told her brother the story of "poor crippled Jim." The man who had "not walked a step in years" could not follow the Union soldiers off the Tillinghast plantation as did most of the other slaves. Before "Sherman's robbers" left, they stripped Jim of his socks and shoes and removed a small knife from his pants pocket. Seeing how the Yankees treated a disabled slave whom she deemed pitiable verified in Sarah's mind how truly evil the Union soldiers were. Still, she wrote, white southerners could not give up hope for a new nation: "Were it not for hope in the future," wrote Sarah, "I would rather that the last brother I have in the world was in his grave. I would far prefer seeing the last one buried than be sure that they were to live victims of Yankee tyranny and taxed to the utmost to pay the debt contracted by Yankeedom." Yankees, she tried to convince David, were the kind of people who "murder their kindred" and "insult their sisters."[41]

Sarah ended her letter to David with a plea: "Come to us as soon as you can, and come with a heart full of love to your country" she begged, "your country that your mother's last efforts, last thoughts, and last prayers were for—your country that your father loved, honored, and hoped for." She reminded her brother, "Your country! that your kindred have laid down so many lives for, that your sisters have worked and prayed for." She was tired of David's opposition to the Confederacy and knew that when David was home with the family he would begin to feel as they did.[42]

In early June of 1865, David's sister Eliza echoed her sister's defense of the Confederacy and attack on the North. The family had recently received a letter from David and were yet again horrified, but "not at all surprised," by David's abolitionist politics: "we all expected that your opinions would be just what they are," she wrote to him. David, they feared, empathized with the argument that all people, including African Americans, deserved self-determination. "I am very sorry that we should differ so widely," lamented Eliza. Nevertheless, she knew that David had received a very different education from her own and had not lived among slaves and slave owners for many years. The North Carolina Tillinghasts "had daily intercourse with the negroes," said Eliza. They therefore, argued David's sister, had "the best opportunity of knowing the falseness of the abolition theory." The Tillinghasts had by that point been abandoned by all but one of their former slaves: "Granny . . . will not desert us as long as she lives," claimed Eliza, because the Tillinghast family had "always treated her with more kindness" than her own children had. "If she had not been a slave, she would probably die in neglect and want," Eliza wrote, "but we will take care of her as long as she lives, and divide our last crumb with her." Eliza claimed that Granny was "now and always . . . as free as any laboring woman could be." In Eliza's mind, Granny loved all of the Tillinghasts "more than she [did] her own children."[43]

Eliza explained the desertion of all the other Tillinghast slaves by arguing that they had been duped by seductive promises by disingenuous Union soldiers. She herself felt that "the abolition of slavery has been the most inhuman" Yankee atrocity committed during the Civil War. Although she knew that David would disagree with her, she tried to convince him that if he knew the truth he would agree with her. "You have been kept in ignorance of many things by the falsehoods Northern papers are filled with," she wrote. If only he could "see the horrors that are enacted among the *freed* negroes," she told him, "you would think the negroes were better off in slavery." As slaves, argued Eliza, African Americans were well fed and "cared for and nursed by their mistresses." Without masters, she said, the ex-slaves were "dying by the thousands with no one to look after them. I *know* this to be true."[44]

Eliza gave David accounts of several former slaves, "crazy like the rest with the idea of freedom," who had lost their families and had no employment. Eventually all of them had been forced to return to their masters and beg to be taken in by them again. She had heard unbearable accounts of "suffering and cruelty" by Union soldiers to the ex-slaves, and claimed that even "the most inhuman masters in the South (and such I think were rare) never practiced such punishments as are inflicted on refractory negroes by the US officers." Even if the soldiers had treated them with respect, there was too little food and not nearly enough opportunity for employment for able-bodied and hardworking African Americans. "God only knows what is to become of the poor wretches, the old, infirm, and helpless, who have been deprived of their protectors," she continued. Under the system of slavery, she claimed, "the young, old, and helpless" as well as the sick were cared for. Under the capitalist system practiced in the North and in England, she added, such dependents had nothing.[45]

Eliza believed that slavery was a morally just institution, allowed by both the Old and New Testaments and "instituted by God." As she reminded her rebellious brother, "I have been taught opinions by my intelligent and Christian parents with the Bible in my hands." On the other hand, she argued, David had come to his own beliefs about slavery with only the evidence of "lying newspapers and by friends who, however good and sincere, know nothing of the institution of slavery." The reporters did not understand the abolition of slavery to be, according to Eliza, "a curse to the negro more than to the master" or understand that liberation would eventually lead to the "extermination of the negro." White southerners did not believe that abolitionists were truly sympathetic to slaves. They were motivated by "hatred and jealousy of the masters," argued Eliza, "not love for the slave."[46]

By the end of the Civil War, the Yankees had "enslaved their Southern [white] brethren" even as they had tried to "free (?) and annihilate the negroes," wrote Eliza. But the Confederacy was not trying to preserve slavery, she claimed: they had "fought not for slavery but for freedom, for our rights as states, for republican governments." The Union would not grant this "freedom" to the white South; federal troops had put down the Confederate protest violently. Because of the repression of southern independence, argued Eliza, the country had become "nothing more than a great military despotism."[47]

Eliza knew that despite her arguments and anger, David was committed to his abolitionist beliefs. "I am aware that nothing I can say will overturn the opinions which you have been forming for years," she wrote to him, "but I hope when you come home and see for yourself, you will in time change your mind." Only residence among them, and isolation from his reformist community in New York, would make David a "true southerner" again. She missed her brother: her heart had been "yearning" for him more than five years. David's family had grown older, but it was not only the years that had aged them. They were "sadly changed" and "altered" by the "sorrow and care" that turned them "from happy careless children" to adults who had "felt the realities of life." The Civil War had been a punishment, Eliza began to think, for the antebellum South's "boastfulness and self-confidence." She knew the privileged life the Tillinghasts had experienced before the war had now ended: "I never expect to be as happy again as I was in my childhood," she wrote. She anticipated "struggling with poverty to the end of my days." Eliza continued, "But this world is not made for happiness, and I can be contented, knowing that it is through much tribulation that we must enter into the kingdom of heaven."[48]

Will sympathized with his sisters' feelings about David's abolitionist leanings: "The injustice that has caused such shedding of blood, and the vandal-like barbarity with which the war was waged by northern troops," he said, "has caused a hatred towards the 'Yankees' wide and deep." He warned that the hatred would "*last* until the children now living and to be born of all the women now old enough to remember this war shall have died." He knew that "whatever government we may live under, henceforth the northern and southern people will be distinct peoples." Nevertheless, Will felt responsible for the solidarity of the family—and specifically responsible for his Deaf brothers. He knew he could not allow David to be estranged from the rest of the family, yet feared that his opinions would cause just that. He advised his brother to stay silent about his beliefs. "When you write again," said Will, "say nothing about political beliefs. It can do no good to talk about things which are now settled and fixed facts." Will recognized that his sisters did not have the cool head that he himself did: "The girls feel so deeply that it only hurts their feelings," Will told David, "and in some measure *alienates* their affections." He concluded, "You may see it is best to let the matter drop." Once again he begged his brother to return to them, at least for a visit, and tried to put a brave face on the destruction of their homeland.[49]

David responded that he would come for a visit as soon as the school session was out: "Only three weeks are between me and you." He intended to fill his trunk with all the goods impossible to get in the South and looked forward to giving gifts to his needy family. Sarah Ann urged David to bring whatever he could to help his brother and sisters: "If you have any money bring it or lay it our way in any way that you think will benefit us most." Although William tried to assure David he need not bring home all his money for the family, he made long lists of goods the family required which they could not obtain in the devastated southern states.[50]

After five years away from his brothers and sisters, David finally came home. He came home an independent man upon whom his family must rely. He visited them for the summer in 1865. When North Carolina's financial situation precluded him from finding high-paying employment in the region, David returned to his teaching job in New York and regularly sent money for his brother Tom to distribute to the family. Soon, David procured a job for a grateful Sarah Ann as head housekeeper at the New York school for the Deaf. David and Thomas began a vineyard in North Carolina, eventually employing their hearing brother Willard to communicate with illiterate clients who could not pass notes with the Deaf brothers. The profits of the vineyard, Thomas hoped, would allow the two Deaf brothers to "lighten the weight" upon eldest brother William and "relieve" the family "from their pecuniary difficulties." By choosing to send the money through his Deaf brother, and by starting a business with his Deaf brother that supported the family, David emphasized the strength and capability of Deaf people. The hearing Tillinghasts had always imagined David and Tom as dependent members, but now they proved they were not only independent but capable of providing for their family.[51]

David's goal was not the destruction of his family's position within the Old South hierarchy, nor was it the destruction of the basic hierarchy itself. His goal was personal: he wanted respect and a self-supporting life. To achieve such a goal required a rupture in his family's definition of a southerner. The Civil War cracked the wall of the Old South's ideology of mastery and dominance. Such fissures allowed (to differing degrees) groups of dependents—former slaves, women, and poor whites—to create new spaces for themselves as independent southerners. The story of David Tillinghast demonstrates that the Civil War also created opportunities for Deaf people.[52]

$\mathcal{C}\!\!\curvearrowright$ Epilogue

DAVID TILLINGHAST RETURNED TO THE SOUTH on his own terms, as a proud and independent man commanding the respect of his family. In 1868 David moved back to his home state as a teacher at the North Carolina school for the Deaf. He brought with him a Deaf wife, Caroline Stansbury, whom he had met at the New York school. Their journey from New York to North Carolina was a difficult one. As David recounted, "On our way south we had to make many changes of [railway] cars. We had to be ferried across rivers." As the train traveled south of Washington, the couple passed "small towns, fields of poor corn, [and] here and there a lean cow tied to a stake." The landscape of the postwar South was nothing like the world to which Caroline was accustomed or the place David remembered. "We saw deplorable scenes of poverty as compared with the prosperity of the north," explained David, and "it made my bride home-sick, so devastated, poverty-stricken and exhausted, did the country seem between Washington and Raleigh."[1]

The move to North Carolina forced David and Carrie to leave a "large circle of friends and acquaintances." In New York, the couple had been surrounded with well-educated Deaf teachers and graduates of the school's advanced class. In Raleigh, there was no such community. Instead, the two began to establish a society of their own, beginning with their signing family members. David and Carrie boarded at the North Carolina school for the Deaf for their first years in North Carolina. They then moved to a house of their own about half a mile from the school. After they were settled, David offered to take in his young hearing brother Willard while he searched for a job in "some good store." In January 1871, another hearing brother, Joseph, was released from Raleigh's insane asylum into David's care. A hearing sister moved into one of the upstairs bedrooms. All three learned to use American Sign Language. By late spring, brother Thomas took a job teaching at the North Carolina school. He brought Marie Clontz, a Deaf North Carolinian, to Raleigh as his wife. The two moved to a house within walking distance of David's residence. In the fall of 1871, David and Carrie rejoiced when the first of their five children was born.[2]

David and Carrie maintained contact with the broader Deaf community. David wrote letters to his friends from the New York school and the couple visited them as often as they could. Sometimes social visits with their old friends happened at national conventions of Deaf educators or Deaf societies. David's involvement with these formal associations of Deaf people helped make up for the isolation he sometimes felt in North Carolina. He retired from the North Carolina school for the Deaf in 1916. David Tillinghast died in 1942, a few days before his 101st birthday.[3]

Like David, Thomas Jefferson Trist created an independent adult life in a signing Deaf community. After eight years at the Pennsylvania school for the Deaf, Trist enrolled in the high class of the New York school. He entered the institution one year before Tom and David matriculated. After three years of advanced classes, Jefferson returned to the Pennsylvania School for the Deaf as a teacher. In 1857 he married Ellen Lyman, a woman from Massachusetts who was a graduate of the American Asylum for the Deaf. The ceremony was performed by Reverend Thomas Gallaudet, one of Jefferson's teachers at the New York school. In Philadelphia, Jefferson and Ellen were surrounded by an active Deaf community. In addition to spending time with the other Deaf teachers and students of the Pennsylvania school, Jefferson was a charter member of the Clerc Literary Association, a Deaf club. He also helped organize St. Ann's Church for the Deaf in Philadelphia. When his wife Ellen died in 1881, he remarried. He chose for his second wife another Deaf woman, Sophia Knabe, a fellow teacher at the Pennsylvania school. Thomas Jefferson Trist taught at the Pennsylvania school for the Deaf until his death in 1890. He had no children.[4]

e⁓

David Tillinghast's eldest son, Joseph Alexander Tillinghast, was hearing. His exposure to the world of his Deaf parents and Deaf aunt and uncle led him to a lifelong connection with the Deaf community and with American Sign Language. He became a prominent educator of the Deaf, a writer about Deaf pedagogy, and the superintendent of a Deaf school. So did his younger brother Edward Stansbury Tillinghast. Their sister Mary also taught in schools for the Deaf. In the generations that followed David and his brother Thomas, Tillinghasts became teachers in Deaf schools throughout the county and the world. Their descendents' continuing commitment to education for the Deaf stands as a tribute to the brothers' struggle for self-determination and community.[5]

NOTE ON SOURCES

In the last thirty years U.S. social historians have tried to recapture the experiences of people traditionally marginalized in the popular narratives of the past. Many scholars lament the multiple "silences" of the current historical account. Finding the hidden "voices" of these historically marginalized groups is the oft-stated goal of social historians. For a historian trying to uncover the experiences of Deaf Americans in the past, the metaphor of "voice" is inappropriate. Nevertheless, the search for sources explicating the views of Deaf people shares many difficulties with the quest that all social historians face.

Finding primary information about early Deaf history is quite a challenge. Because many archives and manuscript collections have not classified their collections with deafness in mind, the historian must often search the collections by proper names of schools or people. Even when archivists have provided subject headings, the keywords are not always obvious to current historians. Because of changing sensitivities about appropriate terminology, manuscripts about Deaf people may be found under *deaf, hard of hearing, hearing-impaired, disabled, special needs, handicapped,* or even *defective.* These are only the more obvious labels.

The majority of the historical information about Deaf men and women has been generated by hearing people. Because many Deaf people in the nineteenth century were not educated, they did not leave written records. Even Deaf people who attended school and learned English often felt uncomfortable using written English except when they were forced to: in communicating with hearing people. Those who did were often from elite families. When Deaf people were communicating with other Deaf—that is, when they were perhaps most willing to discuss their private lives and feelings—they usually preferred face-to-face contact and the use of sign language. Although an indication of a strong community, this fact is unfortunate for historians wanting to eavesdrop on their conversations. Even when

Deaf people did write extensively, their letters were often discarded as unimportant rather than being carefully catalogued in archives and manuscript collections.[1]

Social historians have sought quantitative sources in their efforts to explain the lives of the marginalized. But they are now recognizing the great complexities of such source material. Census records and other statistical materials were typically created and shaped by hearing officials unaware of Deaf cultural attitudes. The listings are not at all complete. Often census takers on their door-to-door circuit did not ask if Deaf people lived in the household. The parents of Deaf children did not always think it important or relevant to volunteer such information. Other parents tried to hide their Deaf children. Even when they were properly counted, it is unclear how often pupils in "asylums" were accurately listed as students, or how often Deaf adults were correctly listed by occupation. The assumptions of census takers that Deaf people were objects of charity rather than fully responsible adults calls into question the accuracy and completeness of their collected data.

Other sources of information about young Deaf students were created by the superintendents and teachers. Residential school administrators wrote yearly or biannual reports to state legislatures in order to solicit funds. These reports are a rich resource for exploring attitudes toward the Deaf, but they rarely offer insight into the perspective of the pupils and their Deaf teachers. The majority of the teachers who published articles were hearing. Although they were intimately acquainted with Deaf children and adults, these teachers often understood them in a framework of benevolent paternalism, pity, and sometimes antagonism.

Even when the historian does find primary sources written by Deaf people, the sources do not necessarily provide unbiased information. For example, school newspapers were popular in the latter part of the nineteenth century and offer a glimpse into the lives of pupils. But the newspapers were edited by teachers of both English and printing. The pupils knew what they could and could not say. Indeed, even many letters written from residential school pupils to their relatives or friends were originally class assignments. Textbooks for the Deaf often provided sample letters closely resembling manuscript letters of Deaf children to their hearing parents. Often teachers helped pupils create the letters by supplying subjects, formulating attitudes, and offering grammatical help. Even when teachers suggested no changes, the pupils knew their letters would be read by a teacher; this fact clearly shaped their manuscripts.[2]

The historian can find a few remarkable collections of letters between Deaf family members, but even these sources are problematic. They tell only about the experiences of elite educated Deaf people who acquired fluency in English. These pupils were extensively educated at some of the most prestigious schools in the country. Many of the manuscript collections are from families with other Deaf members. Having an extended Deaf family, while not necessarily recognized as a marker of elite status by the hearing community, was highly valued by the Deaf community. Families that had more than one Deaf child were perhaps more likely to learn to communicate with their children. Even if they did not, the siblings had each other; they could understand not only the sign language of their sibling, but his or her emotions and values as well. The younger children in such a family grew up learning the visual language of American Sign Language just as hearing children could absorb spoken English. This position, while extremely valuable for the individual child, was not the norm and therefore limits the historian's ability to generalize.

By discussing the problematic nature of sources in Deaf history, I do not at all intend to suggest that it is an impossible endeavor. On the contrary, the historian who considers the complexities of these sources can read them more deeply and learn a great deal more about the historical experiences and attitudes of Deaf people themselves. While the answer may be incomplete, it will offer us a chance to look into the otherwise hidden lives of Deaf community members from the past.

Introduction

1. John Hampden Chamberlayne to Martha Chamberlayne Dabney, 13 April 1877, Chamberlayne Papers, Library of Virginia, Richmond, VA. The Chamberlaynes were an elite family from Richmond. Edward Pye Chamberlayne, born in 1821, was almost twenty years older than his hearing younger brother. "Ham" Chamberlayne, born in 1840, became a newspaper editor and politician in Norfolk and Petersburg, Virginia. When Edward was nine years old, his family enrolled him at the first residential school for the Deaf in America, the American Asylum for the Deaf in Hartford, Connecticut. He attended for two years, was absent for one year, then returned in the fall of 1833 for a final year at the school. He left in 1834 when the American Asylum threatened to sue his family for unpaid tuition. ASD Admissions Register, 1830 and 1850, American School for the Deaf Archives, West Hartford, CT. In 1835, he attended the New York school for the Deaf for one year. "List of Pupils of the New York Institution," *American Annals of the Deaf and Dumb* 6, no. 4 (July 1854). The next year, when Edward had already completed his education, his brother Hartwell was born. Soon the family realized that just like Edward, Hart could not hear. The boys' father, Lewis W. Chamberlayne, joined with others to successfully lobby the state of Virginia to form its own school for the education of the Deaf. Hart attended the Virginia school for three years (starting in 1846) and taught there for many more. R. Aumon Bass, *History of the Education of the Deaf in Virginia* (Staunton, VA: Virginia school for the Deaf and the Blind, 1949), esp. pp. 33–35, 196–99, and 223–24. For more about Hartwell Chamberlayne, see Chapter 10, note 23. For more about Deaf people being hit by trains, see Jack R. Gannon, *Deaf Heritage: A Narrative History of Deaf America* (Silver Spring, MD: National Association of the Deaf, 1981), 71–73.

2. John Hampden Chamberlayne to Martha Chamberlayne Dabney, 13 April 1877, Chamberlayne Papers, Library of Virginia.

3. Ibid.

4. Ibid.

5. Ibid.

6. Ibid.

7. Audiologically deaf people are a diverse group, divided by degree of hearing loss, age of onset, and more significantly, style of communication—be it some form of

signing (itself a spectrum), speaking and reading lips, or writing. In this book I am talking about a subset: those who were born without hearing or lost hearing at an early age and who embrace ASL and the cultural model of deafness.

Deaf activists and scholars have begun capitalizing Deaf when referring to cultural identification. Most elderly people who lose their hearing late in life continue to rely on spoken language and are firmly connected to hearing culture. Although these people may be physically deaf, they are not culturally Deaf. Neither is the cultural identification of Deaf applicable for those mainstreamed deaf children who choose never to learn American Sign Language or associate with the Deaf community.

Douglas Baynton asks, "At what precise point do deaf people become Deaf?" Because of the complicated and often elusive nature of the cultural identity of Deaf people in the past, historians have handled capitalization in a variety of ways. Baynton's solution, along with that of most historians, is not to try "to make the distinction" and therefore to routinely use the lowercase. Douglas C. Baynton, *Forbidden Signs: American Culture and the Campaign Against Sign Language* (Chicago: University of Chicago Press, 1996), 12. Nicholas Mirzoeff suggests that hearing authors should not use such capitalization: "despite being deaf in one ear, . . . I [cannot] call myself Deaf and have therefore decided to retain the conventional orthography." Nicholas Mirzoeff, *Silent Poetry: Deafness, Sign, and Visual Culture in Modern France* (Princeton, NJ: Princeton University Press, 1995), 7. When referring to group cultural identity, Paul Preston capitalizes *Hearing* as well as *Deaf*. Paul Preston, *Mother Father Deaf: Living Between Sound and Silence* (Cambridge, MA: Harvard University Press, 1994), esp. 15–17. Since in this book I am talking about a conscious Deaf identity but not a conscious identity among hearing people, I have chosen not to follow his lead. Susan Burch capitalizes except when she is specifically referring to a noncultural audiological meaning of deafness. Susan Burch, *Signs of Resistance: American Deaf Cultural History, 1900 to 1942* (New York: New York University Press, 2002). Because her study analyzes an already established Deaf community, teasing apart the distinctions between the two meanings of the word is much easier for her than it is for a historian studying the formation of identity in children. Like Baynton, I have decided not to try to determine the moment when people go from being deaf to being Deaf. Unlike him, I have decided to always capitalize when discussing individuals, culture, and community. Whether or not prelingually deaf individuals identified themselves as Deaf people, hearing culture consciously associated them with other prelingually deaf people who used ASL and were part of the Deaf community.

Harlan Lane, Robert Hoffmeister, and Ben Bahan come to the same conclusion, arguing that children are born Deaf not because of outside definition but because of an essential link to Deaf culture: "Where there are cultures whose members have a characteristic physical condition, all the children with that constitution are seen as the rightful recipients of that culture to some degree." They continue, "How could Deaf children start out in hearing society when they do not speak the language of that society and have not become, through the language, acculturated to it? No, they are Deaf, even though they are frequently not allowed to take possession of the Deaf heritage until either they attend school with Deaf peers or are old enough to make their own decisions." Harlan Lane, Robert Hoffmeister, and Ben Bahan, *A Journey into the DEAF-WORLD* (San Diego: DawnSignPress, 1996), 160–161. Also see pages 401–402.

The capitalization of *Deaf and Dumb, Mute,* and so on was a relatively common nineteenth-century practice by both the Deaf community and hearing people. Readers should remember that during the nineteenth century, nouns (such as *Sister* or *Book*) were frequently capitalized and therefore the use of *Deaf* in primary documents does not necessarily imply a chosen cultural identity.

Often nineteenth-century Deaf people did not even use the word *Deaf* at all. Many people embraced the term *Mute* and labeled themselves thus in order to emphasize the fact that they did not speak rather than emphasize that they could not hear. Likewise, the nineteenth-century Deaf community often labeled hearing people "speaking persons." Their choice of labels points out their understanding that use of speech was a more significant marker than the ability to hear. Some Deaf people today are embracing the label "mute" for the same reasons.

8. The importance of ASL's visual mode is shown by the way space is used to communicate meaning. For example, in ASL, time is explained spatially (signing backwards and forwards from the signer's body to indicate past and future) rather than through verb tense. Likewise, nouns can be located in space and then that space pointed to in order to refer to that same noun. This usage is equivalent to English pronouns.

The body of literature on American Sign Language is voluminous. See, for example, William C. Stokoe, *Sign Language Structure: An Outline of the Visual Communication Systems of the American Deaf* (Buffalo, NY: Buffalo University Press, 1960); Lynn A. Friedman, ed., *On the Other Hand: New Perspectives on American Sign Language* (New York: Academic Press, 1977); Edward Klima and Ursula Bellugi, *The Signs of Language* (Cambridge, MA: Harvard University Press, 1979); Harold Poizner, Edward Klima, and Ursula Bellugi, *What the Hands Reveal About the Brain* (Cambridge, MA: Massachusetts Institute of Technology Press, 1987); Ceil Lucas, ed., *The Sociolinguistics of the Deaf Community* (New York: Academic Press, 1989); Susan D. Fischer and Patricia Siple, eds., *Theoretical Issues in Sign Language Research* (Chicago: University of Chicago Press, 1990); Clayton Valli and Ceil Lucas, *Linguistics of American Sign Language: An Introduction* (Washington, DC: Gallaudet University Press, 1995); Karen Emmorey and Harlan Lane, *The Signs of Language Revisited: An Anthology to Honor Ursula Bellugi and Edward Klima* (Mahwah, NJ: Lawrence Erlbaum Associates, 2000).

Historian Jill Lepore summarizes, "Not unlike parent and child spoken languages, like British and American English, French Sign Language and American Sign Language (ASL) today are mutually intelligible. A deaf American can manage to converse with a deaf Frenchman in much the same way that a hearing New Yorker can talk with a hearing Yorkshireman: it can be done, although not without effort. But a deaf American cannot understand a deaf Englishwoman or a Nicaraguan, just as that hearing New Yorker cannot be expected to understand a Russian without first learning the language." Jill Lepore, *A is for American: Letters and Other Characters in the Newly United States* (New York: Alfred A. Knopf, 2002), 104–105. Douglas Baynton suggests the difference is more akin to the difference between Spanish and Italian. Baynton, *Forbidden Signs,* 13.

French Sign Language (LSF) is a combination of the signed language in common use in eighteenth-century Paris and a manually coded version of spoken French. For more information about French sign language, see Renate Fischer, "Abbé de l'Epee and the Living Dictionary," in John Vickrey Van Cleve, ed., *Deaf History Unveiled:*

Interpretations from the New Scholarship (Washington, DC: Gallaudet Unversity Press, 1993), 13–26; Sophia Rosenfeld, *Revolution in Language: The Problem of Signs in Late Eighteenth-Century France* (Palo Alto, CA: Stanford University Press, 2001); and Jonathan Ree, *I See a Voice: Deafness, Language, and the Senses—A Philosophical History* (New York: Metropolitan Books, 1999), 141–206. For information about the connection between French educational sign language and American Sign Language, see Joseph D. Stedt and Donald F. Moores, "Manual Codes on English and American Sign Language: Historical Perspectives and Current Realities" in *Manual Communication: Implications for Education,* ed. Harry Bornstein (Washington, DC: Gallaudet University Press, 1990); and James Woodward, "Historical Bases of American Sign Language" in *Understanding Language through Sign Language Research,* ed. Patricia Siple (New York: Academic Press, 1978).

9. At various places and times in world history, Deaf people were not allowed to marry, vote, or sit on juries. During the 1920s, many U.S. states prohibited Deaf people from receiving driver's licenses. Activists maintained that Deaf people, because of their superior visual acuity, were in fact competent drivers with better records than hearing drivers. The laws were eventually overturned. Susan Burch, *Signs of Resistance,* 155–165. Despite the recent passage of civil rights legislation in the United States, such as the Americans with Disabilities Act, discrimination in employment, educational opportunities, entertainment, and other areas still persists.

10. Roger J. Carver says, "As one enters into the world of the Deaf, disability as a factor in their lives ceases to exist." Quoted in Susan Wendell, *The Rejected Body: Feminist Philosophical Reflections on Disability* (New York: Routledge, 1996), 28. Harlan Lane and many others who experience Deaf culture insist that "because there is a deaf community with its own language and culture, there is a cultural frame in which to be deaf is not to be disabled." He goes on to say, "The deafness of which I speak is not a disability but rather a different way of being." Harlan Lane, *The Mask of Benevolence: Disabling the Deaf Community* (New York: Vintage Books Random House, 1992), 21.

James Charlton agrees that deafness is made by society rather than by a medical condition, but he insists on using the vocabulary of disability when talking about the Deaf community: "Deaf people are considered disabled although many deaf individuals insist they do not have a disability. People do not get to choose whether they have disabilities. Most political activists would define disability as a condition imposed on individuals by society." In other words, all disability, not just deafness, is a cultural construct. James I. Charlton, *Nothing About Us Without Us: Disability, Oppression, and Empowerment* (Berkeley: University of California Press, 1998), 8. Also see Lennard J. Davis, *Enforcing Normalcy: Disability, Deafness, and the Body* (New York: Verso, 1995).

The field of American disability history, a relatively new area of study, has both influenced Deaf history and been inspired by it. For a recent overview of the field, see Catherine J. Kudlick, "Disability History: Why We Need Another 'Other'" in the *American Historical Review* 108, no. 3 (June 2003), 763–793. A wonderful introduction to the breadth and creativity of the field of disability history is Paul K. Longmore and Lauri Umansky, *The New Disability History: American Perspectives* (New York: New York University Press, 2001).

11. There are a multitude of introductions to the history of the South. One especial-

ly accessible text is William J. Cooper Jr. and Thomas E. Terrill, *The American South: A History* (New York: McGraw-Hill, Inc., 1991). A new and fascinating approach is that of Mark M. Smith, *Listening to Nineteenth-Century America* (Chapel Hill: University of North Carolina Press, 2001).

12. Source limitations led me to focus primarily on elite white males. See the essay on sources at the that precedes these notes for more information.

Historians of the Deaf experience have analyzed everything from late-nineteenth-century teaching policy to workforce participation during the Second World War. The vast majority have explored the experiences of powerful Deaf community leaders. As Robert Buchanan carefully notes in his pathbreaking study of twentieth-century work patterns, "This study focuses on the most highly educated and professionally successful white males, who dominated leadership positions in most deaf associations." Robert Buchanan, *Illusions of Equality: Deaf Americans in School and Factory, 1850–1950* (Washington, DC: Gallaudet University Press, 1999), xvi–xvii. The childhood experiences and inner lives of even the most powerful community leaders are rarely mentioned.

With few exceptions, studies of Deaf history focus on evidence from the late nineteenth and early to mid-twentieth century. The most central turning point in Deaf history, as most historians see it, is the shift from sign-based education, called manualism, to speech-based education, called oralism. Readers will find information about the rise of oralism in almost every study of Deaf history. Especially useful analyses are John Vickrey Van Cleve and Barry Crouch, *A Place of Their Own: Creating the Deaf Community in America* (Washington, DC: Gallaudet University Press, 1989); Baynton, *Forbidden Signs*; Richard Winefield, *Never the Twain Shall Meet: Bell, Gallaudet, and the Communications Debate* (Washington, DC: Gallaudet University Press, 1987); Harlan Lane, *When the Mind Hears: A History of the Deaf* (New York: Random House, 1984); and Jack Gannon, *Deaf Heritage.*

Because the postbellum shift to oralism challenged the fundamental values of the Deaf community, and because manualism is a system heartily endorsed by the Deaf, the antebellum period has been portrayed by many historians of the Deaf as a golden age— a time not only of manualist pedagogy (using sign language in the classroom) but respect for American Sign Language and for Deaf people. A recent example of belief in the "golden age" can be found in Rebecca Anne Rourke Edwards's dissertation. She summarizes her argument: "Antebellum manualists were the . . . last [generation] to treat the deaf as social equals." Manualists, she argues, saw Deaf people as "valuable teachers, as competent citizens, as good christians [*sic*], and as loving parents."

This assumption of a golden age for the Deaf is not easy to support with evidence. The vast majority of antebellum schools were headed by hearing men who saw their responsibility as caring for those who could not care for themselves. While there were a few exceptions, most hearing teachers stated plainly that they did not believe that the Deaf could ever be the equals of hearing. Deaf teachers' salaries were lower than their hearing counterparts' salaries, and they were not treated as peers by hearing instructors. But Edwards dismisses such arguments as simply "minor quibbles." As she states, "Social equality did not mean . . . equality of outcome." Rebecca Anne Rourke Edwards, "Words Made Flesh: Nineteenth-Century Deaf Education and the Growth of Deaf Culture" (Ph.D. diss., University of Rochester, 1997), 364, including note 12.

13. David Tillinghast to Eliza Tillinghast, 26 April 1869, Tillinghast Family Papers, Manuscript Department, Perkins Library, Duke University, Durham, NC (hereafter cited as DU). The literature on southern mastery, masculinity, and the culture of honor undergirds this argument. See especially Drew Gilpin Faust, *James Henry Hammond and the Old South: A Design for Mastery* (Baton Rouge: Louisiana State University Press, 1982); Steven M. Stowe, *Intimacy and Power in the Old South: Ritual in the Lives of the Planters* (Baltimore: Johns Hopkins University Press, 1987); Stephanie McCurry, *Masters of Small Worlds: Yeoman Households, Gender Relations, and the Political Culture of the Antebellum South Carolina Low Country* (New York: Oxford University Press, 1995); Peter Bardaglio, *Reconstructing the Household: Families, Sex, and Law in the Nineteenth-Century South* (Chapel Hill: University of North Carolina Press, 1995); Bertram Wyatt-Brown, *Southern Honor: Ethics and Behavior in the Old South* (New York: Oxford University Press, 1981); Kenneth S. Greenberg, *Honor and Slavery: Lies, Duels, Noses, Masks, Dressing as a Woman, Gifts, Strangers, Humanitarianism, Death, Slave Rebellions, the Proslavery Argument, Baseball, Hunting, and Gambling in the Old South* (Princeton, NJ: Princeton University Press, 1996); and Edward Ayers, *Vengeance and Justice: Crime and Punishment in the Nineteenth-Century Antebellum South* (New York: Oxford University Press, 1983).

Chapter 1

1. "Twelfth Annual Report of the Officers of the Georgia Institution for the Education of the Deaf and Dumb, 1861" (Cave Spring, GA: Georgia Institution for the Education of the Deaf and Dumb, 1861), 12; "Proceedings at the Laying of the Corner-Stone of the Tennessee Institution for the Deaf and Dumb" (Knoxville, TN: Jas. C. and John L. Moses, Register Office, 1848), 9. Society's image of deafness as a lamentable condition can be found in many institutional reports, including "First Annual Report of the Board of Trustees and Officers of the Alabama Institution for the Education of the Deaf and Dumb, 1861" (Montgomery, AL: Montgomery Advertiser Book and Job Printing Office, 1861), 11; "Annual Report for the Kentucky Institution for the Education of the Deaf and Dumb, 1853," unpaginated typescript, Volta Bureau; "Tenth Annual Report of the Officers of the Georgia Institution for the Education of the Deaf and Dumb, 1859" (Cave Spring, GA: Georgia Institution for the Education of the Deaf and Dumb, 1859), 11.

References to the misfortune of deafness and the unfortunate condition of Deaf people are extremely common. See for example, S. B. Cheek, "Some Suggestions in Reference to the Enterprise of Deaf-Mute Instruction in the United States," *American Annals of the Deaf and Dumb* 7, no. 3 (1854): 167; "Eighth Annual Report of the Commissioners of the Georgia Asylum for the Education of the Deaf and Dumb, 1857" (Cave Spring, GA: Georgia Asylum for the Education of the Deaf and Dumb, 1867), 7; "First Biennial Report of the Commissioners and Superintendent of the Missouri Asylum for the Deaf and Dumb, 1853–54" (Jefferson City, MO: J. Lusk, Public Printer, 1854), 7. The final quote in the paragraph is from the "Twelfth Annual Report of the Officers of the Georgia Institution for the Education of the Deaf and Dumb, 1861," 11.

My purpose here is not to describe the true condition of Deaf people in the antebellum United States, but to show the assumptions of the surrounding culture that were almost certain to affect the upbringing, education, and adulthood of Deaf people. The construction of deafness tells us a great deal about concerns and fears of the society. As Douglas Baynton points out, "The metaphors of deafness . . . are projections reflecting the needs and standards of the dominant culture, not the experiences of most deaf people." He goes on to say that hearing people "saw deafness through their own cultural bias." Douglas Baynton, "'A Silent Exile on This Earth': The Metaphorical Construction of Deafness in the Nineteenth Century," *American Quarterly* 44, no. 2 (1992), 236–237. Both this article and his book *Forbidden Signs* discuss American nineteenth-century cultural meanings of deafness in detail.

2. John R. Burnet, *Tales of the Deaf and Dumb, with Miscellaneous Poems* (Newark, NJ: Printed by Benjamin Olds, 1835), 7, 13. Burnet was himself Deaf. Deafened at the age of eight, he relied primarily on written English until the age of twenty-two, when he learned ASL at the New York School for the Deaf. Guilbert C. Braddock, *Notable Deaf Persons* (Washington, DC: Gallaudet College Alumni Association, 1975), 2.

3. For examples of the use of the phrase "the children of silence," see: "First Annual Report . . . of the Alabama Institution for the Education of the Deaf and Dumb, 1861," 13; "Fourth Annual Report of the Commissioners of the Georgia Asylum for the Education of the Deaf and Dumb, 1853" (Cave Spring, GA: Georgia Asylum for the Education of the Deaf and Dumb, 1853), 5; "Annual Report of the Trustees and Officers of the Louisiana Institution for the Education of the Deaf and Dumb, 1858" (Baton Rouge, LA: Printed at the Office of the Institution, 1858), 8. For discussions of the impact of a world without sound, see "First Annual Report . . . of the Alabama Institution for the Education of the Deaf and Dumb, 1861," 30; "Fourth Annual Report . . . of the Georgia Asylum for the Education of the Deaf and Dumb, 1853," 8; "Fifth Annual Report of the Commissioners of the Georgia Asylum for the Education of the Deaf and Dumb, 1854" (Cave Spring, GA: Georgia Institution for the Education of the Deaf and Dumb, 1854), 5; "Annual Report of the Trustees and Officers of the Louisiana Institution for the Education of the Deaf and Dumb, 1856" (Baton Rouge, LA: Printed at the Office of the Institution, 1856), 6.

4. "Report of the Board of Trustees and Officers of the Alabama Institution for the Education of the Deaf and Dumb, 1862–63" (Montgomery, AL: Montgomery Advertiser Book and Job Printing Office, 1863), 7; "Annual Report of the Trustees and Officers of the Louisiana Institution for the Education of the Deaf and Dumb, 1853" (Baton Rouge, LA: Printed at the Office of the Institution, 1853), 16; "Annual Report for the Kentucky Institution for the Education of the Deaf and Dumb, 1848," unpaginated typescript, Volta Bureau; "Tenth Annual Report of the Officers of the Georgia Institution for the Education of the Deaf and Dumb, 1859," 11–12; "Annual Report of the Trustees and Officers of the Louisiana Institution for the Education of the Deaf and Dumb, 1853," 16; "First Annual Report . . . of the Alabama Institution for the Education of the Deaf and Dumb, 1861," 13; "Proceedings at the Laying of the Corner-Stone of the Tennessee Institution for the Deaf and Dumb," 13; "First Annual Report . . . of the Alabama Institution for the Education of the Deaf and Dumb, 1861," 30 (Although presented in quotation marks in the report, the poem is not attributed to a particular author); "Third Annual Report of the Commissioners of the Georgia Asylum for the Education of the Deaf and

Dumb, 1852" (Cave Spring, GA: Georgia Asylum for the Education of the Deaf and Dumb, 1852), 12. Another source compared uneducated Deaf people to out-of-control nature: they were "soil untilled" and "overgrown with weeds and briars." Burnet, *Tales of the Deaf and Dumb*, 10.

5. "First Annual Report . . . of the Alabama Institution for the Education of the Deaf and Dumb, 1861," 30, 13, 11; "Third Annual Report . . . of the Georgia Asylum for the Education of the Deaf and Dumb, 1853," 12; "Fourth Annual Report . . . of the Georgia Asylum for the Education of the Deaf and Dumb, 1853," 8; "Proceedings at the Laying of the Corner-Stone of the Tennessee Institution for the Deaf and Dumb," 13.

6. "First Annual Report . . . of the Alabama Institution for the Education of the Deaf and Dumb, 1861," 11, 30; Burnet, *Tales of the Deaf and Dumb*, 14; "Proceedings at the Laying of the Corner-Stone of the Tennessee Institution for the Deaf and Dumb," 13.

7. "Report . . . of the Alabama Institution for the Education of the Deaf and Dumb, 1862–63," 7; "Ninth Annual Report of the Commissioners of the Georgia Asylum for the Education of the Deaf and Dumb, 1858" (Cave Spring, GA: Georgia Asylum for the Education of the Deaf and Dumb, 1858), 10; "Annual Report for the Kentucky Institution for the Education of the Deaf and Dumb, 1852," unpaginated typescript, Volta Bureau; "Proceedings at the Laying of the Corner-Stone of the Tennessee Institution for the Deaf and Dumb," 14. Another observer stated that the Deaf were in the "sad condition of foreigners in the bosom of their native states." "Annual Report for the Virginia Institution for the Education of the Deaf and Dumb and the Blind, 1846" in *Journal of the House of Delegates*, 1845–46, Doc. No. 20, 5. Further analysis of the American use of the metaphor of foreignness can be found in Baynton, *Forbidden Signs*, 15–35.

8. Burnet, *Tales of the Deaf and Dumb*, 8, 13; "Third Biennial Report of the Trustees of the Tennessee Institution for the Education of the Deaf and Dumb for 1848–49" (Nashville, TN: W. F. Bang and Co., 1849), 18, 6; *Southern Literary Messenger*, 1835, 1:136; "Fourth Annual Report . . . of the Georgia Asylum for the Education of the Deaf and Dumb, 1853," 5; Joseph D. Tyler, "The Duty and Advantages of Educating the Deaf and Dumb and the Blind: A Sermon Preached in Christ Church, Staunton" (Staunton, VA: Kenton Harper, Printer, 1843), 5; "First Annual Report . . . of the Alabama Institution for the Education of the Deaf and Dumb, 1861," 11, 13.

9. "First Annual Report . . . of the Alabama Institution for the Education of the Deaf and Dumb, 1861," 30–31; "Report of the Board of Trustees of the Tennessee Deaf and Dumb School, 1853" (Knoxville, TN: Printed by A. Blackburn and Co., 1853), 6; "Third Biennial Report . . . of the Tennessee Institution for the Education of the Deaf and Dumb for 1848–49," 19; "Third Annual Report . . . of the Georgia Asylum for the Education of the Deaf and Dumb, 1852," 12; "Tenth Annual Report of the Officers of the Georgia Institution for the Education of the Deaf and Dumb, 1859," 24; "Sixteenth Annual Report of the South Carolina Institution for the Education of the Deaf and Dumb, and the Blind, 1864" (Columbia, SC: Evans and Cogswell, State Printers, 1864), 14. Interestingly, metaphors often rely not just on hearing and sight but other senses as well: see references to taste in such phrases as "intellectual food" and "the very crumbs of knowledge" in this paragraph, and references to touch in phrases like "cold embrace" in the preceding one.

10. Gen. 1:1–5, 14–19.

11. "Report . . . of the Tennessee Deaf and Dumb School, 1853," 7; "Report of the North Carolina Board of Directors of the Deaf and Dumb Asylum, 1850," 6–7; Tyler, "The Duty and Advantages of Educating the Deaf and Dumb and the Blind," 16; "First Annual Report . . . of the Alabama Institution for the Education of the Deaf and Dumb, 1861," 13, 30; "Twelfth Annual Report of the Officers of the Georgia Institution for the Education of the Deaf and Dumb, 1861," 11–12. Douglas Baynton, using predominantly northern sources, suggests that the antebellum world usually described deafness as "an affliction that isolated the individual from the Christian community." On the other hand, the postbellum world emphasized deafness as a "condition that isolated people from the national community." Douglas Baynton, "'A Silent Exile on This Earth,'" 216–217. See further discussion of religious separation in Baynton's book *Forbidden Signs*, esp. 15–22 and 49–50. In the South, religious and social isolation were emphasized in both the antebellum and the postbellum periods.

12. S. B. Cheek, "Some Suggestions in Reference to the Enterprise of Deaf-Mute Instruction in the United States," *American Annals of the Deaf and Dumb* 7, no. 3 (1854): 172; "First Annual Report . . . of the Alabama Institution for the Education of the Deaf and Dumb, 1861," 11; "Second Annual Report of the Commissioners of the Georgia Asylum for the Education of the Deaf and Dumb, 1851" (Cave Spring, GA: Georgia Asylum for the Education of the Deaf and Dumb, 1851), 7; "Third Biennial Report . . . of the Tennessee Institution for the Education of the Deaf and Dumb for 1848–49," 20. See also the discussion of "undeveloped" moral thinking in "Second Biennial Report of the Board of Trustees of the Tennessee Institution for the Education of the Deaf and Dumb for 1846–47" (Nashville, TN: Printed by W. F. Bang and Co., Banner Office, 1847), 16.

13. "First Annual Report . . . of the Alabama Institution for the Education of the Deaf and Dumb, 1861," 30; "Tenth Annual Report of the Officers of the Georgia Institution for the Education of the Deaf and Dumb, 1861," 20; Burnet, *Tales of the Deaf and Dumb*, 8; "First Annual Report . . . of the Alabama Institution for the Education of the Deaf and Dumb, 1861," 31; "Third Biennial Report . . . of the Tennessee Institution for the Education of the Deaf and Dumb for 1848–49," 19; "Ninth Annual Report . . . of the Georgia Asylum for the Education of the Deaf and Dumb, 1858," 10.

14. "Seventh Biennial Report of the Board of Trustees of the Tennessee School for the Deaf and Dumb, 1857" (Knoxville, TN: Printed by Kinsloe and Rice, 1857), 11; "Third Annual Report . . . of the Georgia Asylum for the Education of the Deaf and Dumb, 1852," 13; "Annual Report . . . of the Alabama Institution for the Education of the Deaf and Dumb, 1863," 10; Burnet, *Tales of the Deaf and Dumb*, 14.

15. "Annual Report for the Kentucky Institution for the Education of the Deaf and Dumb, 1853," unpaginated typescript, Volta Bureau; "Third Annual Report . . . of the Georgia Asylum for the Education of the Deaf and Dumb, 1852," 4; "First Biennial Report . . . of the Missouri Asylum for the Deaf and Dumb, 1853–54," 7; "Second Annual Report . . . of the Georgia Asylum for the Education of the Deaf and Dumb, 1851," 4; Burnet, *Tales of the Deaf and Dumb*, 14; "First Annual Report . . . of the Alabama Institution for the Education of the Deaf and Dumb, 1861," 41; "Annual Report for the Kentucky Institution for the Education of the Deaf and Dumb, 1851," unpaginated typescript, Volta Bureau; "Annual Report for the Kentucky Institution for the Education of the Deaf and Dumb, 1852," unpaginated typescript, Volta Bureau. Administrators at the

Kentucky School suggested that uneducated Deaf people had "vicious tempers and habits." "Annual Report for the Kentucky Institution for the Education of the Deaf and Dumb, 1845," unpaginated typescript, Volta Bureau.

16. "Annual Report of the Trustees and Officers of the Louisiana Institution for the Education of the Deaf and Dumb, 1854," 7; "Annual Report for the Kentucky Institution for the Education of the Deaf and Dumb, 1848," unpaginated typescript, Volta Bureau; "Fourteenth Annual Report of the South Carolina Institution for the Education of the Deaf and Dumb, and the Blind, 1862," 10; "Report of the Trustees of the Tennessee Institution for the Deaf and Dumb, 1852" (Knoxville, TN: Printed at the Knoxville Register Office, 1852), 7; "First Annual Report . . . of the Alabama Institution for the Education of the Deaf and Dumb, 1861," 41; "Second Biennial Report . . . of the Tennessee Institution for the Education of the Deaf and Dumb for 1846–47," 16; "Annual Report . . . of the Alabama Institution for the Education of the Deaf and Dumb, 1863," 7.

17. William Dufton, *The Nature and Treatment of Deafness and Diseases of the Ear; and the Treatment of the Deaf and Dumb* (Philadelphia: Lea and Blanchard, 1848), 113–114.

18. Ibid., 107, 13. Medicine is still attempting to cure deafness. See Lane, *The Mask of Benevolence,* especially his discussion of cochlear implants on pages 203–238. Two good introductions to the general history of medicine in America are Paul Starr, *The Social Transformation of American Medicine* (New York: Basic Books, 1982); and Judith Walzer Leavitt and Ronald L. Numbers, eds., *Sickness and Health in America: Readings in the History of Medicine and Public Health* (Madison: University of Wisconsin Press, 1997).

19. Dufton, *The Nature and Treatment of Deafness,* 117–118.

20. Ibid., 78–79.

21. Ibid., 78, 108–109, 118.

22. Ibid., 99, 119.

23. S. M. Knapp, "A Case of Congenital Deafness, Relieved by an Operation Performed by the Patient on Himself," in *Western Journal of Medicine* 3 (1841), 95. This journal was published in Louisville, KY. John Washington claimed that he was born Deaf, but also said that his mother felt he could hear until he was almost a year old. The American School for the Deaf has no record of a pupil named John Washington. Antebellum ASD Admissions Registers, American School for the Deaf Archives, West Hartford, CT.

24. Knapp, "A Case of Congenital Deafness," 96; Dufton, *The Nature and Treatment of Deafness,* 80, 118.

25. Knapp, "A Case of Congenital Deafness," 96. From my reading of Deaf history sources, I think it was extremely unusual for Deaf people to seek medical cures for their deafness. Why exactly John Washington wished to cure his deafness is not discussed in the brief article. Knapp does suggest that Washington had recently ended his relationships with both his father and an authority at the American Asylum due to arguments. Perhaps his sudden lack of community drove him to the decision.

26. S. M. Knapp, "A Case of Congenital Deafness," 97.

27. Ibid., 97–98.

28. Ibid., 98.

29. Ibid.

30. Ibid., 99–100.

31. Ibid., 100.

32. Ibid., 100–101.

33. See, for example, J. H. Norwood to Samuel Tillinghast, 9 August 1836, Tillinghast Family Papers, DU; "Annual Report for the Kentucky Institution for the Education of the Deaf and Dumb, 1853," unpaginated typescript, Volta Bureau.

34. 1834 commonplace book, Hugh Blair Grigsby Papers, Virginia Historical Society, Richmond, VA. For more on folk medicine, see Charles E. Rosenberg, ed., *Right Living: An Anglo-American Tradition of Self-Help Medicine and Hygiene* (Baltimore: Johns Hopkins University Press, 2003).

35. David Brown, "Cures for Deafness: Columbian Restoratives for the Hearing, and Remedies for Various Other Diseases," 1835 Broadside, Virginia Historical Society. For further discussion of tonics advertised by broadside and the like, see James Harvey Young, *American Health Quackery* (Princeton, NJ: Princeton University Press, 1992).

Chapter 2

1. Burnet, *Tales of the Deaf and Dumb,* 13. This view of deafness was not shared by Burnet. He was merely describing society's views and parental responses.

2. J. H. Norwood to Samuel Tillinghast, 9 August 1836, Tillinghast Family Papers, DU. Samuel Willard Tillinghast, Tom's father, had a mercantile business in Fayetteville, North Carolina. For a brief introduction to the Tillinghast family, see Van Cleve and Crouch, *A Place of Their Own,* 48–59.

3. William Tillinghast to Thomas Tillinghast, 2 December 1845; Tillinghast Family Papers, DU. Cousin B. Huske wrote to Thomas, "Your Ma was here to dinner today and Brother David. He is entirely Deaf, so his Ma told me, caused from a cold, and I hope he will soon be well." B. Huske to Thomas Tillinghast, 17 February 1846, Tillinghast Family Papers, DU. The fact that he was born hearing is confirmed in William Norwood to Jane Tillinghast, 9 June 1846, Tillinghast Family Papers, DU: "As he was not born deaf, I trust that there may be found some means of relieving him." He was beginning to speak in April 1845: David "often talks about Tommy." Jane Tillinghast to Thomas Tillinghast, April 1845, Tillinghast Family Papers, DU.

4. William Tillinghast to Thomas Tillinghast, 2 December 1845; Robina Norwood to Jane Tillinghast, 6 December 1845, both in the Tillinghast Family Papers, DU.

5. Jane Tillinghast to Samuel Tillinghast, 13 October 1845, Tillinghast Family Papers, DU.

6. Robina Norwood to Jane Tillinghast, 21 March 1846, Tillinghast Family Papers, DU.

7. Ibid.

8. Ibid.

9. Robina Norwood to Jane Tillinghast, 9 July 1846; Lydia Norwood to Robina Norwood, 1846 or 1847, both in the Tillinghast Family Papers, DU.

10. Thomas Tillinghast to Jane Tillinghast, 28 May 1846; Thomas Tillinghast to Jane Tillinghast, 30 October 1846, both in the Tillinghast Family Papers, DU.

11. Virginia Trist to Nicholas Trist, 8 September 1829, Nicholas Philip Trist Family Pa-

pers, Southern Historical Collection, Wilson Library, University of North Carolina, Chapel Hill, NC (hereafter cited as SHC); Virginia Trist to Nicholas Trist, 7 October 1829; Martha Randolph to Nicholas Trist, 26 October 1829; Virginia Trist to Mrs. Jefferson Randolph, 29 March 1830, all in the Nicholas Philip Trist Family Papers, SHC. Nicholas Philip Trist, a Louisiana planter, became a political official, serving as State Department clerk, consul to Cuba, and chief negotiator of the treaty ending the Mexican War in 1847. During that negotiation, Nicholas Trist defied a presidential recall and was therefore removed from political office by the Polk administration. He married Virginia Jefferson Randolph, Thomas Jefferson's granddaughter. The family lived at Monticello for a brief time. Nicholas and Virginia had three children: Martha Jefferson Trist (Pattie), Thomas Jefferson Trist (Jefferson), and Hore Browse Trist (Browse). Pattie and Browse were hearing. For more about Nicholas Trist, see Robert W. Drexler, *Guilty of Making Peace: A Biography of Nicholas P. Trist* (Lanham, MD: University Press of America, 1991); Dean B. Mahin, *Olive Branch and Sword: The United States and Mexico, 1845–1848* (Jefferson, NC: McFarland & Co., 1997); and Wallace Ohrt, *Defiant Peacemaker: Nicholas Trist in the Mexican War* (College Station, TX: Texas A&M University Press, 1997).

12. C. [Randolph] to Jane Randolph, April 1830; Virginia Trist to Nicholas Trist, 23 December 1829; Virginia Trist to Jane Randolph, 30 March 1830, all in the Nicholas Philip Trist Family Papers, SHC.

13. Unidentified in "Miscellaneous" folder [Virginia Trist to Dr. Togno?, December 1835]; Virginia Trist to unidentified, 16 January 1831, both in the Nicholas Philip Trist Family Papers, SHC.

14. Virginia Trist to unidentified, 16 January 1831; Virginia Trist to Jane Randolph, 9 January 1831; Unidentified in "Miscellaneous" folder [Virginia Trist to Dr. Togno? December 1835]; Virginia Trist to Jane Randolph, 30 March 1830, all in the Nicholas Philip Trist Family Papers, SHC.

15. Virginia Trist to Jane Randolph, 9 January 1831; Virginia Trist to Jane Randolph, 8 May 1831; C. [Randolph] to Jane Randolph, 9 April 1831, all in the Nicholas Philip Trist Family Papers, SHC.

16. Virginia Trist to Jane Randolph, 18 March 1832, Nicholas Philip Trist Family Papers, SHC.

17. Sister to Virginia Trist, 16 January 1831, Nicholas Philip Trist Family Papers, SHC. It is true that hearing children sometimes begin to speak late. For a fascinating contemporary discussion, see Thomas Sowell, *Late-Talking Children* (New York: Basic Books, 1998); and *The Einstein Syndrome: Bright Children Who Talk Late* (New York: Basic Books, 2002).

18. Unidentified in "Miscellaneous" folder [Virginia Trist to Dr. Togno? December 1835]; Virginia Trist to sister, 16 January 1831, both in the Nicholas Philip Trist Family Papers, SHC.

19. C. [Randolph] to Virginia Trist, 29 May 1831, Nicholas Philip Trist Family Papers, SHC. Many years later, Virginia Trist reported to a healer that her infant son was definitely not congenitally Deaf. "That his hearing was perfect then, no one much with him has ever doubted," reported Virginia. "The proofs were that I had a cold, disturbed him by my coughing, and frequently woke him. The door of my chamber creaked and always disturbed him." She continued, "When he was a few hours old he was so much startled

by a slight noise, perhaps a sneeze, I forgot what, but I remember the remark of the servant standing by, who said, 'the child hears well.'" Unidentified in "Miscellaneous" folder [Virginia Trist to Dr. Togno?, December 1835], Nicholas Philip Trist Family Papers, SHC. Perhaps these remarks reflect the family's unwillingness to be tainted with the stain of inherited defect. Thanks to Douglas Baynton for suggesting this interpretation.

20. Samuel Ackerly to Nicholas Trist, 2 August 1831, Nicholas Philip Trist Family Papers, SHC; Unidentified in "Miscellaneous" folder [Virginia Trist to Dr. Togno?, December 1835], Nicholas Philip Trist Family Papers, SHC.

21. Unidentified in "Miscellaneous" folder [Virginia Trist to Dr. Togno?, December 1835], Nicholas Philip Trist Family Papers, SHC.

22. Nicholas Trist to Virginia Trist, 24 May 1833 ("Good boy" is from a section of the letter dictated to Nicholas by his daughter Martha); Nicholas Trist to Virginia Trist, 27 May 1833; Nicholas Trist to Virginia Trist, 29 May 1833, all in the Nicholas Philip Trist Family Papers, SHC.

23. Nicholas Trist to Virginia Trist, 29 May 1833; Virginia Trist to Nicholas Trist, 29 May 1833; Virginia Trist to Nicholas Trist, 1 June 1833, all in the Nicholas Philip Trist Family Papers, SHC.

24. Nicholas Trist to Virginia Trist, 31 May 1833, Nicholas Philip Trist Family Papers, SHC.

25. Ibid.; Nicholas Trist to Virginia Trist, 18 February 1835, Nicholas Philip Trist Family Papers, SHC.

26. Hannah Lawrence to Frances Lawrence, 9 July 1852; Henry Lawrence to Frances Lawrence, 20 December 1852; Henry Lawrence to Frances Lawrence, 6 March 1853, all in the Brashear-Lawrence Family Papers, SHC. Henry Lawrence was a merchant in New Orleans before becoming a sugar planter in Plaquemines Parish, Louisiana. He married Frances Brashear, daughter of a large landholder from St. Mary Parish. The couple had six children, four of whom were Deaf.

27. Virginia Trist to Nicholas Trist, 16 December 1835, Nicholas Philip Trist Family Papers, SHC.

28. Ibid.

29. Ibid.

30. Ibid.

31. Ibid.; Virginia Trist to Nicholas Trist, 25 December 1835, Nicholas Philip Trist Family Papers, SHC.

32. Virginia Trist to Nicholas Trist, 25 December 1835; Virginia Trist to Nicholas Trist, 4 January 1836, both in the Nicholas Philip Trist Family Papers, SHC.

33. Nicholas Trist to Virginia Trist, 5 May 1836, Nicholas Philip Trist Family Papers, SHC.

34. Virginia Trist to Nicholas Trist, 31 March 1836; Nicholas Trist to Virginia Trist, 5 May 1836; Nicholas Trist to Virginia Trist, 25 May 1836, all in the Nicholas Philip Trist Family Papers, SHC.

35. Virginia Trist to Nicholas Trist, 27 May 1836, Nicholas Philip Trist Family Papers, SHC.

36. Virginia Trist to Nicholas Trist, 18 June 1836, Nicholas Philip Trist Family Papers, SHC.

37. Ibid.

38. Ellen Galt Martin to Elizabeth S. Martin, 23 August 1842, Elizabeth S. Martin Papers, SHC. Born in 1825, Ellen was the daughter of John and Clarinda Martin of New Orleans, Louisiana. She was deafened at the age of four or five due to a bout with measles. Before enrolling at the Pennsylvania school for the Deaf in 1836, she was a pupil for four months at the Kentucky school for the Deaf. She remained at the Pennsylvania school for four years. ASD Admissions Register, 1840, American School for the Deaf Archives, West Hartford, CT.

39. Ellen Galt Martin to Elizabeth S. Martin, 23 August 1842, Elizabeth S. Martin Papers, SHC.

40. Ibid. Ellen attended the American school for the Deaf for one year from 1840 to 1841. She joined the school's "first class"—that is, its advanced class—and also received private lessons in French from Laurent Clerc. ASD Admissions Register, 1840, American School for the Deaf Archives, West Hartford, CT. Clerc, the Deaf man who came from France to help Thomas Hopkins Gallaudet found America's first residential school for the Deaf, is a folk hero in the Deaf community. Information about Laurent Clerc can be found in many works of Deaf history. One fictionalized account is found in Lane, *When the Mind Hears*. Appropriate for young adult readers is Cathryn Carroll, *Laurent Clerc: The Story of His Early Years* (Washington, DC: Gallaudet University Press, 2002). Also see the video *Laurent Clerc, 1785–1869* (Allison Park, PA: DeBee Communications, 1996). Clerc taught Ellen written French (and perhaps French sign language), not spoken French.

41. Ellen Galt Martin to Elizabeth S. Martin, 23 August 1842, Elizabeth S. Martin Papers, SHC.

42. Ellen Galt Martin to Elizabeth S. Martin, 24 September 1844; Ellen Galt Martin to Elizabeth S. Martin, 23 August 1842, both in the Elizabeth S. Martin Papers, SHC.

43. Ellen Galt Martin to Elizabeth S. Martin, 17 July 1844, Elizabeth S. Martin Papers, SHC. Perhaps the cultural and religious diversity of New Orleans encouraged experimentation beyond traditional medicine. One physician noted the likelihood for people, both southern and northern, to seek out alternative cures for deafness: people "who would not commit a watch to repair to any hands but those of the watchmaker" would turn "unhesitatingly" to quacks who knew nothing of "the anatomy of the ear" or to "the effects which their remedies may produce." Dufton, *The Nature and Treatment of Deafness*, 14. For more information about the mesmerism and spiritualism, see Peter McCandless, "Mesmerism and Phrenology in Antebellum Charleston: 'Enough of the Marvellous,'" *Journal of Southern History* 58, no. 2 (May 1992), 199–230; and Robert S. Fox, *Body and Soul: A Sympathetic History of American Spiritualism* (Charlottesville: University of Virginia Press, 2003). For fascinating discussions of mesmerism in Europe, see Alison Winter, *Mesmerized: Powers of Mind in Victorian Britain* (Chicago: University of Chicago Press, 1998); and Robert Darnton, *Mesmerism and the End of the Enlightenment in France* (Cambridge, MA: Harvard University Press, 1986).

44. Ellen Galt Martin to Elizabeth S. Martin, 17 July 1844; Ellen Galt Martin to Elizabeth S. Martin, 15 July 1847, both in the Elizabeth S. Martin Papers, SHC.

45. Ellen Galt Martin remained unmarried until her death at the young age of

twenty-four. She died in 1849 in New Orleans from cholera. ASD Admissions Register, 1840, American School for the Deaf Archives, West Hartford, CT.

Despite the fears of many hearing parents, Deaf daughters did sometimes marry elite hearing men. Hearing men including Thomas Hopkins Gallaudet and Alexander Graham Bell married women who could not hear. Elite hearing men unconnected to the field of deafness also sometimes married Deaf women. For example, in 1848 at age fifty-seven, Samuel Morse, the inventor of Morse Code, married twenty-six-year-old Sarah Elizabeth Griswold, Morse's Deaf second cousin. As he said, "Her misfortune of not hearing, and her defective speech only excited the more my love & pity for her." Historian Jill Lepore speculates on the reasons why Morse and, by extension, other hearing men might have been interested in marrying Deaf women: "Sarah's deafness spelled dependence, a quality Morse consciously sought in a wife." Lepore concludes, "By marrying a poor, deaf relative, Morse believed, . . . he could be 'doubly & trebly sure' of 'her sincere devoted attention.'" Sarah had attended the New York school for the Deaf from 1833 to 1836 and was defined by the school as having "partial" deafness. She was a proficient speech reader and retained, as Morse said, "defective" speech. There is no evidence that Morse ever learned to sign. Jill Lepore, *A is for American*, 157–161.

Although I was unable to find sources describing the reactions to deafness by yeomen and poor whites, they, like their elite white counterparts, were surely affected by society's assumptions about deafness. Feeling grief because of their children's deafness, such parents probably sought folk remedies and cures from local healers and religious leaders. To a degree, however, the nonelite may have been less concerned about their children's deafness. Because most expected all their sons and many of their daughters to become manual laborers, parents might have known that deafness would not significantly hamper their children's efforts to support themselves.

In addition, state residential schools for Deaf students promised literacy and vocational training to all white Deaf children, not just those from wealthy families. The majority of the nonelite families' hearing children would not receive such training. Literacy allowed Deaf people to communicate via writing with hearing literate folks and would therefore potentially open doors for skilled jobs their hearing siblings would be unlikely to attain. On the other hand, literacy would be of little value in communicating with illiterate poor family members.

Antebellum African American Deaf people, whether free or slave, had no opportunities for formal education in the South. Deafness would not restrict a person's ability to do manual labor, but the inability to hear a master's call or a mistress's summons— or another slave's warning—could put a Deaf slave at great risk. Unfortunately, historians do not have access to much information about the actual experiences of Deaf slaves.

46. "Report of the Officers of the Mississippi Deaf and Dumb Asylum, 1859" (Jackson, MS: Barksdale, State Printers, 1859), 8.

Chapter 3

1. Robina Norwood to Thomas Tillinghast, 12 March 1847, Tillinghast Family Papers, DU; Ex. 4:10–11 from the Authorized King James Version of 1611. Both parents and

educators often expressed their faith in the goodness of God's will. Wrote one school principal, "It must not be overlooked that Heaven has decreed, 'Advantages out of disadvantages arise / Deprivations are blessings in disguise.'" "Tenth Annual Report of the South Carolina Institution for the Education of the Deaf and Dumb, and the Blind, 1858" (Columbia, SC: Steam-Power Press of R. W. Gibbes, 1858), 15. The title of this chapter is from the *Kentucky Mute*, 12 June 1884.

2. "Report of the Virginia Institution for the Deaf and Dumb and the Blind, 1856–58" (Staunton, VA: Press of the Institution, 1858), 20–21; Burnet, *Tales of the Deaf and Dumb*, 16.

3. Burnet, *Tales of the Deaf and Dumb*, 12–13.

4. Ibid., 17.

5. Ibid., 17–18; "First Biennial Report of the Commissioners and Superintendent of the Missouri Asylum for the Deaf and Dumb, 1853–54" (Jefferson City, MO: J. Lusk, Public Printer, 1854), 10; "Annual Report for the Kentucky Institution for the Education of the Deaf and Dumb, 1857," unpaginated typescript, Volta Bureau; "Report . . . of the Tennessee Institution for the Deaf and Dumb, 1852," 20. The majority of the signs suggested by advocates are very similar to the specific signs of American Sign Language. For example, HARD is currently signified in American Sign Language in a way quite similar to that described in the 1850s tract. Facial expression is critically important to ASL, serving as both content and grammar.

6. "Report of the Board of Directors of the Deaf and Dumb Asylum, 1850" (Raleigh: Thomas J. Lemay, Printer to the State, 1850), 7; "Report . . . of the Tennessee Institution for the Deaf and Dumb, 1852," 20; Burnet, *Tales of the Deaf and Dumb*, 19. Currently the ASL sign MILK looks like hands milking—even though most children today have never seen a cow being milked at all, and those who have are more likely to have seen mechanical milking. Home sign depends on a concrete connection between act and the sign, but ASL does not. ASL vocabulary often has historical connections to concrete behavior, but the signs are now arbitrary—that is, their connection to the concrete is no longer important or even apparent. This movement from pantomimic to conventionalized signs is discussed at length in Nancy Frishberg, "Arbitrariness and Iconicity: Historical Change in American Sign Language," *Language* 51 (September 1975), 690–715.

David Tillinghast corroborated the limitations of home sign and the fact that Deaf children themselves often created its vocabulary. In an interview conducted when David was almost ninety years old, he recalled that he "grew up to the age of twelve, absolutely without knowledge of word language, depending for communication with my family on a few crude signs mainly invented by myself." It was at the age of twelve that his older Deaf brother came home from residential school and reconnected with young David, introducing him to American Sign Language. Maud Waddell, "Nearly Ninety, Climbs Mountain and Swims" in *The Silent Worker* 180 (June 1929), 180–181.

For more information about the development of home sign and early sign language, see Lane, Hoffmeister, and Bahan, *A Journey into the DEAF-WORLD*, 39–40, 45–51.

7. Frances Lawrence to Hannah Lawrence, 3 July 1853, Brashear-Lawrence Family Papers, Southern Historical Collection, Wilson Library, University of North Carolina, Chapel Hill, NC; "Report . . . of the Tennessee Institution for the Deaf and Dumb, 1852,"

20; Burnet, *Tales of the Deaf and Dumb,* 20; Paris J. Tillinghast to Thomas Tillinghast, 12 December 1849, Tillinghast Family Papers, DU.

8. Burnet, *Tales of the Deaf and Dumb,* 18. Almost certainly, home sign affected the development of American Sign Language—and continues to shape it. Some hearing advocates did not understand the distinction between home sign and the full language of American Sign Language. Wrote one, "There is no deaf mute of sound mind who is not able to communicate with his own family in regard to all common objects. The language in which these communications are made is the natural language of the deaf and dumb." "Report of the Board of Directors of the Deaf and Dumb Asylum, 1850" (Raleigh, NC: Thomas J. Lemay, Printer to the State, 1850), 7.

9. "Report of the Virginia Institution for the Deaf and Dumb and the Blind, 1856–58," 21; Tyler, "The Duty and Advantages of Educating the Deaf and Dumb and the Blind: A Sermon Preached in Christ Church, Staunton" 11; Virginia Trist to Nicholas Trist, 5 December 1834, Nicholas Philip Trist Family Papers, SHC.

10. Virginia Trist to Nicholas Trist, 25 April 1834, Nicholas Philip Trist Family Papers, SHC.

11. "First Annual Report of the Board of Trustees and Officers of the Alabama Institution for the Education of the Deaf and Dumb, 1861" (Montgomery, AL: Montgomery Advertiser Book and Job Printing Office, 1861), 14, 31; Tyler, "The Duty and Advantages of Educating the Deaf and Dumb and the Blind," 5; "Annual Report for the Kentucky Institution for the Education of the Deaf and Dumb, 1846," unpaginated typescript, Volta Bureau.

12. Tyler, "The Duty and Advantages of Educating the Deaf and Dumb and the Blind," 13; "Biennial Report of the North Carolina Institution for the Deaf and Dumb and the Blind, 1858–1860" (Raleigh, NC: Printed at the Press of the Institution, 1861), 20; "Third Biennial Report of the Trustees of the Tennessee Institution for the Education of the Deaf and Dumb for 1848–49" (Nashville, TN: W. F. Bang and Co., 1849), 18; "Report of the Virginia Institution for the Deaf and Dumb and the Blind, 1850" (Staunton, VA: Press of the Institution, 1850), 7; "Report of the Officers of the Mississippi Deaf and Dumb Asylum, 1857" (Jackson, MS: B. Barksdale, State Printers, 1857), 4.

13. "Report of the Virginia Institution for the Deaf and Dumb and the Blind, 1856–58," 20–21; "First Annual Report . . . of the Alabama Institution for the Education of the Deaf and Dumb, 1861," 13, 31.

14. "First Annual Report . . . of the Alabama Institution for the Education of the Deaf and Dumb, 1861," 41; "Tenth Annual Report of the Officers of the Georgia Institution for the Education of the Deaf and Dumb, 1859" (Cave Spring, GA: Georgia Institution for the Education of the Deaf and Dumb, 1859), 11; "Annual Report . . . of the Alabama Institution for the Education of the Deaf and Dumb, 1862–63" (Montgomery, AL: Montgomery Advertiser Book and Job Printing Office, 1863), 7. For an introduction to the history of southern religion, see the classic study by Donald G. Mathews, *Religion in the Old South* (Chicago: University of Chicago Press, 1979).

15. "Fourth Annual Report of the Commissioners of the Georgia Asylum for the Education of the Deaf and Dumb, 1853" (Cave Spring, GA: Georgia Asylum for the Education of the Deaf and Dumb, 1853), 6–7.

16. "First Annual Report . . . of the Alabama Institution for the Education of the Deaf and Dumb, 1861," 31, 13; "Tenth Annual Report of the Officers of the Georgia Institution for the Education of the Deaf and Dumb, 1859," 11.

17. "First Annual Report . . . of the Alabama Institution for the Education of the Deaf and Dumb, 1861," 31; "Annual Report . . . of the Alabama Institution for the Education of the Deaf and Dumb, 1862–63," 7; "Third Biennial Report . . . of the Tennessee Institution for the Education of the Deaf and Dumb for 1848–49", 20; "Report . . . of the Tennessee Institution for the Deaf and Dumb, 1852", 19; "Annual Report for the Virginia Institution for the Education of the Deaf and Dumb and the Blind, 1846" in *Journal of the House of Delegates*, 1845–46, Doc. No. 20, 1; "Annual Report for the Kentucky Institution for the Education of the Deaf and Dumb, 1853," unpaginated typescript, Volta Bureau; "Annual Report for the Kentucky Institution for the Education of the Deaf and Dumb, 1848," unpaginated typescript, Volta Bureau.

18. "First Annual Report . . . of the Alabama Institution for the Education of the Deaf and Dumb, 1861," 31; Tyler, "The Duty and Advantages of Educating the Deaf and Dumb and the Blind," 13; "Annual Report . . . of the Alabama Institution for the Education of the Deaf and Dumb, 1862," 7.

19. "Annual Report for the Kentucky Institution for the Education of the Deaf and Dumb, 1853," unpaginated typescript, Volta Bureau; "First Annual Report . . . of the Alabama Institution for the Education of the Deaf and Dumb, 1861," 31, 13. For more discussion of citizenship, see "Elevate them to the position of useful citizens," and "Educate them and we have useful men and women, good citizens, and valuable members of society," in "Annual Report . . . of the Alabama Institution for the Education of the Deaf and Dumb, 1862–63," 7 and 10; "made useful citizens," in "Third Biennial Report . . . of the Tennessee Institution for the Education of the Deaf and Dumb for 1848–49," 20; and "useful citizen," in "Fourth Annual Report of the Commissioners of the Georgia Asylum for the Education of the Deaf and Dumb, 1853," 8. For more on the history of citizenship, see Rogers M. Smith, *Civic Ideals: Conflicting Visions of Citizenship in U.S. History* (New Haven, CT: Yale Unversity Press: 1999); and Michael Schudson, *The Good Citizen: A History of American Civic Life* (Cambridge, MA: Harvard University Press, 1999).

20. "The Second Biennial Report of the Board of Trustees of the Tennessee Institution for the Education of the Deaf and Dumb for 1846–47" (Nashville, TN: W. F. Bangs and Co. Banner Office), 16; "First Annual Report . . . of the Alabama Institution for the Education of the Deaf and Dumb, 1861," 41; "Fourth Annual Report of the Commissioners of the Georgia Asylum for the Education of the Deaf and Dumb, 1853," 8; "Annual Report for the Virginia Institution for the Education of the Deaf and Dumb and the Blind, 1846," 1; "First Annual Report . . . of the Alabama Institution for the Education of the Deaf and Dumb, 1861," 13, 31; "Report of the Officers of the Mississippi Institute for the Deaf and Dumb, 1859" (Jackson, MS: B. Barksdale, State Printers, 1859), 5.

21. "Report of the Virginia Institution for the Deaf and Dumb and the Blind, 1852" (Staunton, VA: Press of the Institution, 1852), 9; "First Biennial . . . of the Missouri Asylum for the Deaf and Dumb, 1853–54," 23; "Tenth Annual Report of the Officers of the Georgia Institution for the Education of the Deaf and Dumb, 1859," 11; "First Annual Report . . . of the Alabama Institution for the Education of the Deaf and Dumb, 1861,"

41, 13; "Annual Report for the Kentucky Institution for the Education of the Deaf and Dumb, 1853," unpaginated typescript, Volta Bureau; "Annual Report of the President and Officers of the Texas Institution for the Education of the Deaf and Dumb, 1859" (Austin, TX: John Marshall and Co., State Printers, 1859), 12; "Annual Report for the Kentucky Institution for the Education of the Deaf and Dumb, 1849," unpaginated typescript, Volta Bureau.

Chapter 4

1. J. H. Norwood to Samuel Tillinghast, 9 August 1836, Tillinghast Family Papers, DU. Harvey Prindle Peet was the head of the New York school for the Deaf from 1831 until 1866.

Although residential schools for the Deaf were called institutions, or occasionally asylums, they were not intended to be permanent homes. They were institutions in the sense that universities are institutions. It is worth noting, however, that at the time, the majority of schools for the Deaf were funded not by state education coffers but by the monies the state set aside to fund charities and social welfare.

2. J. H. Norwood to Samuel Tillinghast, 9 August 1836, Tillinghast Family Papers, DU. For a discussion of home-based education in the South among families with hearing children, see Jane Turner Censer, *North Carolina Planters and Their Children, 1800–1860* (Baton Rouge: Louisiana State University Press, 1984), 54–56; and Stowe, *Intimacy and Power in the Old South,* 132–134.

3. J. H. Norwood to Samuel Tillinghast, 9 August 1836, Tillinghast Family Papers, DU.

4. Ibid.

5. Ibid.; Robina Norwood to Jane Tillinghast, 27 December 1839, Tillinghast Family Papers, DU.

6. Jane Tillinghast to Samuel Tillinghast, 4 September 1830, Tillinghast Family Papers, DU.

7. Robina Norwood to Jane Tillinghast, 3 April 1840; Robina Norwood to Jane Tillinghast, 20 August 1841, both in the Tillinghast Family Papers, DU.

8. Robina Norwood to Jane Tillinghast, 20 August 1841; Robina Norwood to Samuel Tillinghast, 22 November 1841, both in the Tillinghast Family Papers, DU.

9. Robina Norwood to Jane Tillinghast, 20 August 1841, Tillinghast Family Papers, DU.

10. Ibid.

11. John Pasteur to Samuel Tillinghast, 30 December 1841, Tillinghast Family Papers, DU. Eunice Ivey is listed as a former pupil in the roster of the New York school reprinted in the *American Annals of the Deaf* 8, no. 4 (1854).

12. Caroline W. Nelson to Samuel Tillinghast, 20 January 1842; John Pasteur to Samuel Tillinghast, 30 December 1841, both in the Tillinghast Family Papers, DU. A family friend wrote to Samuel that although she "was not acquainted with the family," she was pleased with what she saw. "They seem to be a very fine family and is very respectable." Caroline W. Nelson to Samuel Tillinghast, 20 January 1842, Tillinghast Family Papers, DU.

13. John Pasteur to Samuel Tillinghast, 30 December 1841; Caroline W. Nelson to Samuel Tillinghast, 20 January 1842, both in the Tillinghast Family Papers, DU.

14. Caroline W. Nelson to Samuel Tillinghast, 20 January 1842; John Pasteur to Samuel Tillinghast, 30 December 1841, both in the Tillinghast Family Papers, DU.

15. Caroline W. Nelson to Samuel Tillinghast, 20 January 1842; Caroline W. Nelson to Samuel Tillinghast, 20 January 1842, both in the Tillinghast Family Papers, DU.

16. Robina Norwood to Jane Tillinghast, 8 January 1842, Tillinghast Family Papers, DU.

17. Robina Norwood to Jane Tillinghast, 16 May 1842, Tillinghast Family Papers, DU.

18. Virginia Trist to Nicholas Trist, 4 January 1834, Nicholas P. Trist Family Papers, SHC.

19. Virginia Trist to Nicholas Trist, 4 January 1834, Nicholas Philip Trist Family Papers, SHC. Near the end of this letter to her husband, Virginia wrote, "I forgot to say that Mr. Peet has commenced an elementary book for the use of the school, now in manuscript, which when printed he would communicate" to the Trists. A few months later, she reported, "I am told that a series of first books are to be published this year for the Deaf and Dumb children in the New York Institution." Virginia Trist to Nicholas Trist, 4 May 1834, Nicholas Philip Trist Family Papers, SHC. Perhaps she was anticipating the publication of Harvey P. Peet, *Course of Instruction for the Deaf* (New York: New York Institution for the Instruction of the Deaf and Dumb, 1845).

20. Virginia Trist to Nicholas Trist, 2 March 1834; Virginia Trist to Nicholas Trist, 12 December 1833, both in the Nicholas Philip Trist Family Papers, SHC.

21. Virginia Trist to Nicholas Trist, 4 January 1834; Virginia Trist to Nicholas Trist, 29 March 1834, both in the Nicholas Philip Trist Family Papers, SHC.

22. Virginia Trist to Nicholas Trist, 2 March 1834, Nicholas Philip Trist Family Papers, SHC.

23. Virginia Trist to Nicholas Trist, 3 April 1834; Virginia Trist to Nicholas Trist, 2 March 1834, both in the Nicholas Philip Trist Family Papers, SHC.

24. Virginia Trist to Nicholas Trist, 3 April 1834, Nicholas Philip Trist Family Papers, SHC. Also see: "The Mutes have not, as we, the assistance of *sound* in the recollection of proper spelling." Quote from "Annual Report for the Kentucky Institution for the Education of the Deaf and Dumb, 1848," unpaginated typescript, Volta Bureau.

25. Virginia Trist to Nicholas Trist, 3 April 1834; Virginia Trist to Nicholas Trist, 25 April 1834; Virginia Trist to Nicholas Trist, 4 May 1834, all in the Nicholas Philip Trist Family Papers, SHC.

26. Virginia Trist to Nicholas Trist, 4 May 1834, Nicholas Philip Trist Family Papers, SHC.

27. Virginia Trist to Nicholas Trist, 29 March 1834; Virginia Trist to Nicholas Trist, 11 May 1835, both in the Nicholas Philip Trist Family Papers, SHC.

28. "Annual Report for the Kentucky Institution for the Education of the Deaf and Dumb, 1857," unpaginated typescript, Volta Bureau; "Eleventh Annual Report of the Officers of the Georgia Institution for the Education of the Deaf and Dumb, 1860" (Cave Spring, GA: Georgia Institution for the Education of the Deaf and Dumb, 1860), 32. One teacher stated, "We hope to see parents give something like the attention both to the education and discipline that they do to their speaking children." "Annual Report

for the Kentucky Institution for the Education of the Deaf and Dumb, 1857," unpaginated typescript, Volta Bureau.

29. "Report of the Board of Trustees of the Tennessee Deaf and Dumb School, 1853" (Knoxville, TN: Printed by A. Blackburn and Co., 1853), 8. Another suggested, "Much may be done by the parents and friends of such children before they arrive at a proper age to be sent to an institution." "Report . . . of the Tennessee Institution for the Deaf and Dumb, 1852," 19.

30. "Report . . . of the Tennessee Institution for the Deaf and Dumb, 1852," 20; "Annual Report for the Kentucky Institution for the Education of the Deaf and Dumb, 1853," unpaginated typescript, Volta Bureau.

31. "Second Annual Report of the Commissioners of the Georgia Asylum for the Education of the Deaf and Dumb, 1851" (Cave Spring, GA: Georgia Asylum for the Education of the Deaf and Dumb, 1851), 5; "Annual Report for the Kentucky Institution for the Education of the Deaf and Dumb, 1851," unpaginated typescript, Volta Bureau; "Report . . . of the Tennessee Institution for the Deaf and Dumb, 1852," 20.

32. "Annual Report for the Kentucky Institution for the Education of the Deaf and Dumb, 1848," unpaginated typescript, Volta Bureau; "Annual Report for the Kentucky Institution for the Education of the Deaf and Dumb, 1853," unpaginated typescript, Volta Bureau. Some students learned before they came to the institution "to write a good hand and to spell a considerable number of words on their fingers, which thus acquired flexibility, while their memories gained a degree of tenacity which they could not have acquired till they had been here some months had they not been previously instructed." "Report . . . of the Mississippi Institute for the Deaf and Dumb, 1859," 6.

33. "Report . . . of the Tennessee Institution for the Deaf and Dumb, 1852," 20; "Eleventh Annual Report of the Commissioners of the Georgia Asylum for the Education of the Deaf and Dumb, 1860," 32; "Second Annual Report of the Commissioners of the Georgia Asylum for the Education of the Deaf and Dumb, 1851," 5. Another teacher stated, "If it were well and generally understood that it is just as easy to teach a mute *his* letters, as a speaking child its alphabet, and that it is just as easy to teach him the names if things around him, as for a speaking child to learn to spell them in a spelling-book, there, doubtless, would be many more who would attempt to help on the education of these poor unfortunate children." "Annual Report for the Kentucky Institution for the Education of the Deaf and Dumb, 1857," unpaginated typescript, Volta Bureau.

34. "Report . . . of the Tennessee Institution for the Deaf and Dumb, 1852," 20–21; "Annual Report for the Kentucky Institution for the Education of the Deaf and Dumb, 1850," unpaginated typescript, Volta Bureau.

35. "Annual Report for the Kentucky Institution for the Education of the Deaf and Dumb, 1857," unpaginated typescript, Volta Bureau; "Report of the Commissioners and Superintendent of the Missouri Asylum for the Deaf and Dumb, 1859–60" (Jefferson City, MO: J. Lusk, Public Printer, 1860), 13; "Report of the Commissioners and Superintendent of the Missouri Asylum for the Deaf and Dumb, 1857–58" (Jefferson City, MO: J. Lusk, Public Printer, 1858), 22.

36. "Report . . . of the Tennessee Institution for the Deaf and Dumb, 1852," 19; "Annual Report for the Kentucky Institution for the Education of the Deaf and Dumb, 1848," unpaginated typescript, Volta Bureau.

37. "Report . . . of the Tennessee Institution for the Deaf and Dumb, 1852," 20. All of these signs are acceptable ASL vocabulary today.

38. "Report . . . of the Tennessee Institution for the Deaf and Dumb, 1852," 21.

39. For more discussion of the rules and traditions of American Sign Language, see the references cited in note 8 of the introduction.

40. "Annual Report for the Kentucky Institution for the Education of the Deaf and Dumb, 1850," unpaginated typescript, Volta Bureau; "Report . . . of the Tennessee Institution for the Deaf and Dumb, 1852," 21.

41. Hannah Lawrence to Frances Lawrence, 9 December 1852; Hannah Lawrence to Frances Lawrence, 9 July 1852, both in the Brashear-Lawrence Family Papers, SHC.

42. Frances Lawrence to Hannah Lawrence, 3 July 1853, Brashear-Lawrence Family Papers, SHC.

43. Lydia Lawrence to Frances Lawrence, 4 December 1855, Brashear-Lawrence Family Papers, SHC.

44. Ibid.

45. Ibid.

46. 1856 Admissions Record, Archives of the Louisiana School for the Deaf, Baton Rouge, LA; Frances Lawrence to sons Towny, Bob, and Walter Lawrence, 28 December 1860; Henry Lawrence to sister, 2 July 1861, both in the Brashear-Lawrence Family Papers, SHC.

47. Joseph Tyler to Samuel Tillinghast, 17 June 1847, Tillinghast Family Papers, DU.

48. Ibid.; Joseph Tyler to Samuel Tillinghast, 30 April 1850, Tillinghast Family Papers, DU. For the story of a hearing southerner teaching her siblings, see Stowe, *Intimacy and Power in the Old South*, 173–184.

49. Thomas Tillinghast to Samuel Tillinghast, 17 March 1850; Thomas Tillinghast to John Tillinghast, 6 September 1850, both in the Tillinghast Family Papers, DU.

50. Cousin Amelia to Thomas Tillinghast, 26 October 1850; William Tillinghast to John Tillinghast, 8 September 1851; William Tillinghast to John Tillinghast, 1 March 1852; William Tillinghast to John Tillinghast, 22 November 1852, all in the Tillinghast Family Papers, DU; Waddell, "Nearly Ninety," 180.

51. Waddell, "Nearly Ninety," 180.

52. Ibid. For more about *Harper's Magazine*, see Lewis Lapham and Ellen Rosenbush, eds., *An American Album: One Hundred and Fifty Years of* Harper's Magazine (New York: Franklin Square Press, 2000).

53. William Tillinghast to John Tillinghast, 1 March 1852, Tillinghast Family Papers, DU.

54. William Tillinghast to John Tillinghast, 22 November 1852; William Tillinghast to John Tillinghast, 6 September 1852; Robina Norwood to Jane Tillinghast, 27 January 1853; William Tillinghast to John Tillinghast, 4 July 1853, all in the Tillinghast Family Papers, DU.

55. Robina Tillinghast to John Tillinghast, 28 July 1853; Samuel Tillinghast to William Tillinghast, 18 July 1853; William Tillinghast to John Tillinghast, 30 August 1853; William Tillinghast to John Tillinghast, 13 September 1853, all in the Tillinghast Family Papers, DU.

Part II

1. For more complete discussions of the history of the American School for the Deaf, see, among others, Van Cleve and Crouch, *A Place of Their Own*, 29–46; Lane, *When the Mind Hears;* Phyllis Klein Valentine, "A Nineteenth Century Experiment in Education of the Handicapped: The American Asylum for the Deaf and Dumb," *New England Quarterly* 64 (Sept. 1991), 355–375; and Phyllis Klein Valentine, "American Asylum for the Deaf: A First Experiment in Education, 1817–1880" (Ph.D. diss., University of Connecticut, 1993). Also see Gannon, *Deaf Heritage,* xxi–xxiii, 16; and Edwards, "Words Made Flesh."

Before the beginnings of formal Deaf education in America, many elite Deaf people were either sent to Europe or taught by private educators. At least one community (Martha's Vineyard) had such a large percentage of genetically deaf people that the community at large sometimes communicated by a signed language accessible to all its members. Nora Ellen Groce, *Everyone Here Spoke Sign Language: Hereditary Deafness on Martha's Vineyard* (Cambridge, MA: Harvard University Press, 1985). For an account of an attempt to start a private school for the Deaf in Virginia in 1812, see Thomas S. Doyle, "The Virginia Institution for the Education of the Deaf and Dumb (and of the Blind)" (Staunton, VA: 1893), 3–5; Van Cleve and Crouch, *A Place of Their Own*, 21–28.

For a discussion of how Deaf children who had received private tutoring, who grew up in communities with large numbers of Deaf pupils, or who were born of Deaf parents affected the development of sign language and Deaf culture, see Lane, Hoffmeister, and Bahan, *A Journey into the* DEAF-WORLD, 57–58.

2. "A Brief History of the American Asylum, at Hartford, for the Education and Instruction of the Deaf and Dumb" (Hartford, CT: Press of the Case, Lockwood and Brainard Company, 1893), 13; H. Van Allen, "A Brief History of the Pennsylvania Institution for the Deaf and Dumb" (Philadelphia: Printed by Order of the Board of Directors of the Pennsylvania Institution for the Deaf and Dumb, 1893), 3–7.

3. "A History of the New York Institution for the Instruction of the Deaf and Dumb" (New York: Printed at the New York Institution for the Deaf and Dumb, 1893), 11–17; Van Allen, "A Brief History of the Pennsylvania Institution for the Deaf and Dumb," 8–11 .

4. Charles P. Fosdick, "A Short History of the Kentucky School for the Deaf" (Danville, KY: Office of the *Kentucky Deaf-Mute,* 1893), 2–5. Also see James B. Beauchamp, *History of the Kentucky School for the Deaf, 1823–1973* (Danville, KY: Kentucky School for the Deaf Alumni Association, 1973). Southern students were also sent to schools in the North, including the American Asylum for the Deaf. The Connecticut school sent Lewis Weld, a hearing teacher, and three Asylum pupils to give exhibitions throughout the nation. (Lewis Weld was the brother of the prominent abolitionist Theodore Dwight Weld.) Because of their appeals to the legislatures of the states, during the 1830s and '40s Georgia and South Carolina sent Deaf children to the Connecticut school. "Report of the Directors of the American Asylum, at Hartford, for the Education and Instruction of the Deaf and Dumb" (Hartford, CT: Hudson and Co., 1835). One ASD pupil wrote in an annual report to the Connecticut legislature, "An institution for the deaf is necessary in one of the Southern States . . . for mutes to get knowledge." Until one was built, it would be necessary "to go a thousand miles for the sake of

instruction." The student quote is from an essay "By A Young Man Under Instruction 3 1/2 years," in "Report of the Directors of the American Asylum, at Hartford, for the Education and Instruction of the Deaf and Dumb" (Hartford: Hudson and Co., 1839), 24.

5. Bass, *History of the Education of the Deaf in Virginia,* 41–49. Also see Doyle, "The Virginia Institution for the Education of the Deaf and Dumb," 3–5. Years later, after Job Turner had retired from the Virginia school, he was called "perhaps the best known and most generally beloved deaf-mutes in America." He received ordination as an Episcopal priest in 1891. For more of his fascinating biography, see Braddock, *Notable Deaf Persons,* 139–142. The quotation (by J. H. Cloud) can be found on page 149.

6. "Tennessee Deaf and Dumb School: Historical Sketch, 1844–1893" (Knoxville, TN: 1893); E. McK. Goodwin, "The North Carolina Institutions for the Deaf and Dumb and the Blind" (Raleigh, NC: 1893); Wesley O. Connor, "The Georgia School for the Deaf, 1846–1893" (Cave Spring, GA: 1893); *Centennial Celebration: One Hundred Years of Education for the Deaf in Georgia, 1848–1948* (Cave Spring, GA: Georgia School for the Deaf, 1948); N. F. Walker, "History of the South Carolina Institution for the Education of the Deaf and the Blind" (Cedar Spring, SC: 1893); Robert E. Bevill and Larry Vollmar, *History of the Arkansas School for the Deaf : 1850–1975 : 125th Anniversary of Educational Services* (Little Rock: Arkansas School for the Deaf, 1975); Bess Michaels Riggs, *A Brief History of the Education of the Deaf in the State of Arkansas* (Little Rock: Arkansas School for the Deaf, 1934); Henry Gross, "Missouri School for the Deaf and Dumb: A Sketch of Its History, Growth, and Present Facilities" (Fulton, MO: Printed at the Record Office, 1893); H. Lorraine Tracy, "The Louisiana School for the Deaf" (Baton Rouge: 1893); J. R. Dobyns, "The Mississippi Institution for the Education of the Deaf and Dumb" (Jackson, MS: 1893); Robert S. Brown, *History of the Mississippi School for the Deaf, 1854–1954* (Meridian, MS: Gower Printing and Office Supply, 1954); Harris Taylor and J. H. W. Williams, "History of the Texas Deaf and Dumb Asylum" (Austin, TX: Press of Deaf and Dumb Asylum, 1893); and "Texas School for the Deaf: 1856–1956, One Hundred Vital Years of Progress: Origin, Growth, Future" (n.p.: [1956?]); J. H. Johnson, "The Alabama Institute for the Deaf" (Talladega, AL: 1893); Robert Hill Couch and Jack Hawkins Jr., *Out of Silence and Darkness: The History of the Alabama Institute for Deaf and Blind, 1858–1983* (Troy, AL: Troy State University Press, 1983).

7. Discussion of other antebellum southern charitable organizations can be found in Peter Wallenstein, *From Slave South to New South: Public Policy in Georgia in the Nineteenth Century* (Chapel Hill: University of North Carolina Press, 1987); Barbara L. Bellows, *Benevolence Among Slaveholders: Assisting the Poor in Charleston 1670–1860* (Baton Rouge: Louisiana State University, 1993); Peter McCandless, *Moonlight, Magnolias, and Madness: Insanity in South Carolina from the Colonial Period to the Progressive Era* (Chapel Hill: University of North Carolina Press, 1996); Elna C. Green, ed., *Before the New Deal: Social Welfare in the South, 1830–1930* (Athens: University of Georgia Press, 1999); and Elna C. Green, *This Business of Relief: Confronting Poverty in a Southern City, 1740–1940* (Athens: University of Georgia Press, 2003).

8. Governor James Whitfield to the state legislature, quoted in Dobyns, "The Mississippi Institution for the Education of the Deaf and Dumb," 3.

9. Governor James Whitfield to the state legislature, quoted in Dobyns, "The Mississippi Institution for the Education of the Deaf and Dumb," 3–4. Virginia, North Caroli-

na, South Carolina, and Louisiana all had blind students during the antebellum period. Alabama added blind students after the Civil War.

10. Bass, *History of the Education of the Deaf in Virginia,* 42.

11. See Buchanan, *Illusions of Equality,* for a more complete discussion of vocational education in nineteenth-century schools for the Deaf.

Chapter 5

1. "First Annual Report of the Commissioners of the Georgia Asylum for the Education of the Deaf and Dumb, 1850" (Cave Spring, GA: Georgia Asylum for the Education of the Deaf and Dumb, 1850), 8; "First Annual Report of the Board of Trustees and Officers of the Alabama Institution for the Education of the Deaf and Dumb, 1861" (Montgomery, AL: Montgomery Advertiser Book and Job Printing Office, 1861), 31. Information on the history of Deaf education in various countries can be found in Renate Fischer and Harlan Lane, eds., *Looking Back: A Reader on the History of Deaf Communities and their Sign Languages* (Hamburg, Germany: Signum Press, 1993); Van Cleve, *Deaf History Unveiled;* and Carol J. Erting, Robert C. Johnson, Dorothy L. Smith, Bruce D. Snider, eds., *The Deaf Way: Perspectives from the International Conference on Deaf Culture* (Washington, DC: Gallaudet University Press, 1994), 160–305.

2. "Tenth Annual Report of the South Carolina Institution for the Education of the Deaf and Dumb, and the Blind, 1858" (Columbia, SC: Steam-Power Press of R. W. Gibbes, 1858), 12–13.

3. "Report of the Virginia Institution for the Deaf and Dumb and the Blind, 1852" (Staunton, VA: Press of the Institution, 1852), 15.

4. "First Biennial Report of the Commissioners and Superintendent of the Missouri Asylum for the Deaf and Dumb, 1853–54" (Jefferson City, MO: J. Lusk, Public Printer, 1854), 13.

5. "Annual Report for the Kentucky Institution for the Education of the Deaf and Dumb, 1861," unpaginated typescript, Volta Bureau. Douglas Baynton explores how postbellum oralists used similar rhetoric in his *Forbidden Signs,* 36–55.

6. "Annual Report for the Kentucky Institution for the Education of the Deaf and Dumb, 1843," unpaginated typescript, Volta Bureau; "The First Biennial Report of Board of Trustees of the Tennessee Institution for the Education of the Deaf and Dumb, 1844–45" (Nashville: W. F. Bang and Co., Printers, Banner Press, 1845), 24. Rebecca Edwards discusses a call for oralism during the 1840s. See R. A. R. Edwards, " 'Speech Has an Extraordinary Humanizing Power': Horace Mann and the Problem of Nineteenth-Century Deaf Education," in Paul K. Longmore and Lauri Umansky, *The New Disability History: American Perspectives* (New York: New York University Press, 2001), 58–82. Although Mann was a powerful figure in American education as a whole, his position in the world of Deaf education was relatively marginal.

7. "First Annual Report . . . of the Georgia Asylum for the Education of the Deaf and Dumb, 1850," 8; "Annual Report for the Kentucky Institution for the Education of the Deaf and Dumb, 1844," unpaginated typescript, Volta Bureau. Referring to the postbellum period, Douglas Baynton explores how the rise of oralism changed the teaching force. Baynton, *Forbidden Signs,* 56–82.

8. "Annual Report for the Virginia Institution for the Education of the Deaf and Dumb and the Blind, 1846," in *Journal of the House of Delegates*, 1845–46, Doc. No. 20, 6; "Report of the Virginia Institution for the Deaf and Dumb and the Blind, 1852," 15; "First Biennial Report . . . of the Missouri Asylum for the Deaf and Dumb, 1853–54," 14; "Annual Report for the Kentucky Institution for the Education of the Deaf and Dumb, 1845," unpaginated typescript, Volta Bureau; "Annual Report for the Kentucky Institution for the Education of the Deaf and Dumb, 1849," unpaginated typescript, Volta Bureau.

9. "Tenth Annual Report of the South Carolina Institution for the Education of the Deaf and Dumb, and the Blind, 1858," 12; Harvey P. Peet, "Address Delivered in Commons Hall, at Raleigh, on the Occasion of Laying the Corner Stone of the North Carolina Institution for the Instruction of the Deaf and Dumb" (New York: Egbert, Hovey, and Kind, Printers, 1848), 34; "First Annual Report of the South Carolina Institution for Deaf and Dumb, 1854" (n.p.: Carolina Spartan, 1854), 6.

10. "Annual Report of the Virginia Institution for the Education of the Deaf and Dumb and the Blind, 1870" (Richmond: R. F. Walker, Superintendent Public Printing, 1870), 9; "Annual Report for the Kentucky Institution for the Education of the Deaf and Dumb, 1847," unpaginated typescript, Volta Bureau.

11. "First Annual Report . . . of the Georgia Asylum for the Education of the Deaf and Dumb, 1850," 8; "Annual Report for the Virginia Institution for the Education of the Deaf and Dumb and the Blind, 1846," 6. See Daniel Feller, *The Jacksonian Promise: American 1815–1840* (Baltimore: Johns Hopkins University Press, 1995).

12. "Annual Report for the Kentucky Institution for the Education of the Deaf and Dumb, 1843," unpaginated typescript, Volta Bureau; "Annual Report for the Kentucky Institution for the Education of the Deaf and Dumb, 1844," unpaginated typescript, Volta Bureau; "Annual Report for the Kentucky Institution for the Education of the Deaf and Dumb, 1845," unpaginated typescript, Volta Bureau.

13. "Annual Report for the Kentucky Institution for the Education of the Deaf and Dumb, 1849," unpaginated typescript, Volta Bureau.

14. "Tenth Annual Report of the South Carolina Institution for the Education of the Deaf and Dumb, and the Blind, 1858," 13; "First Biennial Report . . . of the Missouri Asylum for the Deaf and Dumb, 1853–54," 13.

15. "Report of the Virginia Institution for the Deaf and Dumb and the Blind, 1852," 15, 17; "First Annual Report . . . of the Georgia Asylum for the Education of the Deaf and Dumb, 1850," 8; "Annual Report of the Virginia Institution for the Education of the Deaf and Dumb and the Blind, 1870," 9.

16. "Tenth Annual Report of the South Carolina Institution for the Education of the Deaf and Dumb, and the Blind, 1858," 12–13; "First Biennial Report . . . of the Missouri Asylum for the Deaf and Dumb, 1853–54," 14.

17. "Tenth Annual Report of the South Carolina Institution for the Education of the Deaf and Dumb, and the Blind, 1858," 13; "Annual Report for the Kentucky Institution for the Education of the Deaf and Dumb, 1849," unpaginated typescript, Volta Bureau.

18. Harvey P. Peet, "Address Delivered . . . on the Occasion of Laying the Corner Stone of the North Carolina Institution for the Instruction of the Deaf and Dumb," 31.

19. "Annual Report for the Kentucky Institution for the Education of the Deaf and Dumb, 1844," unpaginated typescript, Volta Bureau; "Annual Report for the Kentucky Institution for the Education of the Deaf and Dumb, 1847," unpaginated typescript, Volta Bureau; "Twelfth Annual Report of the Officers of the Georgia Institution for the Education of the Deaf and Dumb, 1861" (Cave Spring, GA: Georgia Institution for the Education of the Deaf and Dumb, 1861), 11.

20. "Annual Report of the Virginia Institution for the Education of the Deaf and Dumb and the Blind, 1870," 9; "Annual Report for the Kentucky Institution for the Education of the Deaf and Dumb, 1844," unpaginated typescript, Volta Bureau; "First Biennial Report . . . of the Missouri Asylum for the Deaf and Dumb, 1853–54," 13.

21. "Annual Report for the Kentucky Institution for the Education of the Deaf and Dumb, 1845," unpaginated typescript, Volta Bureau; Burnet, *Tales of the Deaf and Dumb*, 26. Or as one teacher of the Deaf said, Deaf people were "ignorant . . . of all that the human voice could teach." Tyler, "The Duty and Advantages of Educating the Deaf and Dumb and the Blind," 5.

Chapter 6

1. Virginia Trist to Nicholas Trist, 11 May 1835, Nicholas Philip Trist Family Papers, SHC. Surprisingly little has been written about the precollege educations of hearing southerners, especially of southern males. Two books that explore the subject are Censer, *North Carolina Planters and Their Children, 1800–1860*, 42–64; and Stowe, *Intimacy and Power in the Old South*, 122–159.

2. Virginia Trist to Nicholas Trist, 11 May 1835, Nicholas Philip Trist Family Papers, SHC.

3. Virginia Trist to Nicholas Trist, 7 December 1835, Nicholas Philip Trist Family Papers, SHC.

4. Ibid.

5. Nicholas Trist to Virginia Trist, 9 December 1835, Nicholas Philip Trist Family Papers, SHC.

6. Virginia Trist to Nicholas Trist, 4 January 1836, Nicholas Philip Trist Family Papers, SHC.

7. Ibid.

8. Burnet, *Tales of the Deaf and Dumb;* Virginia Trist to Nicholas Trist, 4 January 1836, Nicholas Philip Trist Family Papers, SHC.

9. Virginia Trist to Nicholas Trist, 28 April 1836, Nicholas Philip Trist Family Papers, SHC.

10. Virginia Trist to Mary Randolph, 18 September 1836, Nicholas Philip Trist Family Papers, SHC.

11. Virginia Trist to Mary Randolph, 20 May 1837, Nicholas Philip Trist Family Papers, SHC.

12. Ibid.

13. Virginia Trist to Nicholas Trist, 31 March 1836; Virginia Trist to Nicholas Trist, 18 June 1836; Virginia Trist to Nicholas Trist, 31 March 1836, all in the Nicholas Philip Trist

Family Papers, SHC. Virginia Trist is describing the contemporary ASL sign THINK, not FORGET. Perhaps the sign was used at that time to mean "forget," or perhaps she mistranslated what could in this context easily have meant "think."

14. Waddell, "Nearly Ninety," 180.

15. J.A. Jacobs, *Lessons for the Deaf and Dumb* (Lexington, KY: Printed by William M. Todd and William D. Skillman, 1834), esp. 2; "First Annual Report of the South Carolina Institution for Deaf and Dumb, 1854," 11. For more information on southern textbooks generally, see Neil Vernon Arneson, "Education and Slavery, Sectionalism, Union: The Role of Textbooks and Schools, 1800–1860" (Ed.D. diss., University of Virginia, 1991).

16. J. A. Jacobs, *Lessons for the Deaf and Dumb*, 7; J. A. Jacobs, *Primary Lessons for Deaf–Mutes* (New York: Printed by J. F. Trow, 1860), 1:5; J. A. Jacobs, "Discussion with J. R. Burnet," *American Annals of the Deaf and Dumb* 5, no. 2 (1853): 96; J. A. Jacobs, "On the Disuse of Colloquial Signs in the Instruction of the Deaf and Dumb, and the Necessity of General Signs following the Order of the Words," *American Annals of the Deaf and Dumb* 7, no. 2, (1854): 71. In his fictionalized account, Harlan Lane has Laurent Clerc say that although he himself taught Jacobs methodical signs, Jacob used them far more zealously than Clerc did: Jacobs was "'a disciple more devout than the master.'" Lane, *When the Mind Hears*, 247–248.

17. J. A. Jacobs, *Primary Lessons for Deaf-Mutes*, 1:13.

18. J. A. Jacobs, *Primary Lessons for Deaf-Mutes*, 1:13, 1:5.

19. J. A. Jacobs, *Primary Lessons for Deaf-Mutes*, 1:9, 1:118; 2:267–268; 1:150. Race is discussed in a writing sample entitled "The Races of Men" provided by a student at the South Carolina school for the Deaf. The student attributes racial identity to the Noah story of the Bible. Noah's son Ham laughed at his naked father. "God punished . . . Ham severely" and therefore his descendents became "black negroes." Ham's brother Japhet did not laugh but instead pitied his father. Because God favored his actions, "he was white like our races." J[ames] S. H[agins], in samples of student compositions, "Eleventh Annual Report of the South Carolina Institution for the Education of the Deaf and Dumb, and the Blind, 1859" (Columbia, SC: Charles P. Pelham, State Printer, 1860), 28–35.

20. J. A. Jacobs, *Primary Lessons for Deaf-Mutes*, 1:116, 1:139, 1:142.

21. J. A. Jacobs, *Primary Lessons for Deaf-Mutes*, 1:161, 168–169.

22. J. A. Jacobs, *Primary Lessons for Deaf-Mutes*, 2:215, 2:278–279, 2:297. Residents of the Virginia school for the Deaf were housed in the same town as residents of the state lunatic asylum, and thus their writing samples occasionally refer to them: "We eat pies every Sunday," wrote one Deaf student, age twelve. "At the hospital the crazy persons eat pies every Sunday." "Report of the Virginia Institution for the Deaf and Dumb and the Blind, 1850" (Staunton, VA: Press of the Institution, 1850), 13.

23. J. A. Jacobs, *Primary Lessons for Deaf-Mutes*, 2:244, 2:247. Echoing the same themes, a student at the Virginia school wrote "about a Deaf and Dumb Girl: she was very ignorant. She was always working at home. Her mother was talking with her. She could not hear. Her parents were sorry for her. They loved her. . . . Her mother wished her daughter to go to the Institution. She is learning her lesson." Written by a "young lady" aged twenty-two. "Report of the Virginia Institution for the Deaf and Dumb and the Blind, 1850," 13.

24. "The Ignorant Mutes" by TCC [Catherine Carrender?] in "First Annual Report . . . of the Georgia Asylum for the Education of the Deaf and Dumb, 1850," 14. For a brief discussion of southern hearing students' letters to their families, see Censer, *North Carolina Planters and Their Children, 1800–1860*, 58–59; and Stowe, *Intimacy and Power in the Old South*, 142–153.

25. "Annual Report for the Kentucky Institution for the Education of the Deaf and Dumb, 1862," unpaginated typescript, Volta Bureau. Also see "Annual Report for the Kentucky Institution for the Education of the Deaf and Dumb, 1850," unpaginated typescript, Volta Bureau.

26. Robina Norwood to Jane Tillinghast, 16 May 1842, Tillinghast Family Papers, DU.

27. Ibid.; Robina Norwood to Jane Tillinghast, 25 May 1842, Tillinghast Family Papers, DU.

28. Robina Norwood to Jane Tillinghast, 16 May 1842, Tillinghast Family Papers, DU.

29. Robina Norwood to Jane Tillinghast, 25 May 1842, Tillinghast Family Papers, DU. Margaret Eskridge, a hearing women, served as Matron for the Virginia school from 1839 until 1852. Her husband, George Eskridge, was the school's first steward. Principal Joseph Tyler, formerly a teacher at the American Asylum for the Deaf, was the first head of the Virginia school. He served from 1839 until his death in 1852.

30. Robina Norwood to Jane Tillinghast, 25 May 1842, Tillinghast Family Papers, DU. Silas Long enrolled at the Virginia school for the Deaf in 1840, one year after it opened its doors.

31. Robina Norwood to Jane Tillinghast, 25 May 1842, Tillinghast Family Papers, DU.

32. Ibid.

33. Ibid. For discussion of the early residential school experiences of nineteenth-century Deaf students nationally, see Edwards, "Words Made Flesh," 207–265.

34. Joseph Tyler to Samuel Tillinghast, 20 June 1842; Samuel Tillinghast to Jane Tillinghast, 29 May 1842; Mrs. Eckridge to Robina Norwood, 25 June 1842, all in the Tillinghast Family Papers, DU. In Eckridge's letter she talks about the delight Thomas felt when she read the family's letters. She also conveys Thomas's response: "When I spoke of his Father he stuck his fingers in the armholes of his waistcoat, swelled out his chest and began to walk like him." For another example of adults interpreting letters, see: "I have no doubt that when at home [Thomas] was accustomed to designate each person of his acquaintance by some distinctive sign, by the use of which he spoke of them in their absence. Now, if you ever wish to speak of persons to him in your letters, you need only mention such a person's sign and I can bring that person as accurately to his mind as the person's name would bring him to yours. For instance, had you mentioned the sign by which Thomas was accustomed to designate his cousin Mrs. Beatty, I could have most readily communicated to him her death and any other particular respecting her which you might have wished to make known to him." Joseph Tyler to Samuel Tillinghast, 6 March 1843, Tillinghast Family Papers, DU.

35. William Norwood to Jane Tillinghast, 13 September 1842; Joseph Tyler to Samuel Tillinghast, 1 November 1842, enclosed with Thomas to Jane Tillinghast and Samuel Tillinghast, 2 November 1842; Joseph Tyler to Samuel Tillinghast, 28 December 1842, with addendum by Thomas to Jane Tillinghast and to Samuel Tillinghast, 28 December 1842, all in the Tillinghast Family Papers, DU.

36. Joseph Tyler to Samuel Tillinghast, 6 April 1843, enclosed with Thomas Tillinghast to Samuel Tillinghast, 6 April 1843, Tillinghast Family Papers, DU. Susan Wilcox Harwood attended the Pennsylvania school for the Deaf before her enrollment at the Virginia school in 1840. In 1843 she became a teacher at the school. She remained on the faculty until 1863. Margaret Eskridge, a hearing woman, was the Matron at the Virginia school from 1839 until 1852. For more on the staff of the Virginia school during the nineteenth century, see Bass, *History of the Education of the Deaf in Virginia,* esp. 126–137 and 278–294.

For other examples of student literacy, several annual reports have accounts by pupils, sometimes edited by school staff and sometimes apparently unedited. One author quotes the following sentences given by students at the Board of Examiners' annual public exam: "William is not as high as George." "The cat is as smaller as a pig." "The whale is the most largest of the fish." "A horse is a great deal than a cow." These errors are an indication of the difficulty with English usage, especially idioms, that Deaf pupils had. Considering these sentences as well as many grammatically correct sentences, the Examiners declared that "it will be admitted by all that the performances were truly extraordinary." "The Second Biennial Report of the Board of Trustees of the Tennessee Institution for the Education of the Deaf and Dumb, 1856–57" (Nashville: Printed by W. F. Bang and Co. Banner Office, 1847), 31–32.

37. Thomas Tillinghast to Samuel Tillinghast, 10 January 1844, enclosed with Joseph Tyler to Samuel Tillinghast, 10 January 1844; Thomas Tillinghast to Jane Tillinghast, 11 October 1844, enclosed with Joseph Tyler to Samuel Tillinghast, 11 October 1844; Thomas Tillinghast to Samuel Tillinghast and Jane Tillinghast, 7 December 1844, enclosed with Thomas Tillinghast to siblings, 7 December 1844, and Joseph Tyler to Samuel Tillinghast, 7 December 1844, all in the Tillinghast Family Papers, DU. Although most members of both the Whig and the Democratic parties in the South were planters or small farmers, the Whig party especially appealed to southerners with commercial interests. Since the Tillinghasts ran a mercantile business, it is not at all unlikely that they agreed with Thomas's support of the Whigs. It is even possible that they sent Thomas (who still had limited literacy in English) a copy of a Whig newspaper. For an introductory overview of southern Whigs, see pages 173–182 in William J. Cooper Jr., and Thomas E. Terrill, *The American South: A History* (New York: McGraw-Hill 1991). Also see Michael F. Holt, *The Rise and Fall of the American Whig Party: Jacksonian Politics and the Onset of the Civil War* (New York: Oxford University Press, 2003).

38. J. A. Jacobs, *Lessons for the Deaf and Dumb,* 9; Jacobs, "Discussion with J. R. Burnet," *American Annals of the Deaf and Dumb* 5, no. 2 (1853): 102; J. A. Jacobs, "Discussion with J. R. Burnet," *American Annals of the Deaf and Dumb* 6, no. 3 (1854): 173. Acknowledging the failure of his system caused Jacobs great pain: "I have intensely grieved over the poor results and fruits of my own methods of instructing deaf-mutes." J. A. Jacobs, "The Philosphy of Signs in the Instruction of Deaf-Mutes," *American Annals of the Deaf and Dumb* 7, no. 4 (1854): 197. Despite his recognition that the method of teaching written English with occasional augmentation with individual signs failed many Deaf pupils, Jacobs continued to advocate his method and even published a new edition of his text just a few years after his admission of failure.

39. "Annual Report of the President and Officers of the Texas Institution for the Edu-

cation of the Deaf and Dumb, 1869" (Austin, TX: John Marshall and Co., State Printers, 1869), 6. For discussions of the superiority of ASL as the language of instruction, see for example "Report of the Trustees of the Tennessee Institution for the Deaf and Dumb, 1852" (Knoxville, TN: Printed at the Knoxville Register Office, 1852), 17. Statements can be found in most annual reports that schools taught a wide variety of subjects.

Chapter 7

1. "Report . . . of the Tennessee Institution for the Deaf and Dumb, 1852", 16; "Report . . . of the Missouri Asylum for the Deaf and Dumb, 1857–58," (Jefferson City, MO: J. Lusk, Public Printer, 1858), 21. Douglas Baynton makes a similar point in *Forbidden Signs*, 113–122. The title of this chapter is taken from the "Proceedings at the Laying of the Corner-Stone of the Institution for the Deaf and Dumb" (Knoxville: Jas. C. and John L. Moses, Register Office, 1848), 14.

2. "Third Annual Report of the Commissioners of the Georgia Asylum for the Education of the Deaf and Dumb, 1852" (Cave Spring, GA: Georgia Asylum for the Education of the Deaf and Dumb, 1852), 13–14.

3. Ibid., 14–15. This approach is similar to the one employed by Virginia Trist, discussed in Chapter 4.

4. Ibid., 15–17.

5. "Report of the Board of Directors of the Deaf and Dumb Asylum, 1850" (Raleigh: Thomas J. Lemay, Printer to the State, 1850), 7.

6. See Baynton, *Forbidden Signs*, 120–121. For another analysis of the debates about pedagogical sign languages, see Edwards, "Words Made Flesh," 45–109 and 155–206.

7. "Twelfth Annual Report . . . of the Georgia Institution for the Education of the Deaf and Dumb, 1861," 10.

8. Ibid.

9. Ibid.

10. J. A. Jacobs, "On the Disuse of Colloquial Signs in the Instruction of the Deaf and Dumb, and the Necessity of General Signs following the Order of the Words," *American Annals of the Deaf and Dumb* 7, no. 2 (1854), 69.

11. J. A. Jacobs, *Primary Lessons for Deaf-Mutes*, 1:7. The typical modern sign WEATHER incorporates the W, but the modern sign COLOR does not incorporate a C. Although not typically initialized, RED is sometimes signed with the R handshape rather than the pointer finger. The tradition of initializing signs is older than American Sign Language. The sign language taught in France's national school incorporated first letters. ASL, a linguistic descendant of French sign language, has maintained the practice. Laurent Clerc and Thomas Hopkins Gallaudet changed many of the initialized signs from French initials to English initials. MONDAY was now signed with an M rather than with an L, as it was in France for the French word *lundi*. GREEN was signed with a G rather than a V for the French *vert*. Sometimes ASL continued to use the sign without changing the initial to the first letter of the English word. Many modern ASL words are initialized by the first letter of the French word: the sign WITH is made with two A hands for the French *avec*, the sign OTHER with an A hand for *autre*, the sign GOOD with a B hand for *bon*, the sign HUNDRED with a C hand for *cent*, the sign

SEARCH with a C hand for *chercher,* etc. See Joseph D. Stedt and Donald F. Moores, "Manual Codes on English and American Sign Language: Historical Perspectives and Current Realities," in *Manual Communication: Implications for Education,* ed. Harry Bornstein (Washington, DC: Gallaudet University Press, 1990), 1– 20, especially the discussion on p. 2.

12. Rebecca Edwards suggests that although Deaf education in America began with methodical sign, it was soon discarded in favor of the pedagogical use of natural sign. She claims that in the 1850s, perhaps in response to Horace Mann's proposal for oral teaching of the Deaf, methodical sign was discussed again. See Edwards, "'Speech Has an Extraordinary Humanizing Power,'" 58–82. Douglas Baynton suggests that methodical signs remained in use to a limited degree until the 1850s. Baynton, *Forbidden Signs,* 118–121. From the annual reports I have seen, I would argue that the determination as to which sign system was used in the classroom was based not so much on chronological trends, but rather, it was dependent on the particular beliefs of individual schools and teachers. Also see Harlan Lane's chapter "The Oppression of American Sign Language" in his book *The Mask of Benevolence,* 103–120.

13. J. A. Jacobs, *Primary Lessons for Deaf-Mutes,* 1:15; Jacobs, "Discussion with J. R. Burnet," *American Annals of the Deaf and Dumb* 5, no. 2 (1853), 95 and 102; *The Kentucky Deaf-Mute,* 12 June 1884; J. A. Jacobs, "The Philosphy of Signs in the Instruction of Deaf-Mutes," *American Annals of the Deaf and Dumb* 7, no. 4 (1854): 199; "Annual Report for the Kentucky Institution for the Education of the Deaf and Dumb, 1853," unpaginated typescript, Volta Bureau. Even some Deaf people today are adamant that ASL is not the appropriate language of the classroom. As Frances M. Parsons (formerly a professor at Gallaudet, and a graduate of both a residential school for the Deaf and Gallaudet) claims, "During the early years of Gallaudet in the 19th century, peace reigned as the students and faculty used sign language based largely on English. It stemmed from Laurent Clerc, who taught signs to educators of the deaf in proper English-word-order along with a considerable amount of fingerspelling." Parsons continues, "Laurent Clerc's classic signs in English-word-order is the *true* legacy and heritage" of educated Deaf people. She concludes, "Recently, heated arguments about ASL have accelerated tenfold destroying what little was left of Clerc's signs. . . . If he knew that today's ASL (which still consists of some of his signs, but not in English-word-order) was to be mandatory at Gallaudet [University], [Clerc] would be literally 'whirling in his grave.'" (Parsons further claims that "ASLists" are "brainwashing" young Deaf pupils.) Frances M. Parsons, "Why ASL?" in Frances M. Parsons and Larry G. Stewart, *American Sign Language: Shattering the Myth* (Wilsonville, OR: Kodiak Media Group, 1998), 48–54. While I agree that in the classroom Clerc and Thomas Hopkins Gallaudet used a sign language based partially on the word order of spoken languages, I disagree with Parsons that this pidgin language of instruction is the "*true* legacy" of the nineteenth-century American Deaf community.

14. "Twelfth Annual Report of the Officers of the Georgia Institution for the Education of the Deaf and Dumb, 1861," 9. Interestingly, J. A. Jacobs used the same analogy when arguing a very different point. He pointed out that Deaf people thinking in the order of ASL grammar would be likely to translate English into ASL syntax: "You would

not say that a Latin sentence, interpreted in the order of the Latin words by English words, was translated into English." He continues, "The English boy, in the usual way of learning Latin, selects the Latin words and translates them in the order of the English idiom, making a jargon of the Latin."

15. "Twelfth Annual Report of the Officers of the Georgia Institution for the Education of the Deaf and Dumb, 1861," 9–10.

16. "Annual Report of the Trustees and Officers of the Louisiana Institution for the Education of the Deaf and Dumb, 1869" (Baton Rouge, LA: Printed at the Office of the Institution, 1869), 17; "Fourth Annual Report of the Commissioners of the Georgia Asylum for the Education of the Deaf and Dumb, 1853" (Cave Spring, GA: Georgia Asylum for the Education of the Deaf and Dumb, 1853), 16–18.

17. "Report of the Board of Directors of the Deaf and Dumb Asylum, 1850" (Raleigh: Thomas J. Lemay, Printer to the State, 1850), 8–9; "Annual Report for the Kentucky Institution for the Education of the Deaf and Dumb, 1849," unpaginated typescript, Volta Bureau; "Twelfth Annual Report of the Officers of the Georgia Institution for the Education of the Deaf and Dumb, 1861," 10.

18. "Fourth Annual Report of the Commissioners of the Georgia Asylum for the Education of the Deaf and Dumb, 1853," 18. Perhaps this pattern of adjectives tending to follow nouns grew out of the language Laurent Clerc brought from France, since the French Sign Language of the classroom was partially modeled on spoken/written French which follows the noun-adjective structure. One educator pointed out that it would be easier to teach Deaf pupils French rather than English, "since the construction of its sentences conforms more nearly to the order in which signs naturally place themselves. But of what use would this language be to him in a land where English is spoken?" "Annual Report of the Virginia Institution for the Education of the Deaf and Dumb and the Blind, 1870," 9.

19. "Annual Report for the Kentucky Institution for the Education of the Deaf and Dumb, 1849," unpaginated typescript, Volta Bureau.

20. Virginia Trist to Nicholas Trist, 17 April 1836, Nicholas Philip Trist Family Papers, SHC.

21. "Biennial Report . . . of the Missouri Asylum for the Deaf and Dumb, 1855–56" (Jefferson City, MO: J. Lusk, Public Printer, 1856), 21; Harvey P. Peet, "Address Delivered . . . on the Occasion of Laying the Corner Stone of the North Carolina Institution for the Instruction of the Deaf and Dumb," 34. The annual report continues that sign language was the "medium of intercourse with their friends" and that while writing would be important in educated Deaf people's adult lives, they would "never lay aside signs as an instrument of communicating . . . ideas" to Deaf friends.

22. "Report of the Virginia Institution for the Deaf and Dumb and the Blind, 1850," 11. As Thomas Hopkins Gallaudet said, a pupil at a residential school "finds himself, as it were, among his countrymen." Thomas H. Gallaudet, "The Natural Language of Signs," *American Annals of the Deaf* 1, no. 1 (1848), 58.

Chapter 8

1. For more details about John Jacobus Flournoy's life, see E. Merton Coulter, *John Jacobus Flournoy: Champion of the Common Man in the Antebellum South* (Savannah: Georgia Historical Society, 1942).

2. J. J. Flournoy, "To Free the Independent Yeomenry of the County of Clark," *Southern Banner*, 12 Feb 1835.

3. J. J. Flournoy, "A Defendatory Address, to the Enlightened and Generous Public, of all Parties and all Professions" (n.p., n.d.), 3–4. It is possible that Marcus, born perhaps fifteen years before John Jacobus, was educated at a school for the Deaf in Europe, as were many elite southern Deaf people of that era. The American School for the Deaf cannot confirm that Flournoy ever spent time at the school. Thanks to Gary Wait for checking extensively through the archive's resources for me. American School for the Deaf Archives, West Hartford, CT.

4. The American Asylum was established in 1817. There are many excellent studies of the school's early days. For two of the most comprehensive, see Valentine, "American Asylum for the Deaf"; and Lane, *When the Mind Hears.*

5. McCandless, *Moonlight, Magnolias, and Madness*, 88–89, notes 31 and 34 on p. 340. Flournoy, "A Defendatory Address, to the Enlightened and Generous Public," 3–4.

6. Coulter, *John Jacobus Flournoy*, 6; J. J. Flournoy, *A Vindication of Phrenology: By One of the School: A Resident of Athens, Georgia* (Athens, GA: Whig Office, 1835), 1–8; J. J. Flournoy, "Dr. J. J. Flournoy" *Southern Watchman*, 18 March 1858. Initially, he charged the "immensely opulent" $30 for the cure, the "ordinarily affluent" $10, etc., on down to a base price of $1.50 for laborers. When no one seemed interested, Flournoy offered to send the cure for the price of a postage stamp. Eventually he gave up, since as his biographer said, "People apparently would not be cured of their colds by Flournoy free of charge." For more information on the Pennsylvania Hospital, see Charles E. Rosenberg, *The Care of Strangers: The Rise of America's Hospital System* (Baltimore: Johns Hopkins University Press, 1987); and William H. Williams, *America's First Hospital: The Pennsylvania Hospital, 1751–1841* (Wayne, PA: Haverford House, c. 1976). For information on alternative therapies, see McCandless, "Mesmerism and Phrenology in Antebellum Charleston"; John D. Davies, *Phrenology: Fad and Science, a 19th-Century American Crusade* (New Haven, CT: Yale University Press, 1955); Robert S. Fox, *Body and Soul: A Sympathetic History of American Spiritualism* (Charlottesville: University of Virginia Press, 2003); Rosenberg, *Right Living*; and James Harvey Young, *American Health Quackery* (Princeton, NJ: Princeton University Press, 1992).

7. "Exegesis," *Southern Banner*, 7 Jan 1836; Obituary. *The Forest News*, 17 Jan 1879; A. L. Hull, *Annals of Athens, Georgia, 1801–1901* (Athens: Banner Job Office, 1906), 152–54; J. J. Flournoy, "Advertisement," *Southern Whig*, 15 June 1844. Flournoy's biographer reports that he interviewed a judge who remembered running whenever he saw him. Coulter, *John Jacobus Flournoy*, 85, note 44.

8. Flournoy, "A Defendatory Address, to the Enlightened and Generous Public, of all Parties and all Professions"; Coulter, *John Jacobus Flournoy*, 8.

9. Coulter, *John Jacobus Flournoy*, 9, 8.

10. Ibid., 11–14.

11. Flournoy, "A Defendatory Address, to the Enlightened and Generous Public, of

all Parties and all Professions," 2; J. J. Flournoy, "For the Southern Banner," *Southern Banner,* 23 April 1835.

12. J. J. Flournoy, *Essay on the Rise and Progress of Knowledge in the World, and the Expediency of Educating the Deaf and Dumb* (Athens, GA: Office of the *Southern Banner,* 1834), 11.

13. J. J. Flournoy, *Essay on the Rise and Progress of Knowledge in the World,* 14; Coulter, *John Jacobus Flournoy,* 3. For a copy of the law, see *Acts of the General Assembly of the State of Georgia,* 1840, 284–85.

14. J. J. Flournoy, *Facts Important to Know, Respecting the Constitution of the Federal Government; in a Religious View from the Pen of J. J. Flournoy* (Athens, GA: Offices of the *Southern Banner,* 1837); *An Essay on the Origins, Habits, &c. of the African Race: incidental to the propriety of having nothing to do with NEGROES: addressed to the good people of the United States* (New York: 1835), 4, 8; J. J. Flournoy, *A Reply to a Pamphlet, Entitled "Bondage, A Moral Institution, Sanctioned by the Scriptures and the Savior, &c., &c." so far as it Attacks the Principles of Expulsion with no Defense, however of Abolitionism* (Athens, GA: 1838), 1–10.

15. J. J. Flournoy, *An Essay on the Origins, Habits, &c. of the African Race,* 43, 8.

16. Ibid., 9, 24, 26.

17. Ibid., 28, 22–23, 45; Coulter, *John Jacobus Flournoy,* vi.

18. For more about Hinton Rowan Helper, see Hugh C. Bailey, *Hinton Rowan Helper: Abolitionist and Racist* (Tuscaloosa: University of Alabama, 2003); and Harvey Wish, ed., *Writings of George Fitzhugh and Hinton Rowan Helper on Slavery* (New York: Capricorn Books, 1960).

19. Coulter, *John Jacobus Flournoy,* 43.

20. Ibid., 14–16.

21. Oliver Wendell Holmes, *Professor at the Breakfast Table with the Story of Iris,* 3rd ed. (Boston: Houghton, Mifflin and Company, 1887) 5, 6; Coulter, *John Jacobus Flournoy,* 18. In order to persuade his family to accept this arrangement, he agreed to give his wife and two children most of his slaves and land. At the time of his death, Flournoy had had four marriages end in failure.

22. Coulter, *John Jacobus Flournoy,* 19.

23. "Mr. [J. J.] Flournoy to Mr. [William W.] Turner" 21 Dec 1855, in *American Annals of the Deaf and Dumb* 8, no. 2 (Jan. 1856); "Further Explanations by Mr. Flournoy" 20 Feb 1858, in *American Annals of the Deaf and Dumb* 10, no. 1 (Jan. 1858); "Mr. [J. J.] Flournoy to Mr. [William W.] Turner" 21 Dec 1855. A reprint of some of the debate within the Deaf community, along with insightful commentary, can be found in Christopher Krentz, *A Mighty Change: An Anthology of Deaf American Writing, 1816– 1864* (Washington, DC: Gallaudet University Press, 2000), 161–211. For other historical interpretations, see Van Cleve and Crouch, *A Place of Their Own,* 60–70; Margaret Winzer, "Deaf-Mutia, Responses to Alienation by the Deaf in the Mid-Nineteenth Century," *American Annals of the Deaf* 131 (March 1986), 29–32; Barry Crouch, "Alienation and the Mid-Nineteenth Century American Deaf Community, A Response," *American Annals of the Deaf* 131 (December 1986), 322–324; and Carol Padden and Tom Humphries, *Deaf in America: Voices from a Culture* (Cambridge, MA: Harvard University Press, 1988), 112–114.

24. "Further Explanations by Mr. Flournoy" 20 Feb 1858; "Mr. [J. J.] Flournoy to Mr. [William W.] Turner" 21 Dec 1855.

25. "Mr. [J. J.] Flournoy to Mr. [William W.] Turner" 21 Dec 1855; "Mr. [J. J.] Flournoy to Mr. [William W.] Turner" 3 Oct 1857, in *American Annals of the Deaf and Dumb*, 10, no. 2 (April 1858). Elsewhere he wrote that "the genius of woman is the talent of Satan. She it is, as a *tool*—that brought all our woes; and she it is that MUST be over-mastered!" J. J. Flournoy, "Notice," *Southern Watchman*, 19 June 1856.

26. "Further Explanations by Mr. Flournoy" 20 Feb 1858; "Mr. [J. J.] Flournoy to Mr. [William W.] Turner" 21 Dec 1855.

27. Edmund Booth, "Mr. Flournoy's Project" in *American Annals of the Deaf and Dumb*, Vol. X, No. II, April, 1858. For more about Edmund Booth, see Harry G. Long, *Edmund Booth: Deaf Pioneer* (Washington, D.C.: Gallaudet University Press, 2004); and *Edmund Booth (1810–1905) Forty-Niner: The Life Story of a Deaf Pioneer* (Stockton, CA: San Joaquin Pioneer and Historical Society, 1953); Braddock, *Notable Deaf Persons*, 8–9; Van Cleve and Crouch, *A Place of Their Own*, 64–65; and Lane, *When the Mind Hears*, 232–233. Hartwell Chamberlayne of Virginia, discussed in note 23 of Chapter 10, was in support of Flournoy's plan. See "Letter from H. M. Chamberlayne" 28 June 1858 in *American Annals of the Deaf and Dumb* 10, no. 3 (Aug. 1858). Also see the letters by P. F. Confer and W. M. Chamberlain in the same issue.

28. Reverend William W. Turner, quoted in Krentz, *A Mighty Change*, 211; Reverend Thomas Gallaudet quoted in Krentz, *A Mighty Change*, 211.

29. Edmund Booth, "Mr. Flournoy's Project"; "Mr. [J. J.] Flournoy to Mr. [William W.] Turner" 21 Dec 1855; Letter from John Carlin to Laurent Clerc (nd but after Jan 1858 and before April 1858), in *American Annals of the Deaf and Dumb* 10, no. 2 (April 1858); "John R. Burnet Weighs In," in Krentz, *A Mighty Change*.

30. Letter from John Carlin to Laurent Clerc (nd but after Jan 1858 and before April 1858); "Remarks by Mr. [Edmund] Booth" in *American Annals of the Deaf and Dumb* 10, no. 3 (July 1858).

31. "John R. Burnet Weighs In," in Krentz, *A Mighty Change*, 193–194.

32. Ibid.

33. J. J. Flournoy, *Much Prefatory Declarations* (Athens, GA: 1838), 31.

34. Coulter, *John Jacobus Flournoy*, 16; J. J. Flournoy to Jefferson Davis, 30 October 1862, quoted in Coulter, *John Jacobus Flournoy*, 79.; J. J. Flournoy to Andrew Johnson, 30 May 1865, quoted in Coulter, *John Jacobus Flournoy*, 80.

35. Coulter, *John Jacobus Flournoy*, 29.

Chapter 9

1. "First Annual Report of the Board of Trustees and Officers of the Alabama Institution for the Education of the Deaf and Dumb, 1861" (Montgomery: Montgomery Advertiser Book and Job Printing Office, 1861), 5, 24.

2. Couch and Hawkins, *Out of Silence and Darkness*, 33.

3. "First Annual Report . . . of the Alabama Institution for the Education of the Deaf and Dumb, 1861," back cover; Couch and Hawkins, *Out of Silence and Darkness*, 34;

"Report of the Board of Trustees and Officers of the Alabama Institution for the Education of the Deaf and Dumb, 1862–63" (Montgomery, AL: Montgomery Advertiser Book and Job Printing Office, 1863), 10.

4. "Annual Report of the Board of Commissioners of the Georgia Institution for the Education of the Deaf and Dumb, 1860" (Cave Spring, GA: Georgia Institution for the Education of the Deaf and Dumb, 1860), 3. Alabama Principal Johnson's loyalty to the Confederacy was above reproach by the state legislature. In 1862 he resigned from the army and returned to the Deaf school. It is unclear if he was dismissed because of "an injury that prevented further military service" or because the institution's board of directors "urged Johnson to return to assist in keeping the school open" (Couch and Hawkins, *Out of Silence and Darkness*, 34). Johnson joined other Talladega residents to form a Battlefield Relief Association to collect food and supplies for southern troops. Along with other Masons in the city, Johnson raised thousands of dollars to feed imprisoned Confederates in northern jails. Rumors circulated that he filled the Alabama Deaf school's massive columns with gunpowder, silver, and his neighbors' valuables in order to protect them from theft by the Union troops (Couch and Hawkins, *Out of Silence and Darkness*, 35). Johnson's image as Confederate hero is confirmed by this story: "Dr Johnson came into possession of a new hypodermic syringe. He had heard great claims for it as a painkiller, but he was somewhat afraid to use it until he was sure that the results would not be injurious. One night one of the Yankees had a severe earache. Knowing that Dr. Johnson had practiced medicine, he went to him and asked him if there was not something he could do to ease the pain. Dr. Johnson told him about the hypodermic and the man said he was willing to try anything. It gave him so much relief he told his friends about it and the next night three or four more came to see Dr. Johnson. After Dr. Johnson saw that it would not do any harm, but would do good, he told them 'no,' he was not going to waste any more in the 'd___ Yankees.'" J. S. Ganey, "Fact, Fiction, or Fancy," Alabama file, Volta Bureau.

5. "Annual Report . . . of the Georgia Institution for the Education of the Deaf and Dumb, 1860," 5–6; "Annual Report . . . of the Georgia Institution for the Education of the Deaf and Dumb, 1860," 7. The Louisiana school also dismissed the superintendent of the institution. His removal from office may have involved suspected abolitionist politics, although the annual reports are unclear: "The Board took action for the removal of the then General Superintendent, J.S. Brown. It is not deemed necessary to go into a recital of the causes which led to this action; suffice it to say that it was thought by the majority of the Board, that the well-being of the Institution demanded a change in the superintendence of its affairs." "Ninth Annual Report of the Trustees and Superintendent of the Louisiana Institution for the Education of the Deaf and Dumb, 1861" (Baton Rouge: Louisiana Institution for the Education of the Deaf and Dumb, 1861), 5.

6. "Annual Report . . . of the Georgia Institution for the Education of the Deaf and Dumb, 1860," 7; Letter from Milledgeville, 29 Dec 1859, *The Chronicle and Sentinel,* quoted in "Annual Report . . . of the Georgia Institution for the Education of the Deaf and Dumb, 1860," 8.

7. "Annual Report . . . of the Georgia Institution for the Education of the Deaf and Dumb, 1860," 7–8.

8. Ibid., 5–6, 9.

9. Ibid., 9–10.

10. Ibid., 20.

11. Ibid., 11–12. For information about the politics of the Gallaudets, see Valentine, "American Asylum for the Deaf."

12. "Annual Report of the Virginia Institution for the Education of the Deaf and Dumb and the Blind, 1870" (Richmond: R. F. Walker, Superintendent, Public Printing, 1870), 9. Also see Baynton, *Forbidden Signs,* 15–35. The story of David Tillinghast chronicled in the following chapter illustrates this feeling of disconnection between southern families and their Deaf members during the Civil War.

13. "Annual Report for the Kentucky Institution for the Education of the Deaf and Dumb, 1862," unpaginated typescript, Volta Bureau.

14. During the postbellum period, Connor finally became superintendent of the school. *Centennial Celebration: One Hundred Years of Education for the Deaf in Georgia, 1848–1948* (Cave Spring, GA: Georgia School for the Deaf, 1948).

15. "Annual Report of the Board of Commissioners of the Georgia Institution for the Education of the Deaf and Dumb, 1860" (Cave Spring: Georgia Institution for the Education of the Deaf and Dumb, 1861), 5.

16. "Eighteenth Annual Report of the South Carolina Institution for the Education of the Deaf and Dumb, and the Blind, 1866" (Columbia, SC: Evans and Cogswell, State Printers, 1866), 13.

17. "Fourteenth Annual Report of the South Carolina Institution for the Education of the Deaf and Dumb, and the Blind, 1862," 133.

18. "Sixteenth Annual Report of the South Carolina Institution for the Education of the Deaf and Dumb, and the Blind, 1864," 11.

19. Ibid., 15; "Eighteenth Annual Report of the South Carolina Institution for the Education of the Deaf and Dumb, and the Blind, 1866," 9–10.

20. "Annual Report of the Virginia Institution for the Education of the Deaf and Dumb and the Blind, 1867–69" (Richmond: R. F. Walker, Superintendent Public Printing, 1869), 8; *Centennial Celebration;* "Biennial Report of the Board of Directors and Officers of the Arkansas Deaf Mute Institute" (Little Rock, AR: Mitchell and Bettis, State Printers, 1870), 11; "Tenth Biennial Report of the Board of Trustees of the Tennessee Deaf and Dumb School, 1867," 10.

21. "Twelfth Annual Report . . . of the Louisiana Institution for the Education of the Deaf and Dumb," 8; "Eleventh Annual Report . . . of the Louisiana Institution for the Education of the Deaf and Dumb, 1867," 5.

22. "Twelfth Annual Report . . . of the Louisiana Institution for the Education of the Deaf and Dumb," 8; "Eleventh Annual Report . . . of the Louisiana Institution for the Education of the Deaf and Dumb, 1867," 5.

23. "Annual Report . . . of the Georgia Institution for the Education of the Deaf and Dumb, 1868," 4; *Centennial Celebration;* Bass, *History of the Education of the Deaf in Virginia,* 80. The engraved windowpane has been removed and is now framed.

24. Brown, *History of the Mississippi School for the Deaf,* 23; Dobyns, "The Mississippi Institution for the Education of the Deaf and Dumb," 9. In addition to the school building itself being destroyed, information about the school stored there was also de-

stroyed. Wrote the school institution historian: "The buildings of the Deaf Institute were among those destroyed, and the school records and other papers were lost in the flames." Brown, *History of the Mississippi School for the Deaf,* 20. The destruction is confirmed by a postbellum annual report: "Among the disasters occasioned by the late war, may be mentioned the destruction of the former Institution, together with the records and papers pertaining to it, and so far as the writer is informed, nothing remains from which to obtain official data of its former history and condition." "Annual Report of the Board of Trustees and Superintendent of the Mississippi Institution for the Deaf and Dumb, Session of 1872" (Jackson, MS: Kimball, Raymond, and Company, State Printers, 1872), 3. Many of the Virginia School for the Deaf's papers were also destroyed: "The war in its consequences deprived the Institution of many of those papers and reports which are most essential to present a complete and satisfactory account" of the history of the school from the origin through the war. "Annual Report of the Virginia Institution for the Education of the Deaf and Dumb and the Blind, 1867–69," 5.

25. "Thirteenth Annual Report of the President and Officers of the Texas Institution for the Education of the Deaf and Dumb" (Austin, TX: Printed by John Marshall and Company, State Printers, 1869), 6; "Tenth Biennial Report of the Board of Trustees of the Tennessee Deaf and Dumb School, 1867," 10.

26. "Annual Report . . . of the Georgia Institution for the Education of the Deaf and Dumb, 1868," 4, 16; "Eleventh Annual Report . . . of the Louisiana Institution for the Education of the Deaf and Dumb, 1867," 7.

27. "Eleventh Annual Report . . . of the Louisiana Institution for the Education of the Deaf and Dumb, 1867," 7. The Louisiana Institution thought that Alabama and Arkansas "might be induced into the same arrangement" to which Mississippi agreed. "Eleventh Annual Report . . . of the Louisiana Institution for the Education of the Deaf and Dumb, 1867," 10.

28. "Report of the North Carolina Institution for the Deaf and Dumb and the Blind from September 1, 1862, to September 1, 1864," 3 and 11. For more on the teaching of printing skills in Deaf schools throughout the nation, see Van Cleve and Crouch, *A Place of Their Own,* 164–168.

After the Confederacy surrendered, the North Carolina school did close for one semester, "owing to the unsettled condition of the country" and a "want of necessary funds." "Report of the North Carolina Institution for the Deaf and Dumb and the Blind from September 1, 1865, to September 1, 1866," 7. The school had depended upon payment for printing done by the school for the Confederate government. Now that the Confederacy had collapsed and its monetary notes were worthless, the North Carolina school knew the debts could not be repaid. "Report of the North Carolina Institution for the Deaf and Dumb and the Blind from September 1, 1865, to September 1, 1866," 10. The only salvation for the school was the generosity of the officers and troops of the occupying army of the United States. The principal wrote, "They have uniformly manifested a willingness to render me every assistance consistent with their official duties, and in so doing have shown an interest in the success of the Institution highly laudable and praiseworthy." "Report of the North Carolina Institution for the Deaf and Dumb and the Blind from September 1, 1865, to September 1, 1866," 15.

Chapter 10

1. The title of this chapter is from the Biennial Report of the Kentucky Institute for the Education of the Deaf and Dumb (Frankfort, KY: JB Major, State Printer, 1861), 9.

2. Sarah Tillinghast to David Tillinghast, 21 Jan 1860, Tillinghast Family Papers, DU. Why the Tillinghasts did not consider enrolling David in the North Carolina school for the Deaf is unclear. Beginning his education before the building of the North Carolina school, Tom Tillinghast graduated from the Virginia Institution for the Deaf. The family then decided to send both boys to the New York school. Tom finished his additional education and came home before the war. Perhaps the Tillinghasts decided to keep David at the New York institution because of their fears about the future prospects of the North Carolina school.

3. Sarah Tillinghast to David Tillinghast, 6 May 1861, Tillinghast Family Papers, DU.

4. Ibid.

5. Ibid.

6. David Tillinghast to Sarah Tillinghast, 13 May 1861, Tillinghast Family Papers, DU.

7. John Tillinghast to David Tillinghast, 14 May 1861, Tillinghast Family Papers, DU.

8. David Tillinghast to Sarah Tillinghast, 13 May 1861, Tillinghast Family Papers, DU.

9. John Tillinghast to David Tillinghast, 14 May 1861; William Tillinghast to David Tillinghast with addendum, by Eliza Tillinghast to David Tillinghast, 20 May 1861, both in the Tillinghast Family Papers, DU.

10. William Tillinghast to David Tillinghast, 21 Dec 1861, Tillinghast Family Papers, DU. For more on Deaf individuals who were involved in the war effort, see Tom Harrington, "Deaf or Hard of Hearing Persons in U.S. Civil War Military Service," available at <http://library.gallaudet.edu/dr/faq-us-civil-war.html>. Also see Gannon, *Deaf Heritage*, 10.

11. David Tillinghast to William Tillinghast, 18 July 1862, Tillinghast Family Papers, DU.

12. Ibid. The shortage of hearing men that occurred during the Civil War seems to have paved the way for the hiring of Deaf teachers. Between 1859 and 1866, the New York Institution hired fifteen Deaf teachers and nine hearing teachers, three of whom were women. Compare this to the preceding period, 1850 and 1858, when the school hired seven Deaf teachers and fifteen hearing teachers. From the school's founding in 1818 until 1849, the school hired only ten Deaf teachers and twenty-seven hearing teachers. The increased hiring of Deaf teachers ended after the Civil War. Between 1867 and 1893, there were only fifteen deaf teachers but forty hearing teachers.

13. John Tillinghast to David Tillinghast, 9 November 1862, Tillinghast Family Papers, DU.

14. William Tillinghast to David Tillinghast, 13 January 1863 and undated older letters; William Tillinghast to David Tillinghast, 14 April 1863, both in the Tillinghast Family Papers, DU. Unfortunately William's letter to David is not in the archives. It is referred to in the 13 January 1863 letter. Although David appears not to have written, it is

important to remember that the only reason historians have his siblings' letters to him is that David saved them all.

15. William Tillinghast to David Tillinghast, 13 January 1863 and undated older letter; Robina Tillinghast to David Tillinghast, 27 January 1863; Sarah Tillinghast to David Tillinghast, 20 April 1863, all in the Tillinghast Family Papers, DU.

16. John Tillinghast to David Tillinghast, 9 November 1862, Tillinghast Family Papers, DU.

17. William Tillinghast to David Tillinghast, 13 January 1863 and undated older letter; Robina Tillinghast to David Tillinghast, 27 January 1863; William Tillinghast to David Tillinghast, 14 April 1863; Sarah Tillinghast to David Tillinghast, 20 April 1863, all in the Tillinghast Family Papers, DU. On the backs of many family letters are back-and-forth notes showing that hearing family members sometimes communicated with Deaf members via writing.

18. William Tillinghast to David Tillinghast, 13 January 1863 and undated older letter, Tillinghast Family Papers, DU.

19. William Tillinghast to David Tillinghast, 14 April 1863, Tillinghast Family Papers, DU.

20. William Tillinghast to David Tillinghast, 14 April 1863, Tillinghast Family Papers, DU.

21. Sarah Tillinghast to David Tillinghast, 20 April 1863; Sarah Tillinghast to David Tillinghast, 6 June 1863, both in the Tillinghast Family Papers, DU.

22. William Tillinghast to David Tillinghast, 14 April 1863; Sarah Tillinghast to David Tillinghast, 6 June 1863, both in the Tillinghast Family Papers, DU.

23. Sarah Tillinghast to David Tillinghast, 20 April 1863; Hartwell M. Chamberlayne to Thomas Tillinghast, 21 November 1863, both in the Tillinghast Family Papers, DU. Born in 1836, Hartwell Chamberlayne was the younger brother of Edward Pye Chamberlayne, discussed in the introduction. He was admitted to the Virginia school for the Deaf in 1847. His father endowed the Chamberlayne Gold Medal in order to honor Hartwell. It was awarded to worthy students from 1848 to 1896. After three years at the Virginia school, Hartwell Chamberlayne attended the American school for the Deaf in Connecticut for one year, then in 1851 enrolled at the New York school, where he attended advanced classes before graduating. After many years as a farmer, Chamberlayne joined the faculty at the Virginia school for the Deaf in 1890 and taught until his death in 1905. ASD Admissions Record, 1850, American School for the Deaf Archives, West Hartford, CT; "List of Pupils of the New York Institution," *American Annals of the Deaf and Dumb* 6, no. 4 (July 1854); Bass, *History of the Education of the Deaf in Virginia,* 129, 278, 297.

Hart Chamberlayne married a schoolmate and fellow Virginian, Elmena A. McDearmon. The couple had six children. Bass, *History of the Education of the Deaf in Virginia,* 129. They named one of their sons after Hartwell's Deaf brother Edward Pye. Hartwell Macon Chamberlayne to brother, 24 July 1872, Chamberlayne Family Papers, Virginia Historical Society, Richmond, VA. Another son was named Thomas Gallaudet, after one of Chamberlayne's teachers at the New York school who was also the rector at St. Ann's Church for Deaf-Mutes in New York City. "Obituary of Thomas Gallaudet

Chamberlayne," 21 May 1894, clipping in Bagby Family Papers, Virginia Historical Society, Richmond, VA. Thomas Gallaudet was the son of Thomas Hopkins Gallaudet, the founder of the American School for the Deaf. For more information about Thomas Gallaudet, see Otto Benjamin Berg and Henry L. Buzzard, *Thomas Gallaudet: Apostle to the Deaf* (New York: St. Ann's Church for the Deaf, 1989).

Hartwell Chamberlayne published an article about Deaf peddlers, "Vagrancy among Deaf-Mutes," in *American Annals of the Deaf and Dumb* 11 (1859), 86–89. The article is reprinted in Lois Bragg, ed., *Deaf World: A Historical Read and Primary Sourcebook* (New York: New York University Press, 2001), 237–238.

24. Sarah Tillinghast to David Tillinghast, 6 June 1863; Thomas Tillinghast to David Tillinghast, 6 June 1863, both in the Tillinghast Family Papers, DU.

25. Sarah Tillinghast to David Tillinghast, 6 June 1863; Thomas Tillinghast to David Tillinghast, 6 June 1863; Note from Thomas Tillinghast to David Tillinghast, appended to William Tillinghast to David Tillinghast, 8 June 1863, all in the Tillinghast Family Papers, DU. A few months later William reinforced his beliefs about the dependence of his Deaf brothers by telling David that Thomas was unable to live alone "as he is subject to asthma and mute too." William Tillinghast to David Tillinghast, 13 October 1863, Tillinghast Family Papers, DU.

26. Sarah Tillinghast to David Tillinghast, 6 June 1863; William Tillinghast to David Tillinghast, 22 January 1864, both in the Tillinghast Family Papers, DU.

27. Thomas Tillinghast to David Tillinghast, 6 June 1863, Tillinghast Family Papers, DU.

28. Thomas Tillinghast to David Tillinghast, 6 June 1863, Tillinghast Family Papers, DU.

29. David Tillinghast to brother, 26 August 1863; David Tillinghast to brother, 15 October 1863, both in the Tillinghast Family Papers, DU. "Thrice years old" is the "age" of the class, not the pupils. In other words, the students had attended school for three years. David may have been given charge of the class due to the difficulty obtaining hearing male teachers during the war years. Earlier, New York Principal Harvey Peet had argued that Deaf teachers were "not qualified to carry forward a class of Deaf Mutes, successfully, for over a period of three or four years." He continued, "If I have anything to do with the controlling management of the Institution, I will never allow a deaf mute to go forward with the same class beyond three years." These quotes are from the Proceedings of the 1853 Convention of American Instructors of the Deaf, quoted in Donald F. Moores, "Review of: *Mask of Benevolence*," in Frances M. Parsons and Larry G. Stewart, *American Sign Language: Shattering the Myth* (Wilsonville, OR: Kodiak Media Group, 1998), 102. For more on the hiring of Deaf teachers, see Valentine, "American Asylum for the Deaf: A First Experiment in Education, 1817–1880," 155–204.

30. David Tillinghast to brother, 15 Oct 1863; David Tillinghast to Robina Tillinghast, 7 March 1864, both in the Tillinghast Family Papers, DU. Hearing teachers in general had college degrees while Deaf teachers did not. For more on the low salaries of Deaf teachers, see Baynton, *Forbidden Signs*, 60–61.

31. John Witschief to David Tillinghast, 21 September 1863, Tillinghast Family Papers, DU. John Witschief enrolled at the New York school in 1845. He spent the next ten years at the school, where his Deaf younger brother Peter also was educated. "List of Pupils of the New York Institution," *American Annals of the Deaf and Dumb* 6, no. 4

(July 1854), 195; "Thirty-seventh Report of the New York Institution for the Instruction of the Deaf and Dumb" (Albany, NY: Charles Van Benthuysen, 1856), 37.

32. John Tillinghast to David Tillinghast, 15 July 1863; William Tillinghast to David Tillinghast, 8 August 1863, both in the Tillinghast Family Papers, DU.

33. William Tillinghast to David Tillinghast, 8 August 1863; David Tillinghast to brother, 26 August 1863, both in the Tillinghast Family Papers, DU.

34. David Tillinghast to brother, 15 Oct 1863, Tillinghast Family Papers, DU.

35. David Tillinghast to Robina Tillinghast, 7 March 1864, Tillinghast Family Papers, DU.

36. William Tillinghast to David Tillinghast, 21 March 1864, Tillinghast Family Papers, DU.

37. David Tillinghast to Robina Tillinghast, 7 March 1864; William Tillinghast to David Tillinghast, 18 June 1864, both in the Tillinghast Family Papers, DU. Although there is a period of several months with no letters, suggesting the family members were all together, one letter written almost one year later states that David had not yet been home at all during the war. In it, Sarah begged her brother to visit them, stating that she would embrace "this first opportunity" to see him. Sarah Tillinghast to David Tillinghast, 12 March 1865, Tillinghast Family Papers, DU.

38. Sarah Tillinghast to David Tillinghast, 12 March 1865, Tillinghast Family Papers, DU. For more about Sherman's march through North Carolina, see John Gilchrist Barrett, *Sherman's March through the Carolinas* (Chapel Hill, NC: University of North Carolina Press, 1996); and Jacqueline Glass Campbell, *When Sherman Marched North from the Sea: Resistance on the Confederate Home Front* (Chapel Hill: University of North Carolina Press, 2003).

39. Sarah Tillinghast to David Tillinghast, 12 March 1865; Sarah Tillinghast to David Tillinghast, 3 May 1865, both in the Tillinghast Family Papers, DU.

40. Sarah Tillinghast to David Tillinghast, 3 May 1865, Tillinghast Family Papers, DU.

41. Ibid.

42. Ibid.

43. Eliza Tillinghast to David Tillinghast, 8 June 1865, Tillinghast Family Papers, DU.

44. Ibid.

45. Ibid.

46. Ibid.

47. Ibid.

48. Ibid.

49. William Tillinghast to David Tillinghast, undated [1865], Tillinghast Family Papers, DU.

50. David Tillinghast to William Tillinghast, 5 June 1865; Sarah Tillinghast to David Tillinghast, 12 March 1865; William Tillinghast to David Tillinghast, undated [1865], all in the Tillinghast Family Papers, DU.

51. Sarah Ann Tillinghast to Emily Tillinghast, 4 April 1868; Sarah Ann Tillinghast to Joseph Tillinghast, May 1868; Thomas Tillinghast to William Tillinghast, 27 September 1867, all in the Tillinghast Family Papers, DU.

David recommended Sarah Ann to Principal Peet arguing that she was well suited for the job because of "her familiarity with the use of the manual alphabet and her knowledge of many natural signs, acquired in her intercourse with me before I came to school." David to sister, 27 January 1868, Tillinghast Family Papers, DU. She wrote to her siblings about her situation. "Truly this is a wonderful establishment!" She was excited by the lovely living quarters and the generous meals: "dessert every day—fresh meat *at every meal.*" But she did not stop teasing northerners just because of her position. When given a multitude of keys to the institution, Sarah Ann said, "Now I can get behind every lock in the house. Ain't it a pity I ain't a prying yankee—couldn't I have fun?" Sarah Ann Tillinghast to Emily Tillinghast, 4 April 1868; Sarah Ann Tillinghast to Joseph Tillinghast, May 1868, both in the Tillinghast Family Papers, DU.

More about the hiring of the men's hearing brother Willard can be found in David Tillinghast to Thomas Tillinghast, 15 October 1867, Tillinghast Family Papers, DU. For letters that include money from David, see for example David Tillinghast to Thomas Tillinghast, 16 December 1865; David Tillinghast to Thomas Tillinghast, 2 February 1866; David Tillinghast to Thomas Tillinghast, 26 March 1866; David Tillinghast to Thomas Tillinghast, 1 May 1866; David Tillinghast to Thomas Tillinghast, 6 June 1866; David Tillinghast to Thomas Tillinghast, 18 June 1867, all in the Tillinghast Family Papers, DU.

52. It is clear that David did not reject his family's racial views. As one of his siblings stated, "I was very glad you showed your Southern raising by taking the side you did about the darkies doing menial work. I believe that God in his wisdom put the negroes in the south to do the menial work because the climate is such that it kills white women or worse than kills them." Sibling to [David Tillinghast], 5 May 1866, Tillinghast Family Papers, DU.

Epilogue

1. Maud Waddell, "Nearly Ninety," 180–181. Caroline Stansbury was a pupil at the New York School for the Deaf when David Tillinghast was a member of the faculty. The daughter of Judge George A. and Evelyn Goodell Stansbury, Caroline grew up in Baldwinsville, New York. David and Caroline were married in 1868. Rose C. Tillinghast, *The Tillinghast Family, 1560–1970* (n.p.: 1972), 150.

2. Emily Tillinghast to Joseph Tillinghast, 17 October 1868; David Tillinghast to Eliza Tillinghast, 26 April 1868; David Tillinghast to Willard Tillinghast, 18 November 1869; David Tillinghast to William Tillinghast, 3 January 1871; Joseph Tillinghast to William Tillinghast, 4 January 1871; Thomas Tillinghast to Robina Tillinghast, 10 March 1871; Thomas to Emily, 9 October 1971, all in the Tillinghast Family Papers, DU. By 1880, Robina Tillinghast had joined David's household as well. From 1880 United States Census: Raleigh, Wake, North Carolina, Roll T9-984, Enumeration District 266, Image 0597.

For examples of the ways in which David Tillinghast missed the Deaf community of New York, see David Tillinghast to Henry Winter Syle, 5 November 1872, 28 May 1873, 21 August 1873, 2 April 1874, and 19 September 1877, all in box 7, folder 17, Rev. Henry Winter Syle Collection, 1832–1975, Gallaudet University Archives, Gallaudet University, Washington, DC. For more about Syle, an important member of the national Deaf community of the nineteenth century, see Braddock, *Notable Deaf Persons*, 110–112.

3. David was active in the 1870s effort to erect a memorial for Laurent Clerc in New York's Central Park. For more information about his involvement with formal associa-

tions of Deaf people and issues of importance to the Deaf community, see David Tillinghast to Henry Winter Syle, 5 November 1872, 19 December 1872, 21 August 1873, 1 October 1873; 19 September 1877, all in box 7, folder 17, Rev. Henry Winter Syle Collection, 1832–1975, Gallaudet University Archives, Gallaudet University, Washington, DC.

Occasionally David did express his frustration with the isolation he felt in Raleigh. It sometimes seemed that surrounding him were only the young pupils just beginning their education and a handful of other Deaf people whose education was not nearly as extensive as David's own. As he wrote, "I long for more intelligent congenial society than I can find here. Constant contact with deaf mutes so far below me in culture I fear drags me down." David Tillinghast to Henry Winter Syle, 19 September 1877 in box 7, folder 17, Rev. Henry Winter Syle Collection, 1832–1975, Gallaudet University Archives, Gallaudet University, Washington, DC.

For more about the lives of adult Deaf Americans during the nineteenth century, see Edwards, "Words Made Flesh," 264–303.

4. "List of Pupils of the New York Institution," *American Annals of the Deaf and Dumb* 6, no. 4 (July 1854); Record of the Marriages, Baptisms, and Funeral Services performed by Rev. Gallaudet at St.Ann's Church for Deaf-Mutes, Gallaudet University Archives, Gallaudet University, Washington, DC; ASD Admissions Register, 1836, American School for the Deaf Archives, West Hartford, CT; Braddock, *Notable Deaf Persons,* 19–21; Thomas Jefferson Trist to Henry Winter Syle, undated, in box 7, folder 21, Rev. Henry Winter Syle Collection, 1832–1975, Gallaudet University Archives, Gallaudet University, Washington, DC. Braddock writes on page 21 that Trist "was a crusader for the right of the deaf to take active part in any undertakings begun for their benefit, and resented any denial of representation to them in public meetings or projects." Rev. Henry Winter Syle, discussed in the previous note, was a member of the clergy at St. Ann's, the church Trist attended. Reverend Thomas Gallaudet was the son of Thomas Hopkins Gallaudet, founder of the American School for the Deaf. For more information about Thomas Gallaudet, see Berg and Buzzard, *Thomas Gallaudet.*

5. Rose C. Tillinghast, *The Tillinghast Family, 1560–1970,* 148–150; Van Cleve and Crouch, *A Place of Their Own,* 57–59.

Note on Sources

1. For an excellent discussion of why there are so few texts in English by nineteenth-century Deaf people, see Krentz, *A Mighty Change,* vii–xiii and xxii–xxix. As Krentz points out on page xiii, Deaf writers who wrote in English "sought to express their views in the language of hearing people. To say they did so despite great challenges does not begin to convey the heroic proportions of their accomplishment."

2. Authors of the annual reports published by state schools for the Deaf often selected samples of students' writing, be they letters home or classroom essays, to provide evidence to government officials of student progress. Rebecca Anne Rourke Edwards is perhaps the only historian to date to use these valuable sources extensively. However, she assumes they adequately represent the reality of Deaf beliefs and actions. Edwards, "Words Made Flesh." For a discussion of the use of copybooks by hearing pupils from the nineteenth century, see Steven M. Stowe, *Intimacy and Power in the Old South,* 141–142.

INDEX

Marianne Jewell Memorial Library
Baker College of Muskegon
Muskegon, Michigan 49442